Edward Dowling

Australia and America in 1892

A contrast

Edward Dowling

Australia and America in 1892
A contrast

ISBN/EAN: 9783337311759

Printed in Europe, USA, Canada, Australia, Japan

Cover: Foto ©ninafisch / pixelio.de

More available books at **www.hansebooks.com**

Published by Authority of the New South Wales Commissioners
for the World's Columbian Exposition, Chicago, 1893.

AUSTRALIA AND AMERICA

IN

1892 :

A CONTRAST.

BY

EDWARD DOWLING,

HON. SECRETARY OF THE AUSTRALIAN NATIVES ASSOCIATION AND SECRETARY TO THE LATE
BOARD OF TECHNICAL EDUCATION OF NEW SOUTH WALES.

Sydney :

CHARLES POTTER, GOVERNMENT PRINTER.

1893.

[2s.]

127 183—92 a

CONTENTS.

INTRODUCTION.

In the tribal councils of the North American Indians all present from the youngest to the oldest express their views for the common good, so, in meeting at the World's Fair in Chicago, Australia, the youngest born of England, claims on the score of relationship to take "sweet counsel" with her American sisters. The United States and Canada are noted for the publication of excellent pamphlets disseminating information respecting the resources of those countries ; and the present condition of the British colonies in Australasia cannot be better illustrated to visitors to the Columbian Exposition than by contrast with the relative progress made by the two great English-speaking countries in North America.

The United States, Canada, and Australasia are admitted to be the three wealthiest communities founded in modern times; and a comparison of their respective performances in the industrial race should be profitable to each other and also to representatives who will be found assembled from nearly every other part of the world at the centenary celebration of the discovery of America.

New South Wales has made rapid growth since a previous representation of her resources was made at the Philadelphia Centennial Exhibition, so that an account of her present condition and future prospects should prove of special interest to numbers of persons who visited that exposition seventeen years ago. New South Wales, Victoria, Queensland, and South Australia, the principal colonies on the Australian continent, greatly resemble in their progress and resources the neighbouring states of California, Colorado, Oregon, and Nevada, so that a comparison can approximately be made as to their relative growth during the last decade in pastoral, agricultural, mining, and manufacturing industries. In natural and acquired wealth New South Wales is the wealthiest Australian Colony as in resources and capabilities California is the richest American State, and it should prove instructive to compare the progress made in these two settlements formed about the same time on opposite shores of the Pacific. For many years past there has been considerable commercial intercourse between Sydney and San Francisco, and there should always be direct communication between Port Jackson and the principal harbours of California, Oregon, and British Columbia.

The compiler is an Australian who, after a residence of nearly half-a-century in his native land, visited Great Britain during the celebration of the Jubilee of the reign of Queen Victoria in 1887, and with representatives from many countries saw the foundation stone of an Imperial Institute laid with the object of making the Colonies of the British Empire more

b

united.   In 1890 he made extensive travels through the two great off-shoots
of the mother country in North America ; twice crossing the continent from
San Francisco to New York by the Central Pacific Railroad in the United States,
and from Montreal to Vancouver by the Canadian Pacific route ; staying in
many of the important towns on these long tours, in order to obtain
information respecting the working of Federal Institutions as deputed by the
Australian Natives Association, of which he is Honorary Secretary.   The
comparisons in this pamphlet have necessarily to be made from an Australian
standpoint ; but the writer can claim to be also identified with both great
countries in North America, and so to have American sympathies, as some of
his relatives were among the early Palatine citizens in New York, who, on ,
the separation of the United States from England, left their property in that
city to settle as "United Empire Loyalists" on the banks of the St. Lawrence
in Canada.   Heck Hall at the North-Western University, near Chicago,
was named in honour of one of these pioneers, who has been often styled
" The Foundress of American Methodism," the largest Protestant denomination in the United States ; and the building for the Grand Army of the
Republic, in Monclovia, Ohio, is called " The Ruckel Post," after four of
the writer's cousins (brothers), who were killed in the Northern Army
during the battles of the late Civil War.

Most of the facts contained in the present compilation have been gleaned
from a variety of sources too numerous always to acknowledge in a short
pamphlet ; but the writer tenders his thanks to many persons in Australia,
the United States, and Canada, for their kindness in furnishing him with
books to quote from, and otherwise helping him in preparing for the
publication of this work.   Americans are noted not only for great courtesy
to women, but also for their kindness to travellers ; and Australian visitors
are sure of special attention from their Trans-Pacific kinsmen, who have
always evinced much interest in the welfare of Australasia.

A comparison in which many figures have to be used is not as interesting
to the general reader as personal descriptions of what has been seen ; but
the facts condensed in this pamphlet should afford a surer method for
making a proper comparison than any mere general impressions of a traveller
which may often lead to hasty judgments being made on matters brought
under his notice.   The statistics used may have been originally compiled in
the various settlements from different standpoints, but they nevertheless
present a fairer estimate of the respective conditions of the settlements in
Australasia and North America than would statements made without the aid
of figures or other sufficient data.   Although this pamphlet is published
under the auspices of the New South Wales Commission for the Chicago
Exposition, the writer is solely responsible for the statements contained
therein, which however he has endeavoured in each case to verify by the
latest statistics or last census returns when obtainable, and by quoting from
recognised authorities rather than giving unsupported opinions of his own.

In order to do anything like justice to a subject involving so much observation and comparison, the compiler has had to extend the inquiry much further than was proposed by the Commission; nevertheless the comparison made between the United States, Canada, and Australasia is not as complete as could be wished, as the task is one difficult satisfactorily to perform, especially in the compass of a pamphlet. He has, however, endeavoured as far as possible to avoid making any invidious comparisons or entering into questions of party politics, confining himself principally to discussing matters relating to the material progress of Australasia as compared with similar development in the United States and the Dominion of Canada.

The varied information respecting Australia and America compiled in this publication has been cast into paragraphs complete in themselves, and with the subject-matter so compressed as to be suitable as "clippings" for journalistic "copy," besides being in the form adopted for that purpose by the Department of Publicity of the Columbian Exposition. This compilation has not, therefore, been made of that consecutive and classified character as will be found in more systematic treatises on special subjects issued under the direction of the New South Wales Commission, but reference to the index will enable readers to find information on such general matters as are contained in this publication.

Great Britain and the United States of America have now attained a highly satisfactory position in promoting the material and moral advancement of the world, and appear destined to be the greatest nations of the future, especially if a closer union of the English-speaking races can be brought about before the end of the present century. The great industrial progress made by the United States during the last hundred years places her second only to the whole British Empire in that acquired wealth obtained by developing vast natural resources in an intelligent manner. Figures given in the following review show for the Australasian Colonies even a larger gain in the total amount derived from the principal industries than what has been secured in that grand possession of the British Crown, the Dominion of Canada—notwithstanding the nearness of her eastern provinces to the centres of civilization, their larger population, and their much longer occupation by Europeans. It will also be seen from the statistical tables compiled by the writer that the four British colonies situated near the Pacific shores of the Australian Continent exhibit during the last decennial period greater development in some of the principal industries than the four American States on the opposite Pacific slope; and especially is this the case with New South Wales, which has even surpassed in returns from several great sources of wealth those obtained in a most enterprising way by "the Golden State of California."

Although the population of California still continues larger than that of New South Wales, the total annual amount received from the products of the primary industries of agriculture, stock-raising, dairy-farming, mining, forestry, and fisheries is as great in the Australian Colony as in the American State. New South Wales has within its borders live stock estimated at eight times the number of those contained within the boundaries of California; but, on the other hand, the agricultural crops raised in the Pacific State are three times the value of those grown in the Australian Colony. Dairying is, however, carried on to a much greater extent in New South Wales than in California, owing to the recent starting of a number of butter factories with cream separators, a considerable quantity of whose product is exported to the United Kingdom. There has been a much greater return obtained from the redwoods and other timbers in California than from the excellent hardwoods contained in the forests of New South Wales, several of which would be found as useful to Americans for street-paving as Oregon pine is to Australians for house-fitting. The annual value of the mining products is now more in New South Wales than in California, notwithstanding the much larger output of gold in the American State, as in the Australian Colony there are greater amounts obtained from the silver, coal, tin, and copper mines. The number of hands employed in manufacturing industries in New South Wales is larger than in California, although there is a much greater number of Chinamen employed by manufacturers as cheap labour in San Francisco than is the case in Sydney.

Whilst the population of Australasia increased during the last decennial period 34 per cent., the products have increased 45 per cent., and Mr. Mulhall did not over-estimate the surplus earnings of the people of New South Wales when he credited them at £9 13s. 2d. per head per annum against £6 per head in the United States. Mulhall also reckons the wealth per inhabitant in New South Wales at £483, or £133 more than in California; and the amount for the Australian settlement was made up of the following amounts:—Land, £181; cattle, £25; railways, £27; houses, £92; furniture, £46; merchandise, £23; and sundries, £89.

Australasia should afford much more room for the capital and labour of the enterprising emigrant than even the United States, as the British Colonies in the Southern Seas—covering about the same extent of territory—have only four millions of people, whilst there are about sixty million more to be found within the American Union. The Canadian Dominion has a still larger territory than either Australasia or the United States, and contains magnificent prairie land in the north-west territories, but much of the ice-bound provinces near the Polar regions has hitherto offered little attraction for permanent settlement. There are now only about five millions of people resident in Canada, notwithstanding her comparative nearness to Europe, and that over three centuries have elapsed since the formation of the first settlement, as numbers of Canadians have emigrated even from the maritime provinces to more equable climates in British Columbia, the United States, and elsewhere. There is not much difference observable by the traveller between the manners and customs of the Australians, Canadians, and Americans, as they have generally copied the social practices of the mother country; but each people have points of excellence which are most noticeable by an observant visitor. For example, Americans are mainly distinguished for their love of liberty, for their mechanical ingenuity, and for their great enterprise. Canadians are remarkable for the progress they have made since the confederation of the provinces, for their habits of thrift, for their advanced temperance legislation, and for their humane treatment of the Indians. Australians are proud of having during a century successfully colonised the greater part of the Australian Continent and adjacent Pacific islands, of their having solved several important political problems before other countries, and of the methods of enjoying life found so prevalent among all classes of society by means of outdoor sports. Lord Jersey, the Governor of New South Wales, in recent speeches said : " Australians have the cardinal points of a great people—they had freedom and they had honour, they had loyalty and they had energy. Well, with those four cardinal points, he did not know they need fear the future. * * * Anyone travelling through New South Wales as he had done would see not only assets for the present liabilities, but for those likely to be contracted in the future."

In common with most parts of the world Australasia has been suffering from the financial crisis which commenced with the failure of Baring Brothers, the well-known London bankers, through their losses on loans to South American borrowers, and the consequent greater caution exercised by British capitalists has prevented many public works being undertaken to develop the resources of Australia, and also a number of persons from obtaining employment. Another check to the normal prosperity of the Australasian Colonies has been also recently given through inflation principally caused by "land booming," which had been carried on by private syndicates, leading to a similar depression in real estate to that experienced several times in California, when many of the investment societies had to suspend their operations. The public borrowings of English capital by the Australasian colonies amount to over 200 million sterling; but this money has been mainly spent on such reproductive works as railways, tramways, waterworks, docks, &c., which in the United States and Canada are almost wholly in the hands of private trusts, whose principal object is to obtain good dividends for their shareholders rather than, as is the case with the Australian Governments, to open up the country and study the interests of producers in the far interior. Sir George Dibbs, Premier of New South Wales, during his recent visit to England intimated that the sale of· the railways would pay off the public debt of the colony, and that the expenditure of £1 of borrowed British capital on public works increased the value of the immense public estate yet unsold by five times the amount borrowed. The money loaned to the Australasian Colonies was spent in increasing the security to the investor, especially as the railroads are retained by the Governments and the lands adjoining the lines not handed over as free grants to private syndicates as has been the practice in Canada and the United States. In Canada the private railways companies have received bonuses of Government money and land amounting in value to far more than the public debt of New South Wales, and the United States also granted, up to 1880, 110 million acres to private railroad trusts and a subsidy of £10,970,000 and 23 million acres to the Union Pacific Company alone. The Chief Commissioner of Railways in New South Wales has recently shown that of late years there have been great advances made through working the railroads under non-political management, and that " the average price paid on the debentures raised for railway purposes is about 3·85 per cent., and the return this year is about 3·58 per cent.," so that the present lines should soon return the interest on the cost of construction and management. English capitalists have lent private borrowers in Australasia a further sum of nearly £200,000,000, making a total indebtedness to them of about £400,000,000; but the borrowings of the farmers in ten of the United States amounted in 1890 to £666,000,000, and there is now greater difficulty in obtaining money for mortgages in the Western States, even at much higher rates of interest, than is found for Australian loans in the London market, as it will be seen the latter offer a far better security than even that given by the famous prairie farms of America.

Mr. M. G. Mulhall, the eminent statistician, has estimated the national earnings from agriculture, mining, manufactures, internal transport, house rent, commerce, shipping, banking, and professions to be per inhabitant in Australia, £40 2s.; in the United States, £39; and in Canada, £26. He further reckons the wealth in land, cattle, houses, furniture, railways, ships, merchandise, bullion, &c., per inhabitant to be in Australia, £370; in the United States, £210; and in Canada, £196. The annual accumulation per inhabitant has been found by him to reach in Australia, £17 10s.; in the United States, £8 10s.; and in Canada, £5 10s.

It might be urged that the colonies of Australasia and the two great countries in North America cannot be fairly compared, as the Australian continent was unknown until the end of last century, whilst both the United States and Canada have had European settlements on the territories now occupied by them for over three hundred years. Moreover, the comparative nearness of the eastern states of America to the civilized powers of Europe has been a great means of securing an immense population for the United States, which now numbers fifteen times more than that of the Australasian Colonies. The industrial achievements of 4,000,000 of Australians cannot of course be compared in volume with the work performed by 63,000,000 of Americans during the same time, but in proportion to population the pioneer labours of the English people in Australasia will bear favourable comparison with even those of their American kinsmen, and show far better industrial results than those obtained by the settlers in the first hundred years of colonisation of North America.

Sir George Dibbs not only greatly benefited his health through a late trip to Europe, but he rendered important service to his native land in many ways such as, for example, in endeavouring to obtain the authority of the Imperial Government for permitting trust funds to be invested in Colonial stock, in advocating the coinage of silver at the Australian mints, and in taking the preliminary steps for the consolidation of the debt of New South Wales. The London correspondent of a leading Sydney journal states that " the Premier of New South Wales during his stay in England succeeded in removing erroneous impressions which have existed far and wide with regard to the Australasian Colonies and their position. This is amply proved by the very appreciative references to him, and to the task which he has under-taken, that have appeared in the English press from time to time. If further testimony of the same kind were necessary, it could be found in the very warm reception accorded him in London." Sir George Dibbs returned from Europe by way of America, but, owing to Parliament having been convened during his absence and his presence urgently required in the Legislative Assembly, he was unable to stay long either in Canada or the United States.

At the time of the separation of the North American colonies from the mother country their population was about the same as is now found in the Australasian Colonies, but the latter are much more extensive, as they cover 3,169,000 square miles, against 600,000 square miles contained in the original American States. England tried to thrust her past fiscal policy of protec-tion on the American colonies and lost them, so that no attempt is likely to be made to force her present fiscal policy of freetrade on the Australasian Colonies. The protective encouragement of native industries adopted by the United States as a matter of expediency has not prevented them from now surpassing in home production the British Isles, but the present freetrade policy of the mother country has secured for her a very much larger foreign trade amounting to 10,242,000 tons per annum, or 52 per cent. of the mercantile marine and 63 per cent. of the steam tonnage of the world. All the Australasian Colonies have now copied the protective fiscal policies of the United States and Canada, as New South Wales has recently altered her freetrade tariff so as to encourage local manufacturing and agricultural industries. The total growth of population, trade, and revenue in New South Wales during the last decade has been greater than in the neighbouring colony of Victoria, although the latter has had a protective tariff for a quarter of a century. New South Wales, however, has a much larger territory and greater mineral resources than Victoria, and the late Sir Edward Creasy, in his work on the " Constitutions of the Britannic Empîre," made the following prediction after visiting Australia twenty years ago :—" If the Australian Colonies continue to be separate from each other either as colonies or provinces, or as states, it seems very certain that the most powerful of them will be New South Wales."

There can be no doubt but that New South Wales will be able hereafter to support as many people within her borders as are now to be found in a similar extent of territory in North America, as there are immense deposits of both the precious metals and such economic minerals as coal, tin, copper and iron in the formations of the Australian Colony. The extremes of both heat and cold endured during the year by residents in the Eastern States of the Union are not suffered by residents even in the hottest parts of the Colony, where although the temperature is very high in summer the weather is mild in winter, so that a traveller could camp out at night in the bush all the year round with but little injury to health. There are very few deaths from sunstroke in Australia, and a disastrous heat-wave like that which passed over Chicago, New York, and other parts of America, in July, 1892, has never been experienced by residents on the Southern Continent.

As the heroic work of colonization is much the same in Australasia, Canada, and the United States, the inhabitants of these countries should learn more from each other than from the residents in the ancient kingdoms of Europe, in which the conditions of life are quite different to those obtaining in new lands. For example, if Australiahs, combined with their venturous energy, had the hopeful industry of the Americans and the thriftful temperance of the Canadians, Australasia, with her vast natural resources, might soon be made the centre of Greater Britain; and thus fulfil the patriotic prediction of Wentworth, a distinguished native-born statesman, written when a student at the Cambridge University in 1822, and contained in the following apostrophe to the mother country:—

> May all thy glories in another sphere
> Relume, and shine more brightly still than here:
> May this—thy last-born infant—then arise
> To glad thy heart and greet thy parent eyes;
> And Australasia float, with flag unfurl'd,
> A new Britannia in another world.

Australia and America in 1892 : A Contrast.

AUSTRALASIA AND THE UNITED STATES.

ONE of the greatest triumphs of the Nineteenth Century has been the successful colonization of Australasia, away from the terrible conflicts which have devastated other portions of the Globe. The separation of the United States of America from the Mother Country led the British Government wisely to endeavour to counterbalance the loss, by forming a settlement in 1788 on that eastern portion of Australia which had been discovered by Captain Cook eighteen years previously. The founding of British Colonies at the antipodes of the civilized world has been productive of great good to the human race, as Australasia has providentially afforded prosperous homes to millions of people from the over-crowded countries of Europe.

Although the great Earl of Chatham maintained in the House of Lords that the resistance of the American Colonies to Great Britain was justifiable, he erroneously conceived that when the independence of the United States was acknowledged the glory of England would be at an end, and died in the act of denouncing the separation. When, however, the ministry of William Pitt, ten years after his father's death, caused the British flag to be planted on the shores of Port Jackson, fear of the decay of England through not having an extensive colonial empire was obviated, and a new continent prolific in natural resources was added to the British Empire.

The discovery of New South Wales by Captain Cook in the year 1770, therefore, opportunely supplied on the loss of the American Colonies a new outlet for British population and manufactures, and also another arena for philanthropic experiments in criminal reformation in lieu of the plantations in America which had been long used for that purpose. If the United States had not severed their connection with England it is reasonable to suppose that Australasia would still have been in an almost primeval condition, as the terrible difficulties of her early settlement could not have been well overcome by any European nation other than the one so celebrated for her successes in colonization. It is, therefore, meet that Australia, the youngest daughter of England, should in an especial manner be found congratulating her American sister at the International Exhibition to commemorate the anniversary of the discovery of America.

Four centuries have passed since Spain made conquests in South America, and but one century has elapsed since Great Britain founded the first colony in Australia, so that Oceana is now styled " The New World" as America

A

was in the days of Columbus. The comparative nearness of America to Europe gives that country a great attraction over Australia as a place of settlement, inasmuch as the immigrant to the Antipodes has to traverse 12,000 miles, and unless most enterprising he is generally found choosing the nearer country for his new home. Australia has, however, the much longer experience gained by America in colonization to profit by, whilst that country in her early history had only the precedents of the nations of the old world to follow. Both countries have made wonderful progress, but there was little settlement in America during her first hundred years compared with what has been accomplished in Australia in the same period of time. The history of the early conquest of South America, principally by military adventurers, who, to gratify their desire "for plunder, for power, and for extended rule," sacrificed millions of lives, affords a strange contrast to the more recent peaceful occupation of Australia by the British race. Australians, however, cannot but be.more interested in the progress of the two English-speaking commonwealths in North America than in the settlements in South America, which were colonies belonging to foreign powers until they recently adopted republican forms of government. Canada and the United States can be rightfully claimed as the elder sisters of Australia, the offspring of one common mother whose example and traditions they may.be said to have invariably followed.

Neither the Commonwealth of Utopia as sketched by Sir Thomas More about the time that America was discovered, nor the Oceana of James Harrington which was dedicated to Cromwell as the Lord Protector of the Commonwealth, may ever have an existence in the way outlined by these writers. Nevertheless, many of their ideals of what would be best for the human race have been realised in the three British commonwealths which have been firmly established in modern times on the American and Australian continents. The term "commonwealth" was adopted at the National Australian Convention of 1891, and suggests the democratic idea of the greatest good to the greatest number, in contrast with government under privileged classes such as obtains in the kingdoms or Europe. The designation of Commonwealth, though frequently used by Shakespeare, was discarded on the restoration of Charles II., and has therefore only come again into use in modern times as part of the proposed name for " United Australia."

The Englishman in Australia or America cannot well realise the feeling of the native born in either country who has never seen the lands of which his parents speak. The Australian for example listens from childhood to descriptions of many localities celebrated in the history of the mother land, and a feeling of awe is generally instilled into his mind regarding the historic spots of the old world. When having arrived at maturity, he is often seized with a desire to visit the most famous places in the Mother Country ; but until late years he has been almost debarred from doing so by the distance. Happily, the increased speed of the floating palaces now crossing the seas between Australia and Europe has to a great extent conquered the difficulty in the long ocean voyage which must be undertaken by travellers from the Southern Hemisphere. The small travelling expense now incurred compared with former times enables the tourist to take a trip to England at a less cost than would be paid by an American visiting the same country not many years ago. Owing to the substitution of steam for sailing power the Australian after arriving in the United Kingdom may stay there a couple of months, and return by way of America in about the same time that it used to take vessels in the early days of the colonies to make a single voyage from Australia to Europe. Although the Australian desires to see the ancient cities and magnificent scenery of the Continent of Europe, his chief associations are naturally clustered round the British Isles as the home of his forefathers ; and, like numbers of Americans, he visits with delight the grand cathedrals and ruined castles ever memorable in the history of the Anglo-Saxon and Celtic races, contained as Shakespeare says, in "This blessed spot, this earth, this realm, this England !" The wealthy Australian, if he can stand the English climate—whose winters are most trying even to the returned Briton—is often as partial to living in London as the retired American is in Paris, though this action cannot always be deprecated as being unpatriotic ; and there has been consequently an agitation in Australia for an absentee tax to be levied on those who derive income from property in the Colonies but spend their money elsewhere with little benefit to the country which supplies their wealth.

Although the first aspirations of an Australian are to visit the mother land, his next instinct is to see her great offspring in America, whose history and resources bear a strong resemblance to those of his native country. Australia is like a younger daughter who, although naturally desiring chiefly to meet her mother after a long absence from home, cannot but have strong affection for an elder sister who left the family circle about the time she was born, and whose example she may desire to follow when arrived at sufficient maturity, if considered more conducive to her best interests than remaining as she is. The meeting of Great Britain, the United States, Canada, and Australia at the Columbian Exhibition should partake, therefore, of the character of a birthday re-union in a family who by force of circumstances have been widely separated, rather than that of an assemblage of nations with no strong bond of blood or relationship.

To better illustrate to visitors to the Columbian Exhibition at Chicago the present condition and future prospects of the Australasian Colonies, it has been therefore deemed desirable, in the compilation of this short review, to consider only the English-speaking settlements in North America and Australasia as being three sister commonwealths who owe their existence to one mother land. The growing commercial and social intercourse between the United States, Canada, and Australasia, particularly between San Francisco, Vancouver, and Sydney, should receive a much greater impetus in the Columbian Exposition from the display of the natural products and manufactures of these countries, especially as it has been recently predicted by Mr. A. S. White, the Secretary of the Royal Scottish Geographical Society, "that once the Isthmus of Panama is cut, or otherwise ceases to offer obstacles to shipping, the stream of human progress will partly become diverted into the Pacific, and that the political development of the States on its shores will receive an impulse such as the world has never before experienced."

The Australian traveller finds in every part of America numbers of persons who have relatives in Australasia, owing to part of a family leaving the mother country for the United States or Canada and others preferring to make their home in Australasia. There are, therefore, hundreds of thousands of persons in Australasia and America who are much interested in the welfare of both countries. Though separated by the waters of the Pacific Ocean thoughts of these distant relatives no doubt rise in each other's minds, and a desire to know how their kinsmen are progressing in the land in which each has cast his lot.

Australians travelling to visit the home of their ancestors are reminded of the great nation to which they belong by seeing her outposts in the Pacific Ocean, Indian Ocean, Red Sea and the Mediterranean Sea; and cannot but feel proud of belonging to such an extended Empire, which has been well described by the Earl of Onslow, when Governor of New Zealand, in the following words :—"There is one thing which I think your Governor should remind you of, and that is of the extent and power of Imperial England, of the Empire which possesses the most extensive territory, and the largest population in the world, the greatest wealth, and the greatest commerce of modern times—an empire which conducts under one flag one third of the trade of the Globe, and which waves that flag over every sea and one-eighth of its dry land, while the Queen's sceptre rules over one-fifth of the people of the earth—and yet an empire held together by bonds looser than any that bind together any other empires of to-day, or that have ever united an empire in the past, bonds which can hardly be defined, and which depend almost entirely on sentiment, with a dash of self-interest."

The discovery of America by Columbus inflamed other navigators with an ardent desire to discover that other great continent in the Indian Ocean or the South Pacific, in the existence of which so many of them firmly believed. The Spaniards and Portuguese appear to have led the way, and amongst the most noteworthy explorers was Alonza Mendaña de Neyva, a Spaniard, and his pilot, Fernandes de Quiros, who sailed from Callao, in Peru, in 1568, enduring great hardships, and who, like Columbus, died from anxiety and disappointment caused by the neglect of the Government. Quiros presented a memorial to the King of Spain, in which he enumerated twenty-three islands which he had discovered, besides certain parts of a country which he believed was a portion of the Australian mainland, but his account of these important countries was received with indifference. Dutch explorers made many attempts to ascertain the extent and richness of the great south land, and produced testimony of having landed on the shores of Australia in March, 1606, a few days before Quiros discovered the land which some contend was part of the Australian Continent, and that the crew of the *Duyfhen* were the first Europeans to touch Australian soil. French maps in the British Museum and at the War Office in Paris show that Manoel Godinho de Eredia, a Portuguese, discovered Australia in 1531, all the maps being dated 1555, and the author being the renowned Provençal navigator, Guillaume le Testu. Of English navigators, Dampier was the first to visit the shores of Australia in 1688, and in that memorable year described it in his journal as an island or main continent joining neither Asia, Africa, nor America.

The discovery and exploration of Australia has been accompanied with almost as much romance as that which surrounded the colonization of America ; and authentic accounts of the voyages to Oceana of the early Spanish, Portuguese, Dutch, French, and English navigators, if compiled from the national archives of their respective countries, would be found most interesting reading. The interior of Australia has been now travelled over by gallant explorers, who not deterred by many privations have so opened up the way that enterprising settlers have quickly followed their tracks. Leichhardt and Kennedy, in New South Wales, and Burke and Wills, in Victoria, are examples of enterprising men who led exploring expeditions across the Australian Continent, but unfortunately perished in the wilderness, when trying to open up an unknown country for the benefit of their fellow men.

Neither Australia nor Canada may be able to sustain as dense a population as the United States, owing to the large ice-fields of the one and the tropical heat to be found in parts of the other, but the conditions of life, especially as to longevity, are shown to be as favourable in the southern colonies as in the settlements on the eastern shores of North America. Wide-spread malee scrubs in the interior of Australia now under cultivation were once classed as sterile, and other mistakes made in estimating the capabilities of the soil. Boundless plains stated by explorers to be unfit even for the support of sheep are now often found waving with crops of wheat and corn.

In a recent work on the Physical Geography and Climatology of New South Wales, Mr. H. C. Russell, C.M.G., Government Astronomer, states, with regard to some of the supposed waterless plains of the interior of Australia, which are now being successfully tapped for artesian wells : "The Darling in order to carry off one-tenth of the rainfall for its district should flow 200 ft. wider and 100 ft. deep all the year through. As the river does not approach such dimensions even in summer-time, and sometimes stops running altogether, in flood-time it is clear that the water must to a large extent sink into the ground to flow at some lower level." On the question of the climate of the Colony Mr. Russell shows that from its geographical position, being beyond the limits of tropical heat and yet within the influence of effects from the trade winds, it may expect a most enjoyable climate ; yet Australia generally is credited in works of reference with heat in excess of that due to her latitude. This, he thinks, may be due to a habit of one of her early explorers, "who carried a thermometer and carefully published all the high, and none of the low, readings he got, until fortunately for the Colony the thermometer was broken, and the unfair register stopped." Even Sydney is usually credited to the present day with a temperature about three degrees higher than the true mean—66·2 instead of 62·9—although meteorological observations have been taken and published here for 40 years. Another crude error which Mr. Russell points out is that of inverting Australia on the map of Europe and inferring that the climate is as hot in corresponding latitudes. The temperature of Dubbo corresponds to that of Rome, Bourke to Messina, Toulon to Sydney, Nice to Mudgee, Florence to Inverell, Central France to Bathurst Plains. In the United Kingdom, London corresponds to Bombala, Edinburgh to Kiandra, Plymouth to Cooma, Swansea to Queanbeyan, and the Midland counties to Monaro Plains.

America and Australia, "the heirs of all the ages," are greatly indebted to Europe for their development in civilization, and especially to England for their political institutions, jurisprudence, training in self-government, and for an intellectual inheritance in science, literature, and the arts. Mere material prosperity after all is not the greatest good for the individual or the nation, and the beautiful should be cultivated along with the useful. Both America and Australia have still, therefore, a great deal to learn from the ancient store-houses of art and philosophy to be found in Europe. Although Australia especially has the climate of Athens and Rome, she cannot as yet lay claim to the prestige of great artistic development ; but her bright natural surroundings should enable her hereafter to vie in the fine arts even with the great classic republics of ancient times. Emerson has however wisely said : " I have no expectation that any men will read history aright who thinks that what was done in a remote age, by men whose names have resounded far, has any deeper sense than what he is doing to-day."

A comparison between the relative progress of America and Australasia at the present time may provoke emulation and afford room for congratulation at the great material prosperity given to the two greatest countries founded in modern times. Although the progress of Australia has been retarded by her distance from the great centres of civilization and other circumstances attending early settlement, still her present proud position in the van of British colonies should afford food for grateful reflection.

As the other colonies of the Australasian group are mainly offshoots from New South Wales, it is reasonable that in every review their progress should be noted in connection with that of the parent settlement. The colonies of New South Wales, Tasmania, Western Australia, South Australia, New Zealand, Victoria, and Queensland occupy an area considerably over 3,000,000 square miles, and are nearly equal in extent to the territory now possessed either by the United States or the Dominion of Canada. The population of the Australasian Colonies at the end of 1892 will number about 4,000,000, being about the same as that of the residents in the United States at the time the independence of that country was gained. The trade of the Australasian Colonies is, however, nearly twenty times greater than that of the American States when they declared their independence; and shows the much greater commercial intercourse between nations during the present century obtained by the extensive use of large steamships instead of small sailing vessels. Amongst British provinces the trade of the Australasian Colonies with the United Kingdom is 7½ per cent. of the whole, being only second in importance to that of India, which was 9 per cent., and amounts to more than double that of Canada, which only reached 2¾ per cent., although parts of the latter have been settled by Europeans three times as long, her cities are much nearer the great centres of trading operations, and she has a million more inhabitants. The prosperity of the Australasian Colonies is greatly due to the large area of excellent pastoral and agricultural land, accumulated wealth, invested capital, home manufactures, and foreign trade, which have made the average wealth of the Australian to be greater than that of the inhabitant of any other country. The revenue of the several Governments for the year 1891 was £29,922,987, being more than three times as great as that for Canada, notwithstanding her much larger population. The exports of Australian produce and manufactures to the United Kingdom averaged in 1890 £13 18s. 2d. per inhabitant. These exports consist principally of the produce of the pastoral, mining, and agricultural industries in Australasia, such as wool, tallow, hides, gold, silver, tin, copper, coal, wheat, meat, &c. During 1890 the Colonies conducted a trade between themselves, Great Britain, British possessions outside Australasia, and foreign states, amounting to £133,801,164, or £64,799,178 for exports and £68,001,986 for imports, being an average of £35 10s. 3d. per head of population. The "Statesman's Year-book" shows that in the same year the trade of Canada was only one-third that of Australasia, being £19,879,962 for exports and £25,039,365 for imports, but the trade between the provinces of the Dominion is not counted in the same way as the intercolonial trade of the separate colonies of Australasia. The external trade of the Australasian Colonies with other countries, however, increased from £35,061,282 in 1861 to £75,223,727 in 1890, of which latter amount 74·9 per cent. was with the United Kingdom, 7·3 per cent. was with British possessions outside Australasia, and 7·83 per cent. was with Foreign States. Of late years Canada has conducted a larger import and export trade with the neighbouring United States than with Great Britain. The trade of Australasia with the United Kingdom amounted in 1890 to £56,366,811, being three times as much as the trade of Canada. During the last thirty years the trade of Great Britain with

North America did not develop to anything like the same extent as with Australasia during the same period, so that the young southern colonies have proved of far more commercial value to the Mother Country than the older possessions in North America. The following figures shew the value of the export of domestic produce per inhabitant in the principal countries of the world, and give a comparative idea of the wealth contained in the British colonies of Oceana:—Australasia, £13 8s. 3d.; United States, £2 17s. 9d.; Canada, £3 12s. 7d.; United Kingdom, £7; France, £4 17s. 9d.; Germany, £3 7s. 2d.; Austria and Hungary, £1 11s. 1d.; Italy, £1 4s. 7d.; Argentine Republic, £7 0s. 4d.; Belgium, £9 11s. 6d.; and Chili, £5 10s. 5d.

The present condition and resources of the Australasian Colonies are now attracting great notice in Europe and America, as many writers in Great Britain have recently called attention to the large public debts incurred by the Colonial Governments, which it is alleged are altogether out of proportion to those of other countries. But the fact is overlooked that the amounts borrowed from British capitalists secure good interest, and most of the money has been spent in buying English manufactures, such as railway plant, so that since the difficulty of obtaining loans there has been a large falling off in the imports from Great Britain. These writers also in their comparisons have not sufficiently taken into account the fact that the money borrowed has been principally expended on public works of a reproductive character, and that the state railways alone if sold should pay off all these liabilities.

In a paper read by Mr. R. Giffen, the eminent English Statistician, " On the Rise and Growth of the British Empire," before the Australasian Association for the Advancement of Science, held at Hobart in 1892, he showed that Australian capital wealth is increasing at a much greater rate than the capital wealth of England. He endorsed the estimate of private wealth of Australasia in the same way as that of the United Kingdom to be 1,175 millions sterling, although of course the amount of the growth when compared to that of England is but small.

There is no doubt that much of the wonderful progress in material wealth made in Australasia is due to a progressive policy which has led to incurring a large public debt for improvements so as to properly develop great natural resources, which will doubtless hereafter amply repay the expenditure incurred. The first half-century of Australian colonization was marked by much caution when administered as a Crown colony, and therefore comparatively little progress could be made in opening up the country, but with the increase of population, and under responsible government, the work of settlement has been conducted in a more enterprising manner. Much of the money borrowed in the London market has been expended in England on material required for public and private works, which expenditure has greatly benefited British manufacturers, and has caused a considerable trade to be carried on between the two countries which otherwise would not have been the case. As the Australasian Colonies have immense assets there can be no fear of their not being able to meet any of the monetary engagements entered into, which unfortunately has not been the case in South America and some other foreign countries, where the money of British bond-holders has not been spent to the same extent in erecting public works. England gets one-fifth of her income from outside investments, but British capitalists are also now found chary in speculating in American securities owing to the silver legislation of the United States, so that any excess of American exports that are not paid for by imports from Europe may be met by the price of surrendered American securities without drawing to any great extent on Australian gold, which is usually shipped in exchange by way of San Francisco.

Residents in Europe as a whole know but little of the resources and capabilities of the Australasian Colonies, but this is not altogether to be wondered at considering that complaints have been made that to them even America is comparatively an unknown country, and that absurd mistakes are often made respecting her geography, politics, and customs. For example, the general impression has gone abroad that the interior of the continent of Australasia is one great desert, owing perhaps to misleading descriptions on the early maps, in the same way as thirty years ago in America the country on which the fine city of Denver now stands was considered "a sage bush wilderness only fit for the habitation of Indians." The Great North West, whose rich prairies are now so highly prized by Canadians, was once also stated by travellers to be then "only fit for a preserve for fur-bearing animals."

A review of the productions of colonial literature would show that Australia numbers within her domain many persons of high intellectual power and literary taste. In an age when the late Sir William Hamilton lamented that modern universities teach professional and ignore liberal sciences, there have been men in Australia for whom speculation and the gold fields had no charm, and who in the height of excitement during their first discovery could not be lured from studying the muses and the liberal arts. Australian poets have striven to sing the songs of their native land, and the philosophic De Quincey had a follower who with something of his master's power had unfortunately a worse frailty than even that of the opium-eater. The foundation stone of an Australian literature has been laid, but it yet remains for the poet and the word-painter so to catch the ideal conceptions of the inhabitants and scenery as to give an individuality to the building. A remonstrance uttered by Emerson is applicable as much to Australia as it was to America : " Why should these words Asia, Athenian, Roman, England, so tingle in our ears. Let us feel that where the heart is there the muses, there the gods sojourn, and not in any geography of fame." As may naturally be expected most of the literary men who have as yet published works on colonial subjects came from Great Britain, but the writings of some of the Australian native-born have also secured praise from leading English reviewers. Major Dane, Mr. Gilbert Parker, and other well known American orators have delivered many lectures in Australia on history, literature, and art, and these addresses did much towards promoting a love for these studies among the colonists who heard them.

The pursuit of learning art, and science is encouraged in Australia by many literary and professional societies, which in some instances are affiliated or correspond with similar institutions in the Mother Country. Several of these Australian societies hold a periodical congress at which papers are read by representatives from the different colonies, showing the progress made in the studies in which they are most interested.

Australians, like Americans, are much more prone to travel than the European born, so that railways and steamers in Australasia are generally crowded with holiday excursionists, not only from the towns through the country districts and to neighbouring colonies but also to the Mother Country, where representatives of the sister continents often meet when inspecting the picture and sculpture treasures deposited in rare old historic buildings, only to be found in England and on the continent of

Europe. Australia has had the benefit of the experience in the applied arts gained by all other countries during many centuries, as well as the use of great inventions which are the outgrowth of mechanical science in past times. The results of the great expansion of commercial intercourse, combined with law and order in government, has been specially inherited by Australia and North America from the mother land.

Australia has been hitherto spared the hard discipline suffered by the nations of Europe in terrible wars, pestilence, and famine, but there is no doubt that the struggle for existence will hereafter become more intense as the competition of other countries is felt. The evils endured by Australians from droughts, strikes, and over-speculation have not been worse in the Colonies than similar calamities in America and Europe, which occurred at about the same time. The late miners' strike at the largest silver mine in the world in Broken Hill has been peaceful compared with the outrages at similar strikes at the iron mines in Pittsburg and Idaho.

Owing to scattered populations and other causes there is not the same regular attendance at churches in Australasia as in England, or even in the long-settled States of America, but when the Colonies are older there is no doubt that a more devout spirit will be developed amongst the colonial youths who now are often carried away by the secularism of the times. There is no State Church in Australia and consequently no agitation against the payment of tithes in New South Wales as in the principality after which it is named. Most of the Colonies have been visited from time to time by leading clergymen of the various denominations in Great Britain, and colonial representatives often take a trip to Europe, so that the churches are kept well in touch with those "at home" on all religious questions of the day.

It has been written that "it is a good thing for a man to bear the yoke in his youth," and there can be no doubt than the training necessary for the individual is often required by the nation, but Australia has been singularly exempt from the trials that have sadly afflicted other communities. Australia has had no bitter experience like that of the United States in connection with slavery, except it be a once terrible legacy from England in the Imperial convict system, which however the colonists fought so manfully against that it was discontinued fifty years ago, long before three-fourths of the present generation of Australians were born. The political struggles of the early settlers in New South Wales are now only history to the present generation, who happily live in the golden era of colonial life. The industrial depressions which occasionally pass over the Australian Colonies cannot be considered unmixed calamities, as often good has arisen from them to those who are able to learn from past failures.

Education in Australia and America received considerable attention from the earliest days of settlement, when in both countries besides the elementary schools there were founded grammar and other superior schools, principally in connection with Christian denominations who believed that instruction in secular subjects should be associated with religious training. Both America and Australia are now in some respects in advance of the Mother Country through having complete systems of education leading from the primary school to the University, including the recent addition of kindergarten training for young children, high-schools to prepare for matriculation, and technical schools for apprentices, which have made the level of intelligence amongst all classes of the people equal to the most advanced countries in Europe.

If America had not been colonized by European nations sending their fleets across the Atlantic Ocean, much of that continent might have been taken possession of by Asiatic hordes, who, settling on the Pacific Coast, would be able greatly to retard the progress of Christianity and civilisation in the Western Archipelago, which would have been a great calamity to the world, and especially so to Australasia.

It has been said by an American author that, "as the commerce of the world originated in Asia, was carried to Africa, and thence to Europe, and from Europe to America, the movement can go no further westward, for on the other side of the Pacific is China, which has successfully resisted every attempt of the European to encroach upon her domains." It appears, however, to have been overlooked by this writer that Australia only lies on the other side of the Pacific to America, and that the southern continent is the last link in the chain to complete the circle of civilisation over the world. It is found that the course of the progress of civilisation, like that of the sun, is from the lands of the east to the lands of the west; from the eastern shores of the Mediterranean to the countries of Europe, from Europe to America, from America to Oceana, and thence across the Indian Ocean to the starting point in Asia, "where Delos rose and Phœbus sprang, where burning Sappho lived and sang."

The late Rev. Dr. Lang, to whose memory as a patriot and statesman a public statue has been erected in Sydney, visited the United States from Australia in 1840, and he was so much interested in what he saw that on his return he wrote a work on "Religion and Education in America," in which he defended the separation of Church and State or the voluntary system against the attacks of Captain Marryat. Dr. Lang again visited the Union more than a quarter of a century afterwards, and noted the won-derful advance made during that period, to which he constantly referred in his political speeches. He was so greatly impressed by what he observed in America that it led him in 1851 to publish a work entitled "Freedom and Independence for the Golden Lands of Australia." In this work, which reached a second edition under the title of "The Coming Event," the sentiments of another Presbyterian divine, the Rev. Dr. Witherspoon, who signed the Declaration of Independence, are quoted by Dr. Lang "as to the inherent and indefeasible right of any community, such as a British colony, able and willing to sustain and protect itself, to declare its entire freedom and independence." Dr. Lang, with regard to the probable glorious future of Australia, wrote : "In short, as we are so near the first meridian in Australia as to be almost equally accessible from the eastward as from the westward, for we are actually the ' Far West ' in California, I think we may adopt for Australia, with a slight change of numerals merely, the beautiful lines which the celebrated Bishop Berkeley applied upwards of a century ago to America, not knowing that there was still another Empire of British origin to arise in the world much farther west :—

> "Westward the course of Empire takes its way,
> The first *fire* acts already passed ;
> A *sixth* shall close the drama with a day,
> Time's noblest offspring is the last."

An English University lecturer, in a recent work, says :—" Australia, unlike Canada or the United States, is bound to become a great maritime power, and her destiny as a trading and colonising nation will, and must be, something like our own, possibly on a grander and a vaster scale. She will most certainly regard the island spangled archipelago of the East as her heritage. Hers will be the task of penetrating the mysterious secrets of the

Antartic circle. Hers beyond all doubt the ultimate suzerainty of New Guinea." The position of the continent of Australia and the adjacent islands is referred to in a verse of an Australian Marsellaise :—

> Where is the Austral Fatherland ?
> Behold it here, that mighty land !
> Where Tasman's island sleeps at ease,
> Far north towards the Timor seas ;
> From the great Barrier's coral shoals,
> To where the Indian Ocean rolls ;
> From coral sea to ocean sand—
> That is the Austral Fatherland.

There are many groups of productive islands in the Pacific Ocean which would have remained in a state of nature but for the enterprise of Australians, and they have therefore the greatest right to carry on a commerce with the natives, whom they have raised from cannibalism to comparative civilisation. Fifty years ago Sir George Grey, then Governor of New Zealand, was constantly urging upon the Colonial Office in London the desirability of having an English protectorate over the South Pacific archipelago before other powers had taken possession of any of the groups. England and the United States might then have agreed to undertake a joint protectorate of the islands nearest to Australia and America respectively, making the equator the dividing-line of their several jurisdictions, and many complications with European Powers and the natives could thus have been obviated.

The Australasian Colonies contain within their borders an immense territory, three times the area of the British possessions in India, about the same extent as the United States of America, and not much less than the provinces constituting the Dominion of Canada, asserted by Mackenzie, in his "History of America," "in respect of extent to be the noblest colonial possessions over which any nation has ever exercised dominion," and as prophesied by Lord Dufferin: "within which one of the most intelligent and happiest off-sets of the Englishman is destined to develop into a proud and great nation." The seven Australasian Colonies cover an area of 3,076,768 square miles; of which New South Wales possesses 310,700 ; Victoria, 87,884 ; South Australia, 903,425 ; Queensland, 668,224 ; Western Australia, 979,920 ; New Zealand, 104,235 ; and Tasmania, 26,375. The Fijian Islands, ceded to the British Crown in 1874, contain an additional 7,740 square miles, but this group and other similar British possessions in Oceana are not counted in the area given for the Australasian Colonies. The great island-continent of Australia alone extends over 2,946,953 square miles, the greatest breadth from north to south being 1,965 miles ; greatest length from east to west about 2,600 miles, with a coast line of about 8,850 miles.

Dr. W. P. Cullen, M.P., lecturing before the Australian Natives Association, in Sydney, on the "Federation of the Australasian Colonies," compared their extent with those of the federated states and provinces of North America in the following words :—" People constantly speak of the United States of America as being a larger area than Australia, forgetting that over 500,000 square miles of their territory consists of the frozen wilderness of Alaska. This large tract of country, bigger than New South Wales, Victoria, and New Zealand put together, is almost uninhabitable, being situated some degrees further north than the northermost point of Scotland, and it is severed from the United States by the entire breadth of the Canadian

Dominion. It was only purchased by the States some years back as a dependency from Russia, and has neither part nor lot in her Federal Government. If we exclude Alaska, the United States are smaller in area than Australia with Tasmania. Again, of British North America a tract of nearly 2,000,000 square miles is out in the cold with Alaska, and the balance, comprising the whole of the provinces and districts of the Dominion of Canada, is not two-thirds the size of Australia. United Australia would be considerably larger than European Russia. It will be the largest extent of habitable land united under one free Legislature in the world, with the exception of the large territory of Brazil, and of course excepting the British Empire itself. As to the size of its separate provinces, there are now, and even after the subdivision of Queensland, South Australia, and Western Australia will probably continue to be, immensely larger on the average than the separate States of the American Union. New South Wales alone is almost as large as the original thirteen States of America put together. Texas is the largest of the present States of America, and New South Wales is larger than Texas with half-a-dozen of the smaller States thrown in. This one Colony is nearly five times the average size of the present States of the American Union ; compared with the provinces of the Canadian Dominion, it immensely exceeds them all in area, excepting British Columbia ; compared with the entire Confederation of the German Empire, New South Wales is about half as large again."

Although some of the rivers of New South Wales are subject to occasional floods in the winter time, yet there has never been such a great catastrophe as those which have recently occurred in Kansas and Missouri, when four towns were destroyed and fifty persons fatally injured, with an estimated damage to property of three-quarters of a million sterling. Gales of wind also sometimes blow fiercely on the Australian coast, but there is nothing on the interior plains at all comparable in the damage inflicted on life and property to the blizzards and snow storms which have been cabled as having swept in 1892 the prairies of America.

The Murray River, running along the borders of New South Wales, Victoria, and South Australia, is only surpassed in length by the Missouri, Mississippi, and the Amazon in America, and the Who-hang-ho in China. The Murray, and other colonial rivers are bound to play an important part in the agricultural development of Australia, as the volume of their waters is now running to waste in the ocean, and large quantities can, by locking, be readily conserved for irrigation purposes.

As the waters of the Pacific Ocean roll between the shores of America and Australia, it should be the mission of both countries to make it true to its name as an emblem of peace, by preventing hostile fleets from meeting on its waters and staining it with human blood, as has been the case with the other great waterways of the world.

Owing to its important geographical position on the mainland of Australia, Sydney has been, ever since the commencement of the present century, the central depôt from which operations have been carried on for civilizing the inhabitants of Polynesia. The natives of many groups of islands have accepted the truths of Christianity and benefited by the teaching of the missionaries, not only in religion but also in the industrial arts. There is a considerable trade carried on between Australia and the South Sea Islands, such as the Fijian, Samoan, and Loyalty Groups. Although New Zealand and Tasmania are the only islands enumerated as belonging to the Australasian Colonies, the Fijian Group and British New Guinea have been annexed to the British Crown, and are governed by administrators appointed by the English Government. The Governor of New South Wales is charged with the care of Norfolk Island, on which the descendants of the mutineers of the " Bounty " reside, and of Lord Howe Island, both of which were taken possession of by the Colonial Government at the end of the last century. The arrangements made by the English, American, and German Governments for securing law and order among the natives of the Samoan Group were especially needed, as these islands, from their position in the Pacific Ocean, make suitable coaling stations on the mail route between America and Australia.

Captain Cook discovered the Sandwich Islands, "The Paradise of the Pacific," and was killed there by the natives in 1779, and ever since that time much interest has been taken in its affairs by Australians. Honolulu was often visited by whaling vessels from Sydney in the early days, and of late by miners on their way to the Californian goldfields on their first discovery, and many other travellers to America by the monthly mail steamer from Australia. The late Sir Charles St. Julian (ex-Chief Justice of Fiji) when Hawaiian Consul at Sydney greatly assisted in the preparation of a constitution for the proper government of these islands.

The Hawaiian Islands trade annually amounts to from £900,000 to £1,000,000 in imports, and about twice the amounts in exports principally to the United States,. Honolulu is on the direct mail route between San Francisco or Vancouver and Australia, and will be a convenient point of call for steamers to the Colonies. It is very desirable that cordial relations should always exist between the inhabitants of Hawaii, Australia, Canada, and the United States, especially as there has been intercourse between the inhabitants of all these countries from the earliest days. The large number of Chinese in the Sandwich Islands, and the business transacted by them, renders them formidable competitors with the white races, whom in time they may supplant on the extinction of the native race, now fast dying out through leprosy and other diseases introduced by foreigners. Considering the well-known keen business talents of the American trader, it is surprising to find that much of the business in Honolulu is conducted by Chinese shopkeepers, whose influence has not been much checked by the importation for that purpose of other races.

The area of the Fiji Islands, which were ceded to the British Crown in 1874 is 7,740 square miles. In 1891 the population was 121,180, of whom 2,036 were Europeans, 105,800 Fijians, 7,468 immigrant Indian coolies, 2,267 Polynesian immigrant labourers, and 2,219 natives of Rotuma. It has been suggested to replace the Indian Coolie labour, which is not popular with the planters, with Japanese who are crowded out from Japan, or Kanakas from the other South Sea Islands. The public debt of Fiji was £248,989 ; but there has been of late years a surplus of revenue over expenditure. The imports amounted to £253,049, and the exports were nearly as much again, or £474,334. Fiji is fully capable of becoming the tropical fruit market of the Australasian Colonies, and it now exports to Sydney large quantities of bananas and pineapples. The tea-plant seems to thrive in these islands. Excellent samples of sea island cotton have been grown in Fiji, and if there was a failure of the American crops the staple could be readily produced there. Specimens of tobacco leaf will be shown at the Chicago Exhibition. The number of persons attending worship in the native churches in 1890 was at the Wesleyan Mission 103,829, and at the Roman

Catholic Mission 10,402. The revenue of Fiji for 1891 was £71,249 and the expenditure £60,973, leaving a surplus of £10,276 which goes to a sinking fund to repay the debt and to refund a deduction of salary to officers made during a temporary depression a few years ago.

The United States have considerable interests in the Pacific Ocean, especially at the Sandwich Islands and Samoa, in the promotion of whose welfare they have taken an active part. The American Government has hitherto abstained from annexing any of the islands in Polynesia, but merely obtained sites for coaling stations on a few of the most important. European Powers have undertaken to protect or annex most of the other islands in the Pacific Ocean such for example as Fiji, now under the protectorate of the English, and New Caledonia which is occupied as a penal settlement by the French.

During the last decade the portion of New Guinea not annexed to Holland has been divided between Great Britain and Germany. The Dutch hold the part of the island nearest to their own possessions in Java, whilst the English secured that portion which is situated very near the Australian Continent. The occupation of New Guinea by the British was hastened through the action of Queensland in taking possession even without Imperial authority, and in 1888 the Australian Colonies agreed to pay £15,000 yearly towards its government. Three different Protestant missions are now in operation on that island, under the direction of missionary agencies in Sydney. Bishop Virjus, of the Roman Catholic Mission, recently succumbed to the effects of the malarial fever so prevalent in New Guinea. Chili, Peru, China, and Japan have seaboards on the Pacific Ocean, and therefore have a common interest in its navigation with the United States, Canada, and Australia. The trade of China is, however, less than half, and Chili about a quarter that of Australasia, whilst the commerce of Peru and Japan is comparatively small.

A seizure in Behring Strait of Canadian and American sealing vessels by Russian gunboats, shows that the latter power considers this vast expanse of waters a closed sea, even though the United States now owns the opposite shore of Alaska. and this circumstance evidences the dangers to the peace of the Pacific which may be apprehended from the existence of a great arsenal there. Besides England and America, Germany and France have possessions in Polynesia, and Russia an arsenal at Vladivistok. It is highly desirable that arrangements should be made by the Powers interested, so that the peace of the Pacific Ocean may be preserved from European and Asiatic strifes, by the adoption of a policy similar to that first promulgated by President Munro, "of neither entangling ourselves in the broils of Europe nor suffering the Powers of the Old World to interfere with the affairs of the New." Complications have often occurred in several of the groups of islands in Polynesia, owing to there being no proper understanding between the various Governments concerned; as, for example, in the matter of selling fire-arms and intoxicating liquors to the natives, a thing which is prohibited by the English Government, but carried on by traders belonging to other foreign States, shewing the necessity for a definite protectorate being arranged, as has been done by the three treaty Powers in Samoa, who have recently informed King Malietoa that assistance will be given him by their warships to execute warrants of the Supreme Court. President Harrison has recently accepted England's proposal inhibiting the sale of arms and spirits in the islands of the Pacific, and Australians are much pleased with his action in the matter, as it should remove much of the present unsatisfactory position of British traders and settlers in the New Hebrides.

The French followed the British in colonizing North America, and took pos·session of the valley of the Mississippi, and in that age were excellent colonists, though since not so successful in Algeria, Tahiti, Africa and Tonquin. France lost her colonial interests owing to entanglement in Continental conflicts, though in 1789 the imports to the French colonies were valued at £1,250,000. France has been desirous of securing extensive colonies in the Pacific, as 50 years ago the French Government asked the British Foreign Office how much of the unoccupied area of Australia it claimed, and the reply was "The whole of it!" The French expedition under La Perouse arrived in Botany Bay only a few hours before Port Jackson was taken possession of for Great Britain; and France lost possession of New Zealand by arriving shortly after the British flag had been hoisted there. France gained New Caledonia a short time before its proposed occupation by Great Britain, and there have been complaints of considerable interference with the Protestant missionaries on the adjacent Loyalty Group by the French authorities, who have also taken possession of these islands, after many improvements had been made by resident Englishmen. The French settlement in New Caledonia has now regular steam communication with the Australian continent, but the colonists offer strong objection to foreign convicts landing in numbers on their shores, as many who have escaped are found committing criminal offences, unchecked in Australia by fear of the guillotine or Kanaka policemen of whom they have great dread. A similar objection has been urged by the people of California |to these French récidivistes, who appear sometimes to escape to that side of the Pacific owing to their not being allowed to land in Tahiti or any other French settlement. There are 11,000 convicts in New Caledonia, who produce little for exportation, but about 800 are engaged in the large nickel mines, though their labour is not found to be satisfactory, as a large guard has to be kept, and the amount of work done not very much, so that it is thought the French Government will shortly have to abandon this penal system, as Japanese are now being engaged for these mining works.

Both Macaulay and Carlyle predicted that when the United States were densely populated the conditions of life obtaining there would be similar to those in Europe, but it will take a long time before Australia becomes as thickly inhabited as the present American Union. The population of the Eastern States of America has been largely decreased by the migrations westward, and the Pacific States, owing to their great agricultural and mineral resources, are now the wealthiest portions of America. In the natural course of progress, when the Pacific Slope of America is more populated, numbers of persons may be expected to move over the sea to those Pacific colonies and islands in Australasia which lie in proximity to the American settlements, and are now but sparsely inhabited when compared with the density of population per mile in the United States.

For many years past the City of Sydney has been styled "the Queen of the Pacific," on account of its magnificent natural harbour and commercial greatness. The title has been also given to San Francisco, the "City of the Golden Gate," in view of its excellent situation and wonderful progress. The great emporium of the Pacific has yet to be determined; and in the industrial race New South Wales, with its vast resources and comparatively free ports, will be found a worthy competitor with the famous State of California. Humboldt records that in 1514 Balboa, one of the earliest American explorers, took possession of the Pacific for Castille, by wading into its waters sword in hand; but supremacy on this great natural highway can only now be secured by generous rivalry in trade, as "the life of a nation, not only in a commercial but also in a moral point of view depends on the part it takes in the commerce of the world." Sydneyites believe that the Federal City of Australia should be near Port Jackson, and Mr. Henry Halloran, C.M.G., writes :—

> Within our midst a city vast
> A Southern Washington shall be :
> The heart of banded States that cast
> Their strength within one golden key,
> Records and law, and wealth amassed,
> The Union City of the Free.

The tonnage of shipping per head of population in New South Wales was 4·37, being over twice as much as in Canada, and over eight times as much as in the United States. Only five of the principal ports of Great Britain have a larger tonnage than that of Sydney, so that her extensive wharves are generally lined with large steam and sailing ships. New South Wales, Queensland, and Victoria at present subsidise special lines of splendid steamers for carrying foreign mails so that their capitals may be better brought into direct contact with European nations, and it is very desirable that the Pacific mail service from San Francisco to Sydney should always be continued. Although a postal route between Australasia and the United Kingdom, *via* America had been discussed as far back as 1848, it was not until 1863 that it was established by way of Panama, and there is no doubt but that this line will be reverted to when a waterway is made through the isthmus for mail steamers. In 1869 an arrangement was made for the conveyance of British mails *via* San Francisco, which ended in 1871, but although several experiments were made, it was not until 1875 that a regular service obtained, which has continued up to the present time, but with comparatively small subsidies from the United States Government, although many petitions from American citizens have been presented in the matter. In a memorial from the San Francisco Chamber of Commerce to the United States Congress it was pointed out "that for 22 years the cost of the mail service from America to Australia had been met by the Colonies almost exclusively, and in view of the early termination of the existing contract that the line will almost to a certainty be abandoned unless the United States Government pays its fair share." A recent cablegram from London states that the Imperial Post Office authorities had declined to renew the contract for the conveyance of mails between Great Britain and Australia, except on the rates sanctioned by the Universal Postal Union, but the New South Wales Government has agreed to give £4,000 as subsidy for another year in order that this mail service should not be discontinued. Sir Roderick Cameron, of New York, says by fast steaming the London mails could be delivered in from 25 to 30 days by the American overland route. In 1874, the mails travelling by the San Francisco route between Sydney and London occupied an average of 64 days in transit, but the present time is from 34 to 37 days, which is longer than by the other routes. British mails have been received in Australia in 28½ days from London to Adelaide by the Suez route, and there can be no doubt but this record will be beaten. It remains to be seen, as the distance will be greatly shortened by the proposed Panama or Nicaragua route, whether the American route will be quicker than by the Egyptian Canal. The opening of the Nicaragua Canal, it is stated, should reduce the freight of goods at least three-fourths, give easy communication between the eastern and western states of America, and increase the population of the Pacific States in a wonderful manner, so that the Australasian Colonies will be much benefited by this American under-taking. There can be but little doubt that in the near future the Pacific Ocean will be used to a much greater extent for commercial intercourse between Europe and Australia, and hereafter vie as a commercial route in industrial importance with the Atlantic, over whose waters so much more of the products of the world are now carried, especially if canals can be made profitably through the isthmus connecting North and South America.

Canada, one of the sister countries on the North American Continent, still maintains loyal allegiance to the mother land, although Canadian commercial interests are greatly affected by the fiscal policy of the United States with whom she could carry on most of her trade if she would enter into a com-mercial union adverse to Great Britain. Both Canada and Australasia remain at the maternal side, as they have been treated with greater justice by the parent country than those North American Colonies experienced who so long ago for better or worse set up housekeeping on their own account. The sister countries in North America may be said to have nearly the same extent of territory stretching from the Atlantic to the Pacific, with climate and resources somewhat alike, so that it is interesting to note their progress with that of the younger community, whose home far away on the other side of the Pacific prevents her obtaining that close intercourse with America which has always existed between the United States and Canada, or even participating in any little differences that may arise between them.

The traveller from Australia to the Columbian Exposition will be comfort-ably carried across the American Continent from San Francisco to New York on lines of steam and electric railroads of different companies, who possess immense buildings for union depôts at every centre of population. He can-not but be surprised to find in the centre of the United States a magnificent city like Chicago only half-a-century old, with more lines running into it than any other American town and with over a million inhabitants. Chicago has been twice razed to the ground by fire, but since reconstructed of granite, marble, stone, and other substantial materials, so that owing to its impor-tance and central position it has been considered the most appropriate place on the American Continent in which to commemorate the great discovery made by Columbus. Australasia has cordially responded to the invitation of her go-ahead American relative requesting the "Land of the Southern Cross" to exhibit her natural resources and capabilities for the purpose of comparing them with those from the extensive prairies and mines of America. The products sent from New South Wales should give some idea of the varied wealth contained in the whole of the Seven Colonies of Australasia, which in a true federal spirit " the Mother of the Australias" has undertaken to represent in what will be found to be a typical Australian Court.

Mr. E. M. G. Eddy, who has had great experience in working English railways, has recently made the following comparison between the working of the lines in the United States and New South Wales :—" In connection with travel, our circumstances were different to some extent to the circumstances of the old country, and were more closely allied to America. He would give them a few figures he had carefully worked out in connection with the railways in the United States and he compared these figures, which were for 1890, with our figures for the year just closed on June 30. The gross earnings on each mile of line in America amounts to £1,381 ; our gross earnings amounted to £1,422. In the States the working expenses amounted to £909, while here they were £876. The net earnings were £472 in the States, and £540 here. The percentage of working expenses was in the States 67·79, while in New

B

South Wales it was 61·60. The passenger traffic in New South Wales was of larger proportion to that of America. The percentage of returns to the totals was in New South Wales 37·67 for passengers, and 61·67 for goods. In the United States the figures were 29·41 passengers and 68·23 goods. But there was one great obstacle in this country, and that was that in the States the goods trains haul 156 tons per mile, whereas our trains only haul 51 tons per mile, so that they saw what a great handicap we had with our very big grades, and how necessary it was that they should do something to overcome our natural disadvantages. The service of trains given in this Colony was practically as good as the service in America. The number of trains each way per day was 2·77 for passengers in the States, while in New South Wales it was 2·53. For goods in the States the number of trains was 4·21, and here 3·27. In the States they had 6·98 passenger trains per day, while here there were 5·80. In America they had an advantage over this Colony; their haulage was greater than ours, therefore the expenses were less. In the States the average length of haul was 119 miles, while here it only amounted to 55 miles, but each mile of line with the railways in America dealt with a much greater volume of traffic. The average traffic passing over each mile of line per annum in the States was 487,245 tons, against 109,000 tons in this Colony, so that there was a great development possible with our agricultural produce, which was a great part of the business in the States."

Independence for the Australian Colonies has not been sought by the colonists, as they well know that they would not be able under present circumstances to undertake the great responsibility of maintaining a separate national existence. The free institutions possessed by the Australasian Colonies make them as contented with their lot as residents in the land where triumphant democracy holds sway. The people and institutions of Australasia have had as many critics as Americans in the early days of the United States, and while some of these writers have been too profuse in their praises others have gone to the opposite extreme of denouncing everything colonial. In hasty generalisations modern travellers have sometimes proclaimed that in the United States republican institutions have failed, and that in Australia there is too great a desire to outstrip other countries in industrial competition. Critics have observed lust of wealth and non-observance of the restraints of social life both in Australia and America, but Australian and American travellers have noticed that love of money and want of reverence are not lacking in European countries. There is no doubt that Australians, even more than Americans, are inclined to enjoy life in all its phases, but this is probably induced to a greater extent by the Italian climate of the southern colonies. Moreover, the great natural wealth of Australia distributed amongst a comparatively few inhabitants has permitted a better style of living for the masses than in Europe, or even in some of the Eastern States of America which have been populated by the poorer classes of foreign emigrants.

Even if the Australian Colonies were separated from Great Britain, the influence of the Mother Country over her off-spring could not be lessened, as there would always exist a union of consanguinity which time can never destroy. The prophecies of leading statesmen and political economists at the beginning of the century with regard to the relations between Great Britain and America are just as applicable to the connection of the Mother Land with Australia, but without the disturbing elements which lost the United States to the British Crown.

It is stated that "there is only a silken thread" binding the Australasian Colonies to England, but this bond is much stronger than if rivetted in iron bands, so that a hope of Adam Smith has been realised when he wrote, refering at that time to the United States:—"The same sort of parental affection on the one side and filial affection on the other might arise between Great Britain and her colonies which used to subsist between those of ancient Greece and the mother city from which they descended." That great friend of America, Edmund Burke, also well declared:—"My hold of the colonies is in the close affection which grows from common names, from kindred blood, from similar privileges and equal protection. These are ties which though light as air are as strong as links of iron." At a more recent period that great tribune of the people, John Bright, said, respecting Imperial Federation:—"Colonies should remain attached to and in perfect friendship with the Mother Country, but I am of opinion that any attempt to unite them by political bonds more closely than they are now connected will tend not so much to permanent union as to discord and separation. England will not be governed or in any degree influenced in her polity by Canada, or Australia, or the Cape. The colonies will not allow the interference of England with them, with their laws, or their tariff." These reasonings of Adam Smith, Edmund Burke, John Bright, and other distinguished authorities show that closer political ties with the Mother Country are not absolutely necessary to retain her offspring, as there are already family bonds much stronger in keeping the British household together.

The mission of England to the world is not ended in founding and directing her present magnificent Colonial Empire, but should be continued in interesting herself in the welfare of any country which may have to leave the paternal side to carry another great name amongst the nations of the world. Sir Henry Parkes, although desirous of a perpetual union between England and Australia, has said: "It has always appeared to me—and the more I reflect the more forcibly it appears to me—that there can be no federation except upon a common basis of equality, and there can be no true and lasting federation by a great central power—I will not use the word dominant power—with a number of weaker or inferior powers."

Australia is now altogether too young and inexperienced to take upon herself the responsibilities of leaving the maternal side, and her best interests will be conserved by staying with Great Britain. She must, therefore, be allowed to continue her growth to maturity, when she no doubt will be able properly to choose the kind of union which would be best to contract, if then desirous of quitting the family circle.

The native born in Australia are generally found anxious to avail themselves in every way of the civilization of Europe and North America, and to learn from other countries anything that would be useful to the body politic, so that there are few important mechanical inventions or scientific appliances which are not made known in Australia almost as soon as in America. Recognising that Australia is still a comparatively infant State, her people are not desirous in any way to precipitate separation from the Mother Country, but rather seek the counsel and help of Canada, the United States, and other English-speaking countries whose much longer experience in self-government cannot but afford many lessons in working free institutions in a proper manner, as "Australia is America with a chubby face."

The contented condition of the French Canadian shews that the justice uniformly attending British rule is appreciated by this race as much as by their fellow-colonists who are the descendants of United Empire Loyalists in Ontario, as both are governed by the same laws though printed in a foreign tongue for the use of Frenchmen as well as in the English language. The German race always make excellent colonists, and appear to be well satisfied with their treatment both in Australia and America. Germans in both countries readily intermarry and become excellent citizens by adoption, as they take out certificates of naturalisation more than any other people.

As the great external trade of Australia, notwithstanding her apparent isolation, is carried on waterways controlled by the fleets of European Powers, it is necessary that this sea-borne commerce should be well protected, especially as it is greater in proportion to population than in any other country, and therefore would afford rich prizes for privateers. But the required arrangements for this defence could surely be made with the Mother Country and other British possessions, without the Australasian Colonies entering at present into an elaborate and costly system of Imperial Federation.

Australasia, Canada, Newfoundland, and South Africa are the only British colonies having responsible Governments, which would enable them in a proper manner to vote for entering into Imperial Federation so as to help Great Britain and each other against a foreign power, and to bear a proportion of the expense for the defence of the Empire to which they belong. Sir Charles Dilke has estimated the annual expenditure for defence in the British Empire at £60,000,000, and apportioned the amounts paid for Great Britain at £38,000,000, for India at £20,000,000, and for the Colonies at £2,000,000. It costs yearly over 14 millions sterling to defend at sea the British Empire, of which India pays £254,000 for troopships and harbours, and Australia £91,000 towards maintaining an auxiliary fleet, in addition to expenditure on harbour defences, amounting annually to £793,750, and a debt of £2,065,517 for the works already executed.

Before the Australasian Colonies could join any federation of English-speaking nations, it will be necessary for them to enter into a confederation with each other similar to that of the provinces composing the Dominion of Canada. This union, it is believed, will be consummated before the end of the century, provided no disturbing elements are introduced through the Coloured Labour question which is now provoking much discussion on the Australian continent. A United Australia should help quickly to develop the idea of a future world-wide confederation of the English-speaking races. Resolutions passed at two distinct conferences early in 1890, held in Melbourne by representatives from the Governments of the Australian Colonies and delegates from the Australian Natives Associations, and recent discussions in the several local Legislatures and in the columns of the newspaper press, tend to show that the majority of representative bodies and public men fully believe that the time has arrived for a federal union of the Australasian Colonies on somewhat similar lines to those adopted by the Dominion of Canada and the United States of America. As the great majority of the inhabitants of the Australasian Colonies are either natives of the United Kingdom or their immediate descendants, the difficulty of dealing with a large population of foreign extraction would not occur in founding a federal union of the various British Colonies in the Southern Hemisphere, as was the case in the consolidation of the Canadian provinces, and which want of homogenity is still a discordant factor in working the constitution of the United States. All the Australasian Colonies enjoy representative institutions, which in most of them have worked well for over a quarter of a century, although rocks-a-head are now noticeable by many intelligent observers.

Great as has been the growth of the British Colonies in Australasia, their progress has been somewhat retarded by the want of that federal unity amongst themselves which should be no longer delayed in the best interests of the community, in view of its successful working in the United States and Canada. There can be no doubt but that the voice of Australia is not now listened to in the way it would be if the Colonies presented their requests unitedly instead of singly as at present, and a union amongst themselves would be the first step to entrance into a larger confederation. There is, however, not the same reason for federation in Australasia as in Canada or in South Africa, as the Australian Colonies occupy the whole of the continent, and are far from any foreign nation or hostile tribes who would readily make war against the white races, and less troubled with local dissensions than was Upper and Lower Canada before their union.

Intercolonial freetrade and a common tariff would be the result of a complete federal system, and the hostile customs-houses now existing on the Murray River could be abolished, as they are in the States of the Union and also in the Provinces of the Canadian Dominion. At the present time all the Australian Parliaments levy taxes on protective principles, as New South Wales recently adopted a tariff imposing for that purpose duties upon imports, which are however moderate when compared with those collected in other Australian settlements, in the United States, or in Canada.

The electoral system of most of the Australasian Colonies has been satisfactorily worked during the last quarter of a century on the basis of manhood suffrage and vote by ballot, and their example has been followed in extending the franchise and securing freedom in voting, not only by the Mother Country but also by many of the United States, in which one of the reforms recently adopted has been the " Australian ballot-box," which Mr. Carnegie states " has been found admirably adapted for preventing the possibility of exerting undue influence upon the voter, and completely guarding the secrecy of the ballot." The Legislatures of the Australasian Colonies have been formed on the model of the Imperial Parliament, and consequently are like the Legislatures of the principal Canadian provinces, with an Upper and Lower House, resembling in their powers and procedure the British House of Lords and House of Commons. Unlike the British Parliament, however, the members of the Australian Lower Houses of the Legislature receive an annual reimbursement of the expenses in the discharge of their Parliamentary duties at rates varying in the Colonies from £100 to £300 a year. Similar disclosures of corruption to those which have taken place with regard to railways and public contracts in Canada are prevented in New South Wales by a committee of public works, selected each session from both branches of the Legislature, who have to inquire into the necessity for, and cost of, such undertakings as new lines of railways and any building whose cost is over £20,000. The management of the New South Wales railways is now placed under permanent Commissioners, who are entirely removed from political influence, and are required, as experts, to be responsible for the proper working of the lines.

All the Australasian Colonies, excepting Fiji, now enjoy the benefits of responsible Government, and in New South Wales during the last 25 years the working of free institutions has, on the whole, afforded satisfactory results to the great masses of the people. There have been no glaring charges of corruption proved against administrators of the Government in Australia, owing, perhaps, to the maxim never having been adopted there with regard to the Civil Service, "that to the victors belong the spoils," in the same manner as that principle was once acted upon in the United States. Although in the early colonial days there was much discontent with the way in which the Colonies were governed from Downing-street, there are now comparatively few objections urged against the administration of the Colonial Office, which invariably leaves the Governor to act with his responsible advisers as long as the Constitution is not violated. The lesson learned by the separation of the United States from Great Britain has been beneficial in this regard to Australasia, as she has now no great grievances which require to be redressed, and consequently is well satisfied with the community of interest existing between her and the Mother Country.

The late Mr. (U.S.) Consul Griffin has written : " It should be remembered that New South Wales, and indeed all the Australasian Colonies, have institutions in many respects like those of the United States. For instance, universal suffrage prevails, and the system of public education is practically the same. Moreover, there are no class distinctions in the Colonies, no union of Church and State, and no laws of primogeniture and entail. They have also the right to regulate their institutions in their own way, very few acts of the Colonial Legislatures having ever been disallowed by, or even require the sanction of, the Imperial Government."

There is no existing aristocracy in Australia, and the creation of a House of Lords would provoke almost as much opposition there as it would in America, as when a proposal to that effect was made about 40 years ago it was received with much ridicule by the colonists. At present there is an agitation for " one man one vote," the electoral system which now obtains in the United States, and which is made the chief plank in the platform of the labour parties in the various Colonies, as hitherto electors have votes for every constituency in which they owned property.

The Colonies present a fair field for the trial of representative institutions on the English model, but without the distinction of classes found in the Mother Country. In Australia and America every industry has had to be created within a short space of time, and the people of both countries are so accustomed to rapid progress that they are somewhat inclined to be deficient in the virtue of patience. Australians, however, have much to be proud of in the success obtained by their country in solving burning questions which have agitated other countries for many ages, and there can be no doubt that Australia with America will take a leading part in the great political and social changes which will hereafter take place for the betterment of mankind in all parts of the world.

The Rev. Dr. Roseby, who met a number of American delegates at the first International Independent Conference held in London in 1891 to consider the work of Congregationalism in the world, amongst which was the great results of the labours of the Puritan Fathers who landed on Plymouth Rock from the *Mayflower*, concludes an Australian's impressions of the Old Country with the following words regarding the probable future of his native land :—" We shall be an English people—under which phrase you understand I always include Scotland and Ireland—we shall be English, but English with a difference. We have no desire or ambition to see transplanted to these new lands those features of English political and social life which are the still surviving remnants of less-enlightened and less-happy times. The feudalism, the spirit of caste, the spirit of religious intolerance, the rule of the priest and of the aristocrat—these things we shall never, I trust, permit to take root in the soil of our country. But our State need not be irreligious because it forms no alliance with any particular specially-favoured Church. Nor need there, in the manly intercourse of freemen, be any lack of that lofty and beautiful courtesy which feudalism degraded into a spirit of mean and abject dependence. With a fair field and no favour; with ready access to those great gifts of Nature which are the source of all national and private wealth ; with a system of public education which sees to it that none are left in absolute ignorance, and that the really capable, however humble their rank in life, receive an education fully commensurate with their capacity; with this vast over-shadowing drink system first reduced within narrower limits, and at last abolished altogether ; with statesmen and religious leaders equally endowed with wisdom, with patience, and with courage—we shall see the rise and growth in these Austral lands of a nobler and happier Commonwealth than history has ever seen. Still, while it will be English, it will not be England. Climate counts for something ; the mere size of one's country counts for something. There will be more sunshine in our hearts as there is more blue sky in our firmament. We shall be a brighter and more light-hearted people, more æsthetic, more artistic, than our fathers. The summer of the South will do for us what it did for Greece, what it has done for Italy. But I am sure that by God's grace, we shall never lose the deep religious feeling, the sturdy patriotism, the earnestness of spirit, the capacity for self sacrifice, the well balanced caution and enterprise, that have given to our motherland its high place among the nations."

Although the inventive genius of Americans in the mechanical sciences has been very great, yet more is due in nearly every branch of industry to other nations who still surpass them in many artistic works and scientific processes. Neither America nor Australia can be expected to have perfected their manufacturing industries so as to equal those of European countries which have been the growth of many ages, and have attained a high standard of excellence because special attention has been paid to the various lines for which the several lands are famous. There are, however, many " Yankee dodges " in travelling and business life which should be copied in Australia. The United States is the only nation that has become great without Colonies and without foreign commerce and possessions, but she is now acquiring large financial interests in South America on the mainland and also in the adjoining islands of the Pacific. It has been said that in the United States the population, wealth, internal commerce, exports and imports have increased at a more rapid rate than those of any other nation for a similar period, but it will be seen that in all these respects the ratio of growth in Australasia has been even greater. It has been also asserted that experts believe that the population of the United States would have been as large and more homogeneous without emigration, but the large influx of European population during the past half-century has greatly helped the development of both America and Australia.

At the latter end of the last century both La Perouse and Vancouver visited the Pacific Slope of America and the opposite shores of Australia, and the lands on both sides of the Pacific Ocean first attracted great attention of rival European nations about the same time. Vancouver, in 1791, discovered King George's Sound, and La Perouse with all his crew are believed to have been shipwrecked on one of the islands of the Pacific.

The people of the United States have displayed a great interest in the progress of the Australasian Colonies from the first settlement in Sydney, as is evidenced by the following historical reminiscences:—The first foreign vessel to arrive in New South Wales after the establishment of the colony was the American brigantine "Philadelphia," commanded by Captain Patrickson, who thus early displayed that commercial enterprise which has obtained for the people of the United States the reputation of being a smart trading people. This vessel came into Port Jackson on 1st November, 1792, with a full cargo of provisions which were speedily absorbed by the colonists, who had been disappointed at not receiving the supplies expected from England, and had failed to secure a sufficient crop owing to the want of agricultural knowledge of those who came out in the "first fleet."

Commodore Wilkes, in his account of the extended cruise of the first United States expedition sent out for extensive exploration in 1839, states that he without being observed entered Port Jackson with his fleet during the night, and that the citizens were astonished at seeing the vessels anchored opposite the town in the morning. Although he pronounced New South Wales to be even then "a glorious colony," he relates that he might have destroyed the city in defiance of the insignificant harbour defences, and have sailed out of the harbour without the citizens ever discovering the delinquent. Large batteries and other important defence-works, however, are now to be found on most of the prominent headlands, and the late Anthony Trollope, when visiting Australia, said, "he would like to be a resident gunner so as always to enjoy the beautiful views in front of these forts."

Port Jackson has also been visited from time to time by many vessels of the American navy, one of which was the celebrated warship, "Kearsage," whose contest with the "Alabama" is now as well known to the Australian schoolboy as the battles of Trafalgar and the Nile. The colonists rejoiced that the "Alabama" claims were settled so amicably by arbitration, and a fratricidal war between England and America wisely averted, in a way which has since been also satisfactorily copied in deciding other international disputes. During the American civil war the strong sympathy of Australians was with the Northern States in their attempt to suppress slavery and to preserve the Union. The accounts of the assassinations of Presidents Lincoln and Garfield, were received in Sydney with many demonstrations of sorrow, and the greatest indignation was expressed at public meetings against the murderers of patriotic men, who by genius had risen "from a log cabin to the White House."

The case of the so-called Scotch martyrs, Muir, Palmer, Skirving, Gerald, and Margarot, attracted great sympathy in the United States at the end of last century. A large memorial monument has been erected in Edinburgh by its citizens, on which is placed the following extract from a speech by Muir in the Court of Justiciary :—"I have devoted myself to the cause of the people. It is a good cause—it shall ultimately prevail—it shall finally triumph." These devoted men were banished to Botany Bay in 1794 for "leasing making," or libelling the Government, as members of the society called "Friends of the People," and the prophecy of one of them that the sentence passed would be reversed by posterity has been fulfilled, and nearly all the political rights sought for by them have now been achieved. Muir had a most eventful history, as General Washington interested himself in his case, and a ship was sent from New York to his relief, in which he escaped in 1796, but the vessel was wrecked on the west coast of North America, and Muir and two seamen only escaped. After travelling on foot 4,000 miles he reached Panama, but fell into the hands of the Spaniards, and the vessel in which he was being taken to Europe was captured by the English, but in the encounter he was seriously wounded and had to be sent to the hospital at Cadiz. He journeyed to Paris at the invitation of the French Government, and at Bordeaux he was banquetted, and reached his destination in February, 1798, dying near Paris a few months later. Many persons concerned in the Canadian and Irish rebellions, repressed in the first half of the present century, were also banished to Australia, and several of them on returning home were elected to the Legislatures. A number of Irish political prisoners escaped from Western Australia by means of an American whaler in 1876, amongst whom was a poet whose writings were popular in America, where he resided until his death a few years ago.

The representatives of the Government of the United States have always been very popular in Australia amongst all classes of the people. The late lamented Mr. G. W. Griffin, when United States Consul at Sydney, prepared for the Department of State at Washington many valuable reports on the Australasian Colonies, and did much to promote good feeling and trade between the peoples of America and Australia during his long term of office in New South Wales, and when he left Sydney, in 1891, a presentation of an illuminated address was made by the Mayor to him, in the Town Hall, expressive of admiration of his many and untiring services to both countries.

At the exhibition to commemorate the centenary of American Independence held at Philadelphia, in 1876, many of the productions of New South Wales obtained high awards from the judges, and much information was given to visitors respecting the progress and resources of Australasia, so that large numbers of Americans will now be able to appreciate by personal observation the advances made since that time in the preparation of the colonial products, as shown in the several departments of the Chicago Exposition.

The late Lord Tennyson, Poet Laureate of England, wrote, at the request of the Prince of Wales, a poem to commemorate the opening of the Colonial and Indian Exhibition, held so successfully in London in 1886, and the close family connection between Britain, America, and Australia, has been well described in the following lines :—

> Britain fought her sons of yore,
> Britain failed ; and never more,
> Careless of our growing kin,
> Shall we sin our father's sin.
> Men that in a narrower day,
> Unprophetic rulers they,
> Drove from out the mother's nest
> That young eagle of the west
> To forage for herself alone—
> Britons, hold your own.
>
> Sharers of our glorious past,
> Brothers must we part at last,
> Shall we not, through good and ill,
> Cleave to one another still.
> Britons, myriad voices call—
> Sons be welded, each and all.

Of late years owing to the establishment of the Californian mail service and other causes leading to increased intercourse, the Colonies have received

many accessions to their ranks from among the enterprising citizens of the
United States, and commercial men have brought with them some of the
mechanical novelties for which America has become famous. The departure
of the San Francisco mail-steamer each month from Sydney for eighteen
years has afforded Americans an opportunity of giving hearty farewells to
compatriots visiting their old homes on pleasure or business bent. For many
years past the citizens of the United States resident near Sydney have
celebrated the anniversary of American independence, at receptions held
by the Consul, picnics, dinners, balls, base-ball matches, or in some other
way expressive of their love for their native land, and in most of these
demonstrations they have been heartily joined by numbers of leading
Australians.

The late Right Hon. W. B. Dalley, P.C., said, at a local celebration of the
anniversary of American Independence:—" On this festival day of the
English-speaking peoples of the world—the anniversary of the birthday of
the mighty nation which was the oldest born of the children of England—
we, in one of the most distant parts in the British Empire, are here to commemorate this, one of the greatest events in human history. (Cheers.) To
us the privilege has long been given of rejoicing, as heartily and sincerely as
our brethren in America, that the victory of the freedom and the happiness
of the human race was theirs. For us that Declaration of Independence has
long been one of the greatest charters of the liberty of mankind. We listen
to it to-day as we have read it a hundred times with reverence for its
framers, with a pathetic recalling of their patriotism, and of the melancholy
mistakes of those English statesmen who compelled their offspring into a
revolt in defence of liberty. We cherish to-day as sacred names (among
many others) those of Thomas Jefferson, John Adams, Benjamin Franklin,
John Hancock, and Richard Henry Lee.   *   *   *   Here, in the
capital of one of the greatest of English colonies, it has been celebrated with
joy and gratitude by British citizens, and in the presence and with the
hearty enthusiastic sympathy of the honored representative of his and our
Most Gracious Sovereign who is here to manifest his love, and claim among
you the privileges of brotherhood.   *   *   *   The calamities of
our statesmanship culminating in your loss well nigh overwhelmed England.
But she rose again to be the mother of nations by a swift recognition of her
wrong done to you, and an instant abandonment of the fatal policy which
had snapped asunder the golden chain of love and loyalty that bound you to
her. Henceforth, as one of her later historians said, her work was to be one
of colonization. She was to give to her adventurous children in all parts of
the world the liberty which she refused to you. She was to plant nations
and endow them with freedom. By her splendid atonement for the injury
she had done you, she was to memorialise your victory, and establish beyond
the boundaries of European politics the monument of her new statesmanship
and humanity."

Representatives from New South Wales conveyed Australian congratulations to the American people at the centenary of American independence,
and are again commissioned to do so at the commemoration of the 400th
anniversary of the discovery of America. Australia was, therefore, found
heartily uniting with other countries at the Philadelphia Centennial Exhibition seventeen years ago, to commemorate the fight for freedom which gave
the United States independence, as that struggle also obtained a great
increase of constitutional liberty not only to the residents in the British
colonies, but also to the people of the Mother Country.

The malady often suffered by George III. was a principal cause of the severance of a grand country from Great Britain; but out of evil good may come, and the independence of the United States was highly beneficial to the industrial interests of the world, since it is improbable that Australia would otherwise have been opened up to European civilization. But for the establishment of these British colonies, the Australian continent and the neighbouring islands would most likely have been possessed by those Asiatic races now being crowded out of their homes in the Northern Hemisphere.

It has been predicted that Australasia in another century will have double as many people as Great Britain has now, and that the Island Continent of Australia may hereafter become the centre of a united empire and the main factor in carrying out the great mission of the Anglo-Saxon race in civilizing the barbarous races in Polynesia, Asia, and Africa, countries adjacent to her shores.

It is stated as a singular incident in connection with the history of immigration to Australia that in 1877 four vessels arrived at Sydney bringing 834 immigrants from the United States. The first vessel, the *Anna Boyton*, brought a number from New York City. In the report of the Agent for Immigration the following reference is made to these immigrants : " The immigrants from New York thus introduced appear to be of a most useful description, and as far as information can be obtained the greater portion have readily obtained employment in Sydney."

In 1890 the Single-tax League in Australia invited Mr. Henry George, the " Prophet of San Francisco," whose writings on social and political science have received considerable attention of late years throughout the world, to lecture in these Colonies ; and during a successful tour he made numbers of persons converts to his doctrines of a single-tax on the unimproved value of land. Mr. George, as a representative American, often pleaded for free intercourse between the English-speaking races, and in one of his well-known works used the following terms :—" With a relation so close, ties of blood and language would assert their power, and mutual interests, general convenience, and fraternal feeling might still lead to a pact, which would unite all the English-speaking races in a league, to establish justice, insure domestic tranquility, provide for the common defence, promote the general welfare, and secure the blessings of liberty." Australia has been visited by many American and Canadian evangelists and temperance orators, who have generally lectured to large audiences during their tours through the Colonies, and have performed good service to the cause of religion and total abstinence. More than a quarter of a century ago Bishop Taylor, of San Francisco, held numerous revival services in New South Wales, and more recently the Rev. Joseph Cook and Dr. Clark, of Boston, were welcomed in Sydney. Dr. Clark came in the interest of the Christian Endeavour Society, an American institution, of which there are already many branches in the Australasian Colonies, and which bids fair to be as useful in Australia as it has been in America. The Women's Christian Temperance Union of America has now several lady missionaries visiting Australia (Miss Akerman, Dr. Kate Bushnell, and Mrs. Andrews), and a crusade has been instituted by the local branches of that Society against the liquor traffic, in imitation of that so successfully carried on in many parts of the United States. The Rev. Dr. Lucas, of Toronto, has been lecturing on temperance legislation to large and appreciative audiences in the principal cities of Australasia during the current year. Principal Grant, of the Queen's University, Kingston, Ontario, visited Australasia in 1888, and proved himself to be a keen observer of the lights and shadows of colonial life.

In an interview, recorded in a work on "Oceana," which the historian, Mr. J. Anthony Froude, when he visited Australasia, had with Sir George Grey, whose distinguished services have rendered him most popular throughout the Colonies, that old public servant voiced the wishes of the people of Australasia when he contemplated some eventual, far-off league between the members of the British race scattered over the world, for mutual defence and assistance: "The feelings of kindred," he believed, "to be so strong in us that in some form or other America and the old home would again draw together, and the Colonies would be included in the bond." The free alliance, fiscal or otherwise, of the whole of the English-speaking people would conserve the peace of the world. To reach this goal, however, it would be necessary that the Australian Colonies should first have a federal union among themselves.

Professor Seeley in his "Expansion of England" has called attention to the fact that "the extension of the Anglo-Saxon race over the distant regions of the earth's surface is perhaps the most interesting study and the most momentous fact of modern history, as the English language, literature, trade, and commerce are becoming cosmopolitan." In Australia there is comparatively little intermixture of races, as it is estimated that 95 per cent. of the population are of British descent. The native-born have therefore followed English manners and customs more closely than even the people of the United States and Canada, where a large proportion of the population is of foreign extraction. In Australia there is no French-speaking province like that of Quebec, or many foreign communities using their own languages and millions of coloured voters as there are in the United States.

Sir Henry Parkes (late Premier of New South Wales), who visited America in 1881, afterwards said: "I hope it is no vain opinion of mine that the time may come when even the United States of America and the people of the United Kingdom and their off-shoots may act in some kind of friendly perpetual alliance for carrying on the great work of civilization over the world. There is a promise of unprecedented usefulness for the English people by uniting as one in all parts of the world where our language is spoken. I know well that some of the most eminent, and some of the most experienced, of living Americans entertain the view even that the people of the United States may, at some time or other in the future, again re-enter the bonds of unity with the Mother Country."

New South Wales welcomed with peculiar pleasure the products of the industry of the United States, which were shown at the Australian International Exhibitions held in 1879, 1880, 1887, and 1888. The originality of the exhibits displayed at the first Sydney International Exhibition in 1879 clearly proved that the people of the United States are not content with imitating the productions of other countries, but like to apply the principles of science and art and their acquired experience to invent and design machinery of great ingenuity and superior workmanship, and many of these articles have been largely purchased during the last decade by the colonists from the warehouses of many American manufacturers, who have agents in Australia making strenuous endeavours to push trade for their clients.

Lord Loftus, at the opening of the Sydney International Exhibition of 1879, during his speech in the Garden Palace, said:—"In the name of New South Wales, the elder colony of the Australian group, the once despised and—may I not say?—the now honored, I welcome the representatives of the old heroic nations. I welcome the representatives of the bright daughter lands of England. I welcome all of human brotherhood to our newly raised temple of industry and peace in a new world. In this fair building, which has arisen within a few months, as by the wand of an enchanter, the most renowned and enlightened nations of Europe, the great English-speaking republic of America, and those countries of Asia which are the abodes of an immemorial civilization unite in the radiant bonds of brotherhood, in laying at our feet the rich and ever-varying stores of their conceptive genius and creative power. With them are associated the young and aspiring sister colonies of Australasia, each with upturned gaze fixed upon the sun and forming a glorious purpose to achieve in the highest walks of civilization." In the exhibition ode written by the late Mr. Henry Kendall, an Australian poet, welcome was also given in the following words :—

> Lo! they come—the lords unknown,
> Sons of peace from every zone!
> See above our waves unfurled
> All the flags of all the world !
> North and south and west and east
> Gather in to grace our feast.
> Shining nations let them see
> How like England we can be.
> Mighty nations ! let them view
> Sons of generous sires in you.

In 1888, the 100th anniversary of the foundation of the first European settlement in Australasia was held in Sydney, at which Governors, Ministers, Members of Parliament, and other representatives of the Australasian Colonies were assembled, and a statue of Queen Victoria was unveiled. Australians and Americans are found to exceed even Englishmen in their liking for public demonstration in celebration of national events, but some of the street processions in the United States, such as that on Admission Day in California, extend over several days, and are far more ambitious than even the programme for the Lord Mayor's show in London. The annual demonstrations of the labour societies on Eight Hour Day in Sydney and Melbourne are always highly successful, and much like those to be witnessed on Labour Day in Chicago, where the various trades assemble on the water front and march in procession, with bands playing and banners flying, through the main streets of that city.

Since the year 1876, in which the American Centennial Exhibiton was held, Australia has greatly increased her population, revenue, trade, area under crop, and live stock. Her material progress since that exhibition has been relatively more marked than even that of the United States, whose total growth has been, however, greater than any other country owing to the rapid development of her vast natural resources. Notwithstanding that the railroads in Australia—which have enabled her to compete with the wealthy nations of Europe—have not attained to such gigantic proportions as in the United States, there are now in use twice as many railways as there were in the year 1881. The extension of these lines far into the interior of Australia has rendered possible a tapping of immense mineral resources, and has re-vealed pastoral and agricultural capabilities which otherwise would for many years have remained undeveloped.

The Government Statistican of New South Wales has estimated the total value of industries in the Australasian Colonies to be for agriculture, £23,613,700 ; pastoral, £35,920,600 ; mining, £12,262,900 ; dairy farming,

£10,598,400; forests and fisheries, £4,015,800. The value of private wealth in each colony being as under:—In New South Wales, £412,484,000; Victoria, £344,224,000; Queensland, £118,414,000; South Australia, £99,141,000; Western Australia, £10,619,000; Tasmania, £34,860,000; and New Zealand, £150,192,000. The total value of the labour of primary producers during 1893 in Australasia was £86,411,500 against in Canada the sum of £59,000,000, or £23 2s. 2d. and £11 7s. 7d. per head respectively. The increase of wealth in Australasia during the last decade has been very much larger than in Canada, and the national earnings per head in agriculture, mining, manufactures, internal transport, house rent, commerce, shipping, banking, and professions are estimated by Mr. Mulhall at £40 2s. for Australia, £26 for Canada, and £39 for the United States.

Australia is a noble heritage as it contains unsurpassed natural pastures, good soil, rich mines, unique hardwood forests, and extensive sea fisheries. The great range of climate on the Australian continent enables it to grow readily the commercial plants of the cold region of North America as well as those of the tropical regions of South America. Owing to the varied agricultural, pastoral, and mineral resources contained within the borders of Australia, she should be able, if necessary, like the United States, to feed clothe, and employ all her own people without the necessity of sending to other countries for supplies.

The industrial greatness of America is chiefly due to agriculture, as about half the people live by cultivation of the soil, but the suitability of Australia, and especially of New South Wales, for the production of fine wools has led to the pastoral industry being the principal interest on the Australian continent. Eight bags of American cotton, landed at Liverpool in 1784, and 167 lb. of Australian wool, delivered in London in 1810, were the commencement of industrial prosperity not only to America and Australia but also to the textile manufacturers of the Mother Country. The staple products of Australia and America have been manufactured in England into immense quantities of calicoes and cloths by intricate machinery invented to meet the requirements of the times, and these goods have been distributed over all the world to eager purchasers on account of the excellent quality and cheapness of the fabrics.

The United States has been the best customer for British produce in the century, but in 1891 the exports of the Mother Country were in value only half that of the imports from the American Union. The annual purchases by Australasia of English manufactures have only been surpassed amongst British possessions by those of India.

Great Britain, in 1891, imported raw cotton to the value of £40,000,000, against £70,000,000 cotton goods exported and imported wool to the value of £26,000,000, and exported woollen goods to the same amount. America and Australia are the great providers of raw material to European manufacturers, who but for obtaining the staple for their looms from them could not do so much towards clothing the people of the world. Cotton-growing in America and wool-growing in Australia were commenced about the same time, and both have been unparalleled as remunerative industries. Cotton is by far the most valuable export from the United States. The wool clip of Australia amounts in value to about half that of the cotton crop of the Union. Australian wool is highly prized by American manufacturers, as the finer sorts required by them are not grown in any of the States of the Union.

The stoppage of a main source of supply of cotton during the Civil War in America caused that staple to be commenced to be grown in Queensland and the Fiji Islands. This experiment resulted in cotton being produced which would class with the better grade of Sea Islands; but the satisfactory termination of the American Civil War led to the United States again supplying the European markets. Very fair samples of cotton were shown at the Indian and Colonial Exhibition by South Australia, which, it was reported, would class with some of the better grades of America, and would spin numbers up to 50's, as the staple is even running and clean, and would make a nice weft cotton up to these numbers.

The cotton and tobacco of the United States cannot be grown in Europe, but both these crops could be produced in Australia, perhaps, as readily as in America if similar experience, capital, and labour were available. This is shown by the fact that splendid samples of both these commodities have been obtained from experiments made to test the suitability of the soil and climate for their growth.

American cotton, Australian wool, and Canadian timber, are largely required to supplement the home products used by the manufacturers of Great Britain; otherwise the machinery of her great factories and work-shops would have to remain idle for want of raw material, as the bulk of these articles could not be grown within the borders of the United Kingdom.

There are nearly three times as many sheep in Australasia as there are hogs in the United States. In 1880 the number of sheep in Australasia was 65,915,000, as against 35,193,000 in the United States. In 1890, the number of sheep in Australasia was 116,041,707; in Canada, about 2,500,000; in United States, 42,599,679. There are more sheep in New South Wales alone than in the whole of the United States or the United Kingdom. The annual return of the United States Department of Agriculture gives the number of sheep at the beginning of 1892 as 52,398,000, whilst those of Australia numbered 124,449,952. At the present time there are more than twice as many sheep in Australasia as in the United States, and New South Wales alone had nearly 10,000,000 more than the United States had in 1891. In fact, the number of sheep in Australasia then exceeded the total number of sheep and hogs in the United States by 27,396,707, although the pork industry is a large one in the Union.

The value of Australasian pastoral products in 1890-91 was £35,920,600, of which New South Wales contributed £13,359,800, and this Colony owns one-third of the pastoral property in Australasia. The annual increase of sheep in Australasia from 1861 to 1890 was at the rate of 5·6 per cent., whilst the increase of population was at the rate of 3·9 per cent. The sheep increase of New South Wales was 8·3 per cent., against a population increase of 4 per cent., notwithstanding that many millions of rabbits have eaten much of the grass. There were 88,710 bales of Australian wool shipped in 1891-92 over the previous season.

The Chicago Exposition will afford an excellent point of contact with the representatives of the great producing interests of the world, and samples of the best staples of America and Australia will be placed side by side for comparison. The American manufacturer will see a trophy of the better class of Australian wools in their ordinary market condition, which it is believed cannot be surpassed by any fleeces shown from elsewhere. A flock of Australian merino sheep as well as Australian progeny of American sheep will be sent to Chicago to compete with the American sheep to be exhibited. Every one of the Australasian Colonies is adapted to the production of wool, and the growth of this industry in so short a time is one of the most remarkable industrial triumphs, as it has made Australia the greatest grower of that staple in the world, and the principal source from which the immense manufactories of Great Britain obtain their supplies. The failure of the wool crop in Australia, or the cotton crop in the United States, for one season alone would no doubt be the means of closing most of the mills in Yorkshire and Scotland, and throwing hundreds of thousands of persons out of employment. Nearly half of the exports from New South Wales alone consists of wool, as over £11,000,000 worth is shipped yearly; so that the pastoral industry is now the most important one in the Colony, and the Chief Inspector of Stock estimates the number of its sheep to be 61,831,416, against 55,986,431 in 1890, or an increase of 5,844,985. Australia since 1850 has exported wool to the value of 400 millions against gold to the value of 340 millions, notwithstanding the large fall of late years in the price of the "golden fleece," whilst the precious metal has about the same value as at the time of the first colonial gold discovery. It is estimated that from the Australian wool clip of 1891 113,000 bales of the choicest wools have been secured by American manufacturers, and that something like £2,000,000 worth will go into consumption in the United States and Canada, as there has been a large increase in exports to them during last year.

The over-production of cotton and a land boom have caused a wave of depression in the southern states of America, somewhat similar to that which Australasia is now experiencing through the less profitable character for some time past of the Australian pastoral industry, and the jobbing in real estate which has also taken place in the southern colonies. Cotton-growing in India received an impetus through the American Civil War, and as the mills then erected have largely increased of late years and pay only one-sixth of the wages given in England the employers in Lancashire have recently reduced the payments to their operatives by 5 per cent.

Australian commerce now equals that of the United Kingdom when Queen Victoria ascended the throne, and the great progress made will be seen from the fact that the trade of New Zealand alone since that time has risen from the barter first carried on with savages to the value of ten millions sterling in 1891, and is now conducted with all parts of the world. The value of the external and intercolonial trade per head of the Australasian Colonies is £35 10s. 3d., and the external trade £20 2s. 4d., against £9 6s. 2d. for Canada, and £5 13s. 8d. for the United States. The external trade of the Australasian Colonies is much larger than that of any other English possession, and in this respect they more resemble the commercial position of the British Isles than that of the United States, which, under a policy of protection, tries to supply all their wants within the Union, without having recourse to other countries, and so to prefer internal trade to external commerce. The proposals contained in the manifesto issued by Mr. Grover Cleveland for a modification of the existing protective system by which duties will be removed from purely raw material, such as wool, would do much to promote reciprocal relations between the United States and the Australasian Colonies, and his subsequent election to the Presidential chair shows that his views are shared by the majority of Americans. The American Democratic press now urge the Senate to pass Bills removing all duties on wool and other raw materials embraced in the Bills approved by the House of Representatives last session, and as it stated that President Harrison and several Republican Senators are favourable to the Free Wool Bill now before the Finance Committee it should soon become law.

A mass meeting of Freetraders was held in Sydney on the 14th November, 1892, and the following motion passed :—"That this meeting offers its, congratulations to the American people on the triumphant election of Mr. Grover Cleveland as President of the United States, and regards that event as the opening up of a new epoch of freedom and of human progress." A similar large meeting was also held in Melbourne in support of the " removal in the United States of artificial obstacles to commercial interests." Sir Charles Dilke, an English statesman, who, during the last quarter of a century, has travelled twice round the world, and twice half round the world, and has given great attention to the relations of the English-speaking countries with one another, says in the introduction to his work on " Problems of Greater Britain" :—" I desire to call attention chiefly to the imperial position of our race as compared with the situation of other peoples ; and although the official positions of the British Empire and of the United States may be so distinct as to be sometimes antagonistic, the peoples themselves are not only in race and language, but in laws and religion and in many matters of feeling, essentially one." He also says : " The greatest nations of the old world, apart from us, are limited in territory situate in temperate climes, and France and Germany and the others can hope to play but little part in the later politics of the next century, while the future seems to lie between our own people—in the present British Empire and in the United States—and the Russians, who alone, among the continental nations of Europe are in posses-sion of unbounded regions of fertile lands, outside Europe, but in climates in which white men can work upon the soil. Towards the middle of last century France appeared at one moment to be the colonising power of the future. Her Canada and Louisiana together gave her the whole centre of North America, and India seemed already hers. But now the English-speaking people have conquered India, almost the whole of North America, the greater part of Polynesia with Australasia, and most of the opened parts of Africa." The British Empire has an area of 9,000,000 square miles, revenues amounting to 210 millions sterling, and half the commerce by sea in the world. In the British colonies are to be found the greatest wheat fields, wool pastures, timber forests, and diamond fields on the globe. The British people are amongst the largest producers of gold, silver, coal, iron, copper, and tin. In the semi-tropical colonies of England are produced the finest qualities of tea, sugar, coffee, and tobacco.

Mr. Gardiner G. Hubbard in the last annual Presidential address of the National Geographical Society, delivered in Washington, said :—" England's commerce has increased 500 per cent. in fifty years, and has given wealth to her merchants and employment to her artisans." Much of this progress is no doubt due to the great expansion of the Colonial Empire, and Australians have been amongst the largest buyers of English manufactures, greatly surpassing in this respect even the people of Canada, notwithstanding their greater numbers. Canadians now purchase about 50 per cent. of their goods from the United States, and much less than half their purchases are made in the Mother Country, which is not the case with Australians. Since the difficulty experienced by the Australian Governments in regard to borrowing in London there has been, however, a considerable falling-off in the purchase of English manufactures, and the prices of many of the articles have declined in the Colonies owing to the supply being more than this lessened demand. The imports from Great Britain during the first half of the year 1892 were very much less in value than for the same time in the previous year, and merchant vessels have had to come to Australia in ballast to load for the

C

annual wool clip, a cirumstance almost unknown in the past. This falling-off in trade with Great Britain is shared with the greatest competitor of Australasia in pastoral products, as the British exports to Argentina were reduced from 41 million dollars in 1890 to 22 million dollars in 1891, or by nearly one-half. Sir George Dibbs, when recently in England, reminded her merchants that "almost every shilling that had been raised in England for the construction of public works had been spent in the country, thus finding employment for English manufacturing interests."

Australians are large purchasers of manufactures from Great Britain, as in 1890 they imported goods from there to the value of £28,163,348, against £28,200,563 exports of the Colonies. The trade per inhabitant is larger for Australasia than for any other country, and the increase of commerce from 1881 to 1890 was from £101,710,967 to £132,801,164. Canada does a larger trade with the United States than with the Mother Country, and the proportions in the year 1890, were: imports from Great Britain, 35·70 ; from the United States, 49·60 per cent; and exports to Great Britain 49·98 ; to the United States, 41·88 per cent.

If reciprocal relations were instituted between the United States, Canada, and Australia, neighbouring countries having so many interests in common, the products adapted for exchange, such as fine wool, tin, coal, sugar, shale, on the one hand, and lumber, salmon, oil, plaster, tobacco, &c., on the other, could be bartered in a profitable way between them. Among the advantages of the federation of the Australasian Colonies would be the removal of the tariff restrictions between the several settlements, and a free exchange of products with one another, which would afterwards, perhaps, enable them to institute a system of reciprocity with other countries, similar to that once negotiated by Lord Elgin between Canada and the United States.

The value of the imports and exports from New South Wales to the United States is greater than to any other market, except the Mother Country and the other Colonies. The imports from the United States in 1891 amounted to £1,277,032, and consisted of a great variety of articles such as timber from Maine and Oregon, kerosene oil from Pennsylvania, canned meats from Chicago, preserved fruits from California, salmon from the Columbia River, clocks from Connecticut, and hardware, woodenware, and furniture from the great manufacturing plants in the eastern and central states, some of which can be purchased in Sydney even cheaper than in America. The exports from New South Wales to the States amounted to £2,313,671, or £1,036,628 in excess of imports ; but £1,660,000 worth of these exports consisted of Australian gold coin which should help to relieve the strain on that precious metal in the Union. Mr. Alexander Cameron, the Acting American Consul at Sydney, has, however, recently pointed out that though the returns show that there was in 1891 an excess of imports from the United States over exports to the Australasian Colonies amounting to £1,355,622, it was probably balanced by indirect exchange through Great Britain, as 98.000 bales of colonial wool were purchased for American consumption in the London market, in addition to 8,106 bales sent direct from New South Wales.

Australia, with her extensive sea-board of over 8,850 miles and excellent railways and rivers intersecting the Continent, could readily exchange the tropical and sub-tropical products of some parts of the mainland, not only with the colder colonies of Tasmania and New Zealand, but also with the countries on the other side of the Pacific Ocean.

There is a strong feeling among Australians, especially among the native-born, that border jealousies should be sunk as soon as possible by the adoption of intercolonial free-trade, so as to prevent that irritation being experienced in neighbouring communities which has proved, for example, so prejudicial to friendly relations between Newfoundland and the Dominion of Canada, or led to animosities often ending in war in other countries. Intercolonial freetrade would be as beneficial to settlements in Australia, as the unchecked transportation of goods throughout the whole of their territories is to the United States and to the Canadian provinces, which could not be properly governed if each district had a different Customs tariff.

The principal industries in Australia are the pastoral, agricultural, and mining, and the products obtained from them find a ready and profitable market, principally in England. Manufactures have not received the same ratio of development in Australia as in the Eastern States of America, owing to their being less profitable to the colonists, who can import most articles much cheaper from Europe than they can make them and to the fact that industrial enterprise is held in check by fear of labour troubles.

Sir Charles Dilke states that the greatest rivals in the future of the English-speaking nations will be the Russian people, and has made the following contrast between the British Empire, the United States of America, and Russia: "A comparison between the three great growing powers, of which two are mainly Anglo-Saxon, shows that the British Empire exceeds the Russian Empire slightly in size and vastly in population, and has treble the area of the United States; that its revenue is more than double that of Russia, and nearly three times that of the United States; while its foreign trade greatly exceeds that of the American Union and vastly exceeds that of Russia, although no exact comparison between the British Empire and the United States can be made, inasmuch as it is impossible accurately to distinguish, in all cases, trade between the Empire and foreign countries, from trade which is really carried on between various portions of the Empire itself and is similar to the local trade of the United States. In shipping the British Empire surpasses the whole world, but the manufactures of the United States have gained rapidly upon our own, and already perhaps equal ours, although it is difficult to make a precise comparison, on account of differences of classification. In coal production the British Empire still stands far before the United States, while Russia hardly appears upon the list, and we not only stand second in the extent of our coal measures for future use, but first as regards the possibilities of the supply of coal to shipping for the North Atlantic and for the whole of the Pacific. In the production of gold the British Empire and the United States stand upon a fairly equal footing, and each of them produces nearly double as much as Russia. In silver the United States possesses an overwhelming preponderance. In iron the British Empire and the United States are running a race in which the latter must in the long run win, while Russia is all behindhand. In wheat production our Empire exceeds the production of the United States, and each of them produces nearly as much wheat as Russia; but in maize the United States is far ahead. In wool the British Empire stands first of the three, and has nearly double the production of Russia, which itself exceeds by more than a third that of the United States. In cattle, the United States stands first, the British Empire second, and Russia third; while in horses, Russia stands first, the American Union second, and the British Empire third. In sheep, as in wool production, the British Empire is predominant, and Russia occupies the second place; but in pigs, the order is reversed,

In railway mileage the United States stands altogether first, having more
than double the mileage of the British Empire, and Russia is nowhere in
the race. On the whole, then, we may consider that for the present the
British Empire holds her own against the competition of her great daughter,
although the United States is somewhat gaining on her. Both are leaving
Russia far astern, and it is possible that the growth of Canada and Australia
may enable the British Empire not only to continue to rival the United
States, but even to reassert her supremacy in most points." Whilst addressing
the recent Oriental Congress, Professor Max Müller also well remarked :—
"England has proved that she knows not only how to conquer, but how
to rule. It is simply dazzling to think of the few thousands of Englishmen ruling the millions of human beings in India, in Africa, in America, and
in Australasia. England has realised, and more than realised, the dream of
Alexander—the marriage of the East and the West—and has drawn the
principal nations of the world together more closely than they have ever
been before."

Admiral Sir John Colomb shows that during the thirty-five years from the
first English Exhibition in 1851 to the Colonial Exhibition in 1886, the total
trade of the Empire, including United Kingdom, Colonies, and Dependencies,
amounted to not quite 400 millions sterling, of which that of the United
Kingdom counted for 324 million. In 1886 the total stood at 1,079 millions,
of which the United Kingdom supplied 644 millions, the Dependencies 258
millions, and the Colonies 176 millions. In 1837 the annual revenue of the
United Kingdom was 55 millions, and the annual sea-commerce was valued
at 155 millions. At the present day the revenue is 89 millions, and the sea
commerce 744 millions. But a much larger proportionate growth of sea-
commerce is shown on the side of the outlying portions of the Empire. The
aggregate revenue of these was at the beginning of the Queen's reign 23
millions against 105 millions now ; while the sea-commerce, then under 55
millions, has now risen to 460 millions.

It has been charged against Australians that they are generally in a great
hurry to get rich, and the various crises, caused principally by overtrading,
would appear to support the charge, but these faults are shared with other
new communities, and even numbers of persons in the Stock Exchanges in
London and New York are not free from the charge of gambling in stocks, or by
other means endeavouring to realise wealth more quickly than in ordinary trade.
There is in Australia more general distribution of wealth among the people
than in any other country, and although there are many rich squatters and
landowners their individual wealth bears but a slight ratio to that of the
railway and mining kings of the United States. As a rule, however, even
the American school-boy is well-informed of the relative wealth of the many
millionaires of the United States, as the extent of their riches is often
blazoned by their admirers in the newspapers ; but generally the amount
owned by wealthy Australians is not known until their estates are administered, as they are not forced to disclose the extent of their wealth, there
being no income tax in nearly all the Colonies.

The hospitality of Australians, especially in the country districts, has been
warmly eulogised by many visitors, and it is well known that even the tramp
in the far interior is sure to obtain a meal and shelter at any pastoral station
where he may call on his search for work.

Mulhall, in his "Dictionary of Statistics," has estimated the wealth per
inhabitant to be in Australasia £370, in the United States £210, and in
Canada £196. If, however, the amount of British capital invested in

Australia is deducted the actual wealth belonging to the population would, perhaps, only be about the same as that for the Mother Country. The great proportion of the wealth of Australia consists in real estate, being 61 per cent., exclusive of public works, against 42 per cent. for each country in North America. The municipal and census valuation for the United States and Canada show great advances during the last decennial period, but not to the same extent as in Australia, where the rise in the value of property may be said to have been unparalleled.

The cheapening of the cost of moving produce from country to country makes the value of wheat land in Great Britain only as great as the value of similar land in Australia or America, with the cost of taking wheat from the last-named countries to England added, and as a consequence farms in England have depreciated in value, whilst those in new countries have become more valuable. It has been pointed out that in Australasia the men are 24 per cent. more numerous in proportion to the population than they are in Great Britain, and that there is a very much larger proportion of workers in Australasia should be remembered in considering the indebtedness of that country. The proportion of the male sex is much larger also in Australia than in the United States or Canada, and the percentage of producers between 20 and 40 years—the soldier's age—is also greater.

For some years past the question has been raised as to the policy of obtaining freedom and independence for the golden land of Australia, but it is evident that the time for such an event has not yet arrived, nor are the colonists prepared to undertake such a great responsibility. Dismemberment of the British Empire is now deprecated by the majority of English statesmen, and under the present liberal colonial policy of British Government, which has allowed the full enjoyment of free institutions, many years must elapse before the great majority of Australians would desire to see their country an independent State. It is apparent, however, that—notwithstanding the wonderful intercourse obtained during the present century by means of steam and electricity—no system of Imperial Federation will suit Australians which would again sink the individuality of the Colonies in a British Parliament, or entrust the care of their finance and trade to an assemblage sitting 12,000 miles away.

The Imperial Dependencies have a population of some 300 millions, and a volume of trade of £196,000,000, while the British Colonies have a population of some 20 millions, and a trade of £162,000,000, so that the inhabitants of the latter settlements carry on nearly as much commerce, notwithstanding their much smaller number, and this fact should be remembered in any proposal for Imperial Federation.

The number of insane per 1,000 inhabitants is 2·09 in Australasia, 3·3 in the United States, and 1·8 in Canada. The ups and downs of colonial life are felt more by the Australian than the more contented Canadian, but the strain on the brain is even far greater on the enterprising American, who is found working harder and for longer hours than his compeers on each side of the Pacific. The Medical Superintendent of the Insane has reported that the insane in New South Wales gives a smaller percentage than the number confined in Great Britain, and would be lower still were it not that many weak-minded persons had been shipped by their relatives to Australia, as the proportion of native-born lunatics was less than for other countries. At the Intercolonial Medical Congress of Australasia, held in Sydney in 1892, Dr. Chisholm Ross said :—" The proportion of the insane to the population in this Colony is smaller than in England or Scotland, and remarkably so compared with Ireland. While the proportion of insane in relation to the population in all parts of the United Kingdom is increasing—slowly as regards the two divisions of Great Britain, and somewhat rapidly as regards the sister island—the proportion to population in New South Wales has been practically stationary, and on the whole has rather diminished than increased during the 10 years under consideration. On the whole it must be conceded that the statistics of insanity in New South Wales compare not unsatisfactorily with the statistics of the United Kingdom; but it must be borne in mind that in new countries the general conditions of life are usually more favourable to mental soundness. In these Colonies there is but little real poverty. The number of large cities is not great, so that overcrowding and consequent insanitation are less common. Heredity has not had time to exert its full evil effect; mental poverty through want of training and education is rare. The Australian-born is unemotional to an unusual degree —life is not taken very seriously—self-reliance even to self-assurance is their possession, and the climate of almost all the Colonies undoubtedly lends itself to the acquiring and keeping-up of physical, and therefore, to a large extent, of mental health."

As in New South Wales it is possible to labour in the open air nearly all the year round, the workman has not a long season of compulsory rest caused by inclement weather, and he can, therefore, better afford to take more holidays for recreation than artisans in other countries, who have to work many hours in the summer to make up for the time lost in the winter. On an average the number of days in each year that out-door employment can be followed is much greater in Australia, owing to the climate being more equable than in any of the United States except perhaps California.

Darwin and Herbert Spencer have expressed opinions that the American race should develop a better type of man than the European; and their arguments, founded on biological truths, are applicable to the coming men of Australia, who enjoy similar material and social advantages to those which obtain in the United States, with the additional privilege of being almost wholly descended from more than a million and half British emigrants, who voluntarily left their native land to seek new homes in the better countries situated in the Southern Hemisphere during the past half century.

Australians have shown their physical prowess in many contests against the champions of the Mother Country, and the oarsmen of America had, on several occasions, to succumb to a colonial puller, leaving the championship of the world now in Australia. Of late years, by the formation of large boxing clubs, pugilistic contests have become fashionable on both sides of the Pacific as well as in England; but it cannot be said that these exhibitions redound as much to the credit of their patrons, in any of these countries, as the other manly sports, which happily are far more popular in Australia than fighting with fists, although from the number of colonial boxers who visit the United States Americans may naturally form an opposite opinion.

Lord Sheffield's representative team of English cricketers was recently beaten in Australia, the best twice out of three times; and, notwithstanding the very much larger population contained both in Great Britain and America, Australians hold their own in every department of athletics in the contests between them. The American games of base-ball and polo have been introduced into Australia, but are overshadowed by the greater attractions of horse-racing, cricketing, boat-racing, cycling, swimming, &c., to which the genial climate is favourable for the larger part of the year.

Mr. Gladstone has expressed " a hope that Americans will join in proposed Pan-Britannic games, as these contests should have the effect of making English-speaking countries better known to each other," and especially if physical training could carry with it that higher ideal of human symmetry, which requires " beauty for the body, beauty for the reason, and beauty for the spirit." A team of Australian cricketers and several oarsmen will probably visit Chicago and take part in contests at the carnival held during the Exposition.

Australians are the youngest people in the world estimated at the average age of all living years. The average age of the population of Australasia, excluding New Zealand, is 24·5 ; the average age of males being 25·5, and of females 23·4. Australasia has a force of nearly 700,000 men at the soldier's age, or between 20 and 40—the strongest time of human life, so that a large defence force could be enlisted. The birth-rate per 1,000 inhabitants in Australia is 34·75 and the death rate 14·32 per cent., so that the excess of births over deaths is at the rate of 20·43. The death rate is much smaller than in the United States, Canada, or any other country. The number of deaths from suicide, although less than in the majority of States on the Continent of Europe, is greater than in the United States, perhaps owing to Americans being a very sanguine race, and therefore not greatly cast down by reverses of fortune, which they hope quickly to rise from, and in most cases succeed where a less hopeful race would fail.

There are thirteen offices transacting life business in New South Wales, and of these three have their head offices in the United States. The Australian Mutual Provident Society has investments in the Colonies covering over £10,000,000 sterling, at an average rate of £5 19s. 3d. per cent., while the British capitalists find it difficult to realise 4 per cent. on his investments in the Mother Country. The number of existing policies of this the largest life insurance company in the British Empire increased last year from 101,340 to 109,333, or by about 8 per cent., against an increase of about 3¼ per cent. in population. The Mutual Life Insurance Society of New York has shown the aggressive and progressive characteristics of Americans by showing faith in the prospective development of the Australian Colonies by starting a branch of that successful institution in Sydney. A number of citizens were invited to meet Mr. W. P. Stewart, professional actuary of that Company, on his recent visit to New South Wales, when he said: " We have brought this company into Australia because we believe the Australians to be desirable lives, and because we feel that it is a wiser plan to extend our operations, so that our averages may be great, not alone over numbers, but over countries and broad areas. More than this, we have conceived such a good opinion of your country, and have come to have such a faith in its future, that we have concluded to stay here—to build us a home here, and to seek recognition as one of the permanent institutions of your country. We have purchased what we believe to be the best business site in your city. We have paid a large sum of money for it, and we believe it to be a most excellent investment. We are about to erect a structure that will be in keeping with the character and cost of the land." The Equitable Life Assurance Society of New York is also erecting a Sydney office of trachyte found in the Colony, and the building will be a creditable representative of the renowned structure built by the company in New York

At the general census in 1891 the nationalities of the population in New South Wales were found to have the following percentages :—Australian, 64 ; England and Wales, 13·6; Ireland, 6·6; Scotland, 3·3 ; Germany and

Austria, 0·0; China, 1·2; Scandinavia, 0·3; United States, 0·1; and France, 0·2. By far the largest proportion of the population of Australasia have been born in the Colonies of British parents. The Government Statistician has stated that the population of New South Wales is composed of two-thirds native-born and one-third of British or foreign parentage; and that by far the largest proportion of the inhabitants know no other country than that in which they live, and whose progress is dearer to them than that of any other nation. Many Australians are now found occupying leading positions in the land of their birth, and nearly all the members of the present Cabinet in New South Wales were born in Australasia. The number of immigrants who have arrived in Australasia from the United Kingdom during the years 1815 to 1880 was 1,663,388, being 323,859 less than went to Canada, owing to the latter being much nearer to the Mother Country. Australasia has however received more permanent benefit from immigration than Canada, as it has been found that many who went from Great Britain to the Dominion of late years crossed over the border into the United States; but those who once settle in Australia seldom leave it, and of those few who take a trip to England fewer still care to make it a permanent home, as they cannot endure the coldness of the climate after living at the antipodes for some time.

In the interests of anthropology, now being specially studied by scientists in America, an inquiry, similar to that instituted in England and the United States, respecting the growth and development of the body is about to be made in the public schools of New South Wales, so as to ascertain the characteristics which belong to the Australian type, or any deviations from the British type caused by special circumstances on the development of the race, and the results of this inquiry should prove interesting not only to ethnologists, but also to every people descended from the ancient English stock, who would be naturally interested in conclusions on such questions as those which refer to the beneficial or deleterious influences of colonial habits, customs, systems of education, occupation, and climate. Dr. P. Sydney Jones, in the presidential address given to the recent Intercolonial Medical Congress of Australasia, said, respecting the improvements in sanitation which had been accomplished by the colonists: "Much has been done during the past 40 years to secure to our citizens a purer atmosphere. Public parks and recreation grounds—the very lungs of our cities—have been provided; sewerage and mines have been ventilated; house and street sanitation has been greatly improved; smoke consumption has to some extent been made compulsory; and overcrowding has been rendered illegal. It is no exaggeration to say that tens of thousands of lives have been saved and hundreds of thousands of cases of illness have been prevented by the sanitary Acts. There are few towns of any magnitude which do not now possess an abundant supply of pure water, but 40 years ago there were many places, not only in the Australian Colonies, but in Europe and America, which derived their water supply from an uncertain rainfall collected from the roofs of houses, or, still worse, from wells which, in too many instances, were in dangerous proximity to cesspits or other possible sources of contamination." Diagrams prepared by the Government Statistician show that the expectation of life according to the New South Wales life-table is greater for males for every year of age up to 83 than under the English life-table of Dr. Ogle. Mr. Richard Teece, F.I.A., General Manager of the Australian Mutual Provident Society, has reported, as the result of recent actuarial investigations, that native born Australians apparently display greater vitality than other insurers of European nativity, as in that

Society it is found that the actual deaths among the European born are 69·8 per cent. of the expected, while among the colonial born they are only 58·5 per cent.

The percentage of increase in the population of the whole of Australia and the Pacific Islands during the last decade was much greater than in any other country, twice as much as in South America, and one and a half times as much as in North America, being as follows :—Australasia, 30 per cent. ; North America, 20 per cent. ; South America, 15 per cent. ; Africa, 10 per cent. ; Europe, 7 per cent. ; and Asia, 6 per cent.

Mr. E. G. Ravenstein estimates the population of the world for 1890 to be 1,467,920,000, or 29 per square mile, of whom 360,200,000, or 101 to a square mile, live in Europe ; 850,000,000, or 57 per square mile, in Asia ; 127,000,000, or 11 per square mile, in Africa ; 4,750,000, or 1·4 per square mile, in Australasia and Pacific Islands ; 89,250,000, or 14 per square mile, in North America and West Indies ; 36,420,000, or 5 per square mile, in South America ; and in Polar regions and beyond North limit of cereals, 300,000.

There is ample room in Australia not only for the overflow of population from Great Britain, but also for others of sound European and American races, who would contribute to the artistic, literary, scientific, commercial, and industrial advancement of Australasia. The callings in which the unemployed were brought up show, however, that the present great requirement is experienced farmers and other intelligent workers of the soil, who are not afraid of hard manual labor in clearing forests, which Canadians and Americans know from experience is quite different to preparing treeless prairie land, even though the wood is then available for building and fencing.

It is estimated that the British Dominions cover more than one-sixth of the earth's surface, and contain between one-sixth and one-fifth of its population ; and that the Australasian Colonies cover a little over one-seventeenth of its surface, but contain only a little over one-four hundredth of its population, so that there should be more room in Australia than in any of the other possessions of England for disposing of her surplus population.

Nearly eleven per cent. of emigrants from the United Kingdom for the ten years ending 1890 went to the Australasian Colonies. Out of the total number of emigrants (9,334,096) during the years from 1853 to 1890 from the United Kingdom, 1,374,422 came to Australasia, 982,430 to British North America, and 6,854,960 to the United States. This gives 14·72 per cent. for Australia, 10·53 per cent. for British North America, and 69·49 per cent. for the United States, so that although the Australasian Colonies only secured a fourth of the number that went to the United States, the Southern Colonies obtained nearly half as many emigrants again as Canada. Up to 1890 there were 681,995 immigrants to Australasia assisted by the Colonial Governments by their passages being paid wholly or in part.

Australia is not in want of mechanics, general labourers, and navvies at the present time, owing to a depression in the building and other trades throwing many out of employment, but there is plenty of room for farmers with capital to show colonials how best on " bonzana " farms to till the immense areas of land which will be available for cultivation under the systems of irrigation settlements suggested by the present New South Wales Government, which proposals are also favoured by leading members of the

Opposition. Besides the conservation of the waters of Riverina, there is an immense cretaceous formation which is water bearing, and several artesian wells give 4,000,000 gallons per day, while, through the water furnished by one bore, splendid cabbages have been grown where it was stated no vegetation could ever be produced.

New South Wales threw off almost half a century since the incubus of the Imperial convict system, against which there had been strong protests for many years from the Colonies affected by it. It has been estimated that the number of British prisoners sent to Australia was less than had been previously sent to the plantations in America prior to the Revolution, and in both countries there is little now to remind the traveller that these fair lands were once used for the punishment of British exiles. Vested interests in convict labour were only second in importance in Australia to those of negro slavery in America, but these evils have been entirely suppressed in both countries. Civil war was averted in Australia by timely concessions on the part of the English Government, after many local indignation meetings had been held by anti-transportation leagues numbering amongst their members the leading colonists. Transportation to New South Wales ceased by order of the Queen-in-Council on August 1, 1840, and on an attempt to revive it nine years afterwards the people of Sydney rose against the landing of the prisoners, and held a large indignation meeting, at which speeches were made, and even " cutting the painter " advised by one speaker if the remonstrances of the colonists were disregarded. Owing to this manly resistance of the colonists, and the subsequent agitation for responsible government, free institutions have now been gained in each Australian settlement similar to those granted to Upper and Lower Canada, after similar demonstrations had been conducted in them by patriotic men at much personal risk. A number of Canadians concerned in the political insurrections in the early part of the present century were banished to Australasia, and were noted for their expertness in using the axe, though they found the gum trees much harder to cut than the American soft woods, and one of their leaders on his return home was elected a member of one of the local Legislatures.

For over fifty years, and especially since the granting of representative institutions to the Australasian Colonies, their agents have selected suitable emigrants in Great Britain to be assisted from Government funds by paying part of their passage money to Australasia, but of late years payments for this purpose have been discontinued in the majority of the Colonies.

The excess of immigration over emigration for four decennial periods in the Australasian Colonies numbered between years 1851–60, 584,597 ; from 1861–70, 292,942 ; from 1871–81, 330,230 ; and from 1881–91, 403,297. The number of State-aided immigrants to Australasia up to 1890 was 681,995, including 166,417, who arrived there during the period from 1881–90. There have not been similar complaints as to the quality of these immigrants that have been urged with regard to those who were conveyed to the United States from all parts of Europe through agencies whose financial interest was to obtain as many fares as possible, perhaps without strict inspection of those embarking being enforced. Numbers of the recent emigrants to America from the Continent of Europe willingly accept very low rates from employers, and immigration is consequently becoming in us as much disfavour as in Australia with the native workmen, who wish to retain the present standard payments of wages, and not sink to the payments given by employers in Europe.

During the last fifty years the population of the United States has increased at the rate of about 350 per cent., whilst the number of inhabitants in Australasia has grown at the rate of 1,800 per cent. or a ratio of more than five times as much. Australasia has nearly doubled her population during the twenty years from 1871 to 1891, whilst it took the thirty years from 1860 to 1890 for the United States to double the number of her inhabitants.

The population of Australasia, including the native races, now only reaches a density of 1·28 persons per square mile, against 15·5 persons per mile in the United States, so that there is far greater room for immigrants in the former than in the latter country. The development of population in the settlements in Oceana during the last 50 years has in ratio far outstripped its growth in the Eastern States of the American Union, or the Canadian Provinces. The census of 1891 shows that the Colonies of Australasia have increased their present population at the rate of 3·34 per cent. per annum during the last decennial period, whilst Canada during the ten years only obtained an increase of 1·10 per cent. per annum, so that the growth of British Colonies in Oceana in population has been over three times as much as that in British North America.

The annual rate of increase of population per cent. for the Australasian Colonies was in 1801, 15·13; in 1821, 8·97; in 1831, 8·34; in 1841, 10·28; in 1851, 7·36; in 1861, 11·30; in 1871, 4·39; in 1881, 3·60; and in 1891, 3·34; and the increase during the past decade was higher than shown in even the principal countries of North and South America.

Adam Smith stated that the chief causes of prosperity in all new colonies was "Plenty of good land, and liberty to manage their affairs in their own way." Both Australia and Canada possess immense tracts of arable soil, but it is only during the last half of the present century that they were relieved from the direct supervision of the Imperial authorities in Downing-street, and the benefits of responsible Governments conferred upon them.

A proposal was made by Mr. Edward Gibbon Wakefield, in the early days of Australian colonisation, that every new Colony should set aside a certain part of the proceeds of the sale of Crown lands for the introduction of immigrants, so as to pay their passage money, and these views were adopted in the colonisation of South Australia and New Zealand. A large amount of money has been expended by the Australasian colonies in introducing immigrants, and there are records of 682,000 persons having had a greater part of the cost of their passages paid to Australasia, but a similar policy has not been pursued by the United States, which, from being nearer to Europe and other causes, have been enabled to attract the great mass of immigrants without incurring a similar expenditure.

The great bulk of the immigrants from Europe to Australia and America were of an enterprising and independent spirit, and much of this self-reliance has been imparted to their children. Professor Marshall in his work, entitled "The Principles of Economics," says : "In all ages Colonies have been apt to outstrip their Mother Country in vigour and energy. This has been due partly to the abundance of land and the cheapness of necessaries at their command, partly to the natural selection of the strongest characters for a life of adventure, and partly to physiological causes connected with the mixture of races, but perhaps the most important cause of all is to be found in the hope, the freedom, and the changefulness of their lives."

The formation of an American nationality commenced by the dispatch in 1607 of immigrants to Jamestown, where the first permanent settlement for colonization was made under the charters granted by the English Crown to companies and members of the nobility, so that British colonization in North America commenced nearly two centuries before that in the Australian continent. Sir George Grey says there was a great similarity between the Puritan founders of the New England States and the early settlers of the colony of South Australia.

Neither Canada nor Australia appears to present anything like the attractions for the emigration of other nations than the British that the United States does, no doubt greatly owing to most foreigners preferring when changing from monarchial institutions to live under the most successful democratic constitution in the world. Both of these great British possessions are, however, governed by the voice of the people, and Cardinal Moran, the Roman Catholic Archbishop of Sydney, has recently asserted that no republic gives greater liberty than that now enjoyed by Australians.

The original stream of migration to America was due to people whose desire was to get a comfortable home, who found political or ecclesiastical laws oppressive, whom the Government desired to get rid of owing to their misdemeanours, and those who were carried over from Africa as slaves. It has been estimated that it costs the Home Government £175 to bring up an Englishman to his 21st year, and that Australia has therefore gained in 30 years a population valued at £175,000,000, but the indebtedness of America for immigrants is much greater still, for she has received far larger accessions of population from the countries of Europe; and although many Americans appear to be not well pleased with some of these accessions, yet there can be no doubt that much of the progress of the United States, Canada, and Australia is due to enterprising persons from foreign countries who have settled in their midst.

The number of persons to the square mile in the United Kingdom is 318, in Canada 1·5, in Australasia 1·24, and for the whole of the British Dominions 31·7, in the United States (including Alaska Territory and Indians), 17. Of persons to the square mile, the Continent of America has nearly six times as many as Australasia and Polynesia.

The recently formed "People's Party" in the United States express strong objections to the immigrants now arriving, and at the Republican Convention a plank in the manifesto issued declared that "the time has fully come for the passage of more stringent laws on the subject of immigration than those now in force;" so that there is an evident inclination in the Union to restrict the overflow of population from Europe, and a greater volume of it will no doubt come to Australasia, but the distance will prevent any but the better class of immigrants from coming to it, as has been the case in the past. An unsuccessful attempt was recently made in Queensland to import undesirable Italian labourers, as the Colonists were warned by American experience of the dangers arising from such immigration.

There is no pauperism in Australia, as it is understood among European nations, and no poor law adopted by the Legislature, so that in these respects it resembles the United States, in which, it is stated, "all the paupers are imported ones." Temporary relief, however, is liberally given in Australia to orphans and infirm men and women in benevolent asylums, hospitals, and homes for destitute children, but the normal proportion of this class of the population is, as in North America, found to be very small, although, owing to an unparalleled depression over the world at the present time, there are large numbers of persons out of employment in Australia.

The boarding out of destitute children has supplanted the barrack system for orphans in Australia, and in New South Wales the work of the managing committee has been very successful. There are 1,887 Sunday Schools in New South Wales, with 12,169 voluntary teachers, and an average attendance of 123,524 scholars.

One-half of Australasia has a mean temperature in July, the coldest month, of from 40 to 64 degrees, and the other half from 64 to 80 degrees. In December, the temperature ranges from 50 to above 95 degrees, half Australia having a mean temperature below 83 degrees. The climate of Melbourne has a mean temperature of 57·3, and corresponds with Bathurst in New South Wales, and Washington in America. The heat is less in New South Wales in summer and greater in winter than in the corresponding latitudes in the United States. The climate of Australia is far more equable than that of Canada, as there are not anything like the same extremes of heat and cold in Sydney that there are in Montreal, where the butter melts into oil in summer and an ice palace can be constructed in the winter time. In the hottest part of New South Wales the pioneer squatter will be found enjoying good health, and despite occasional years of drought his flocks largely increase, but a frontiersman would be frozen out in a single winter in much of the extensive ice-bound regions of Canada. The old age to which many of the first Australian pioneers and the earliest native-born colonists have lived, notwithstanding the many privations endured by residents in the beginning of the present century, shows that the climate of New South Wales is as favourable to longevity as that of any part of Canada or the United States. There is nothing, for example, like the exodus of citizens from the heat of summer in the capitals of the Australasian Colonies to that which yearly occurs in New York, and which, in 1890, was so apparent on a second census count of the population being taken when the excursionists had returned to their homes. The large number of fatalities from sunstroke in New York and Chicago in the summer of 1892 has no parallel in the hottest part of Australia, where death from this cause very seldom occurs, notwithstanding that the people are very much exposed to the sun, and take but few precautions against its action.

The Australian rainfall, under 10 inches, extends over 1,254,400 square miles, 10 to 20 inches 876,640 square miles, 20 to 30 inches 480,950 square miles, 30 to 40 inches 257,890 square miles, 40 to 50 inches 170,090 square miles, 50 to 60 inches 49,300 square miles, 60 to 70 inches 57,700 square miles, above 70 inches 14,500 square miles. From the above figures it will be seen that by far the greater part of Australia has a rainfall from 10 to 70 inches, and if this water was properly conserved there should be plenty for man, beast, and plant, notwithstanding the assertion of a recent writer that one-third of the continent is a "No Man's Land," through being waterless. Geographers have marked on the maps the interior of Australia to be an immense desert, and in their description make it only to be surpassed in sterility by the Great Sahara of Africa, but the experiences of settlers have often disproved the accounts of first explorers who sometimes in their travels only passed through inhospitable belts of country. Travellers have lamented that much of the interior of Australia is like the Arizona Desert in the middle of the United States, but from the mountain ranges, rivers, and underground springs in both countries will be obtained reservoirs of waters which, by irrigation and artesian boring, should make the now solitary place bloom with products of the garden and the farm.

The Australasian marriage rate, 7·59 per 1,000, birth rate, 34·75 per 1,000, and death rate 14·03 per 1,000, will bear most favourable comparison with those ruling in other countries, the death rate being smaller than even in the United States and Canada. From 1860 to 1888 there was an excess of births over deaths of 1,427,275 persons, equal to 5·21 per cent. of the total increase. These vital statistics tend to prove that the climates of the Australian Colonies are most healthful and superior to those of the countries of Europe. The annual rate of increase of population per cent. from 1881 to 1891 was 3·34 in Australia, being three times as great as in Canada.

The climate of Australia is a remarkably healthy one, principally owing to the salubrious position of the island-continent, between the Pacific, Southern, and Indian Oceans, giving it the benefit of the sea breezes along a very extensive coast line. Fever and ague, which are so prevalent amongst residents in the North American forests, are not malignant in the Australian bush, except in the tropical or swampy parts of the continent, an exemption which is probably due to the prophylactic properties existing in the vegetation through the perpetual exhalation of volatile bodies from the eucalypti, which may, hereafter, make these gum-trees a greater boon to mankind than even the far-famed cinchona tree.

Dr. Andrew Davidson, of Edinburgh, in a recent work on Geographical Pathology, says :—" Australia presents us with the spectacle of a continent from the pathology of which entire classes of diseases, prevalent in other divisions of the globe, were, until comparatively recent times, completely absent. Thus, the whole class of eruptive fevers—smallpox, scarlet fever, and measles—so fatal elsewhere, where unknown. Epidemic cholera, relapsing fever, yellow fever, whooping-cough and diphtheria were equally absent, as was also syphilis." Deaths from phthisis showed 12·73 per cent. in the Australian Mutual Provident Society against 17·61 in the Mutual Life Society of New York. New settlements are not found contaminated with the emanations through the porous earth caused by the use of millions of inhabitants for many ages, and the soil has not been exhausted by over-tillage, as in old countries like Europe and Asia, so that both Australia and America have good sanitary and agricultural conditions for preserving and sustaining life. Australia is singularly fortunate in never having been devastated by the ravages of cholera in an epidemic like that now prevalent in some European countries, notwithstanding her proximity to the home of the scourge in Asia, and the weekly communication with infected ports through the mail steamers. Although small-pox has been several times introduced, it has been quickly stamped out without much loss of life through the excellent precautions of the Boards of Health at the principal Australian ports.

In no part of the British possessions, with the exception of those parts of Canada where the large number of Scotch emigrants keep to the traditions of their old home, is the Sabbath better observed than in the towns of Australasia. There has been, however, a tendency of late years in Sydney especially to have demonstrations and amusements held on Sunday, but this secularisation of the Sabbath is not carried to nearly so great an extent as in San Francisco, where a large number of processions and out-door sports take place on Sunday. There is little difference in conducting religious services in the churches in England, Canada, and Australia, as the same books are generally used by the denominations. The members of the Church of England in New South Wales have recently selected a bishop from their own clergy, instead of, as hitherto, ordaining a dignitary in Great Britain to fill that position ; so that in course of time the English Church in Australia may become in its management like the Episcopal Church in the United States. There is a spirit of freethought in religious matters abroad in Australia as elsewhere, and the attendance at public worship is not as great as could be desired, but there is recent evidence of revival amongst the churches in home evangelisation and mission work. In both America and Australia the great lesson, however, needs yet to be learnt by many who are inclined to esteem material wealth rather than moral worth—"that a nation's treasure is not its gold, or its flocks, or its territory, or its political influence, or its statescraft, but its good men and holy women."

The abuses arising from the facility with which divorces can be obtained in some of the States of the Union was no doubt one of the reasons why the Queen's assent has been only recently granted to a Bill, which had several times previously been passed by the New South Wales Legislature, to dissolve the marriage tie for other reasons than adultery.

In 1892, besides the Centenary celebrations of the discovery of America, the use of gas, the foundation of Trinity College, and the birth of the poet Shelley, the Jubilee of the American Order of the Sons and Daughters of Temperance was celebrated in Sydney, when those present linked hands with their fellow-members in the United States. It was stated that, during the twenty-eight years the Order has had lodges in Australia, 20,000 men and women have been initiated. The Good Templars, another American institution, has had lodges formed in Australia for over twenty years, and continues to perform aggressive work, though some years ago it was nearly closed by dissensions over the American negro question. The Canadian Temperance Act of 1878 has been so conducive to the promotion of good order and the diminution of crime in that country, that a draft Bill has been prepared by the Local Option League of New South Wales, which has been submitted to the Legislature for adoption. Canada has the lowest drink bill per head in the English-speaking world, and she has 2,000,000 of people under State prohibition by a system of full local option dealing with the use of intoxicating liquors, so that her example is looked to with pride by temperance reformers throughout the British dominions. New South Wales alone spends £5,000,000 yearly in strong drink, and the consumption of alcohol per head of population is in Australasia 2·90 proof gallons, and in the United States 2·65 gallons. The greater abstinence from strong drink in America is, no doubt, greatly due to prohibition laws in some of the States, as for example in Iowa, where after a brief time crime decreased one-half and the authorities were enabled to pay off the State debt. The percentage to population of apprehensions for drunkenness in Australia is 1·5, but the police in New South Wales imprison those under the influence of liquor, whilst in other communities the offender must be both drunk and disorderly before being arrested. The average annual consumption of tobacco in Australia is 2·53 lb.; in Canada, 2·11 lb.; and in the United States, 4·40 lb.; so that the people of the latter use nearly twice as much of the noxious weed as the residents in the British Colonies, owing, perhaps, to the habit of chewing tobacco not being prevalent among Australians. A great proportion of adult male Australians however habitually smoke pipes, but do not use cigars to the same extent as Americans. The annual expenditure per inhabitant for food, clothing, rent, taxes, &c., in New South Wales is £47 6s. 3d.; in Canada, £23 6s. 2d.; and in the United States, £32 16s. 2d.; so that the resident in the Southern community can afford to spend on these necessities twice as much as the Canadian and half as much again as the American.

The consumption of tea and coffee per head in Australia is great, being 115 ounces per annum, against 72 ounces in Canada, and 162 ounces in the United States. Recently the duty on tea has been remitted by the Government of New South Wales, so as to cheapen the breakfast table. The tea plant has not been grown in Australia, although there are districts suitable for its cultivation. Australia depends for its tea supply in the same way as America on China and India, there not being enough cheap white labour in the colonies to compete with Asiatic races in their own country. Tea is grown in the Fiji Islands for local consumption, and samples of it will be shown at the Chicago Exhibition. The coffee berry and cocoa plant could be readily grown on the Australian Continent if sufficient labour were available. The warmth of the climate throughout the year in Australia induces greater thirst in the human body than is generally felt by residents in North America, so that besides much tea, lemon squash and milk with soda are also now largely used by Australians. Americans often consume a great variety of artificial mineral waters and other mixed drinks obtainable in the drug stores for that dyspepsia which is too frequently caused through, in the hurry of business, not taking sufficient time at meals to masticate food properly.

The Australian continent is only one-sixth smaller than the whole of the United States of America, as it measures 1,965 miles from north to south, and 2,600 miles from east to west. It has a great advantage over the United States and Canada, in being entirely surrounded by the Pacific, Southern, and Indian Oceans, and holds a unique position in contrast with nations who are only separated by artifical lines, and in this respect is like Great Britain compared with the kingdoms on the Continent of Europe. Australia has a sea-board of 8,850 miles, which is far larger than the coast lines of either the United States or Canada ; and, contrary to what was supposed on its first discovery, it is endowed with many extensive harbours, several of which, such as Jervis Bay, are still almost in a state of nature.

The continent of Australia alone is only 25,372 miles less than the land surface of the United States, exclusive of Alaska, whose frozen region has hitherto attracted very few inhabitants. Settlement of population in the United States extends over two-thirds of the area, whilst a great part of Australia is but sparsely inhabited, except along the sea coasts and on the margins of the interior rivers. But these settled districts with the back country over which the flocks of the pioneer squatter now range extend over territory almost as large as the settled area of the United States. In the extent over which occupation by pastoralists has spread during the past century, Australia is found to have distanced even North America, notwithstanding the great advantage possessed by the United States and Canada over the Colonies at the Antipodes, in their nearness to the great centres of European population. The absence in Australia of immense navigable lakes, such as those of North America, has made the work of colonization more difficult to the Australian pioneer, who has reclaimed the interior of the Continent only after battling with many natural disadvantages which might appal even the American backwoodsman.

The Australian Colonies fronting the Pacific Ocean have extensive ranges of mountains running a short distance from the sea board almost parallel with the coast, resembling to a great extent the Sierra Nevada Range in California, and the Rocky Mountains in British Columbia. Mount Kosciusko in the Australian Alps is 7,308 feet high, and is snow-capped even in summer like Shasta and other mountains on the Pacific coast of America.

The vast heritage of the British Colonies in Australasia has a comparatively small population of less than 4,000,000 people, who have as yet but slightly developed the great mineral and other natural resources already discovered within its borders. The estimated number of persons to the square mile in the Australasian Colonies on the 31st December, 1891, including aborigines and Maories, was 1·21, and for each Colony respectively it was as follows:—New South Wales, 3·65; Victoria, 12·98; Queensland, 0·59; South Australia, 0·35; Western Australia, 0·05; Tasmania, 5·59; and New Zealand, 6·00. These figures afford a strange contrast to those of 308 per mile, the density of population in the United Kingdom; or 20·06, being that of the United States of America, and are even less than the rate for the Dominion of Canada. About one-third of the population of the two principal Colonies is contained in each of the capital cities of Melbourne and Sydney, the inhabitants of which number 490,902 and 383,380 respectively; and, as regards both numbers and wealth, these cities are entitled to rank with some of the largest in the world. The estimated population of Australasia at the end of 1891 was 3,899,177 persons, with a proportion of 86·61 females to 100 males, who are located as follows:—New South Wales, 1,165,300; Victoria, 1,157,804; South Australia, 325,766; Western Australia, 53,285; Queensland, 410,345; New Zealand, 634,058; and Tasmania, 152,619. At the foundation of New South Wales in 1788, the population of Australasia numbered only 1,030 souls, and increased in 1801 to 6,508, in 1821 to 35,610, in 1841 to 211,095, in 1851 to 430,296, in 1861 to 1,252,994, in 1871 to 1,924,770, in 1881 to 2,742,550, and in 1891 to 3,809,895. The total increase in population from 1881 to 1891 was 1,067,345 against an increase of 504,601 for Canada.

A fine collection of large photographic enlargements by the bromide process, which have been prepared by Mr. Charles Potter, Government Printer of New South Wales, under the direction of the local Commission for the Columbian Exposition, will well illustrate to visitors to it not only the magnificent scenery to be found in New South Wales and the progress of many of its principal towns, but also the present condition of some of the adjacent South Sea Islands. A panorama of the city and harbour of Sydney 21 feet 0 inches x 30 inches will give an excellent idea of the extent of the metropolis of New South Wales, and of some of the manifold beauties of Port Jackson. The photographs of many large buildings recently erected in Sydney afford a strange contrast to the much smaller houses they replace, which are also shown in a series of drawings made in 1842 by Mr. John Rae, late Under Secretary for Public Works. The Government Printing Office in Sydney has obtained from the judges at the various International Exhibitions many high awards for the excellence of the letter-press printing, binding, photography, and other scientific and artistic processes at work in that extensive establishment. Mr. Potter recently visited America so as to obtain the latest improvements in labour-saving machinery now at work in the Government Printing Offices at Washington and Ottawa and in other large typographical establishments, whose operations would astonish Benjamin Franklin if he could once more visit the earth.

Sir George Grey, speaking of the Samoan Islands, said: "It would be far preferable to leave each of these island groups with independent Governments, settling all disputes among themselves by arbitration, and guided, if possible, by a commission of foreign powers. It is clear America is aiming at this line of policy, annexing none of the islands herself, and doing her utmost to preserve the peace of the Pacific. This also is certain to be the policy of all English possessions in this part of the world." However, a

D

London cablegram of 13th November, 1892, announces that—"It is understood that America will shortly declare a protectorate over the Hawaiian
Islands." A census taken in 1891 showed that there were in Samoa 235
British-born subjects, 90 Germans, 12 Americans, and a few of other nationalities, who last year carried on a trade amounting to £105,359, including an
export of cotton valued at £2,200, of copra £25,160, and of coffee £860.
The possession of some of the groups of islands in the Pacific Ocean by
other Powers than the British has been recognised in a neighbourly spirit by
the residents of Australia ; but the proximity of the French penal settlement
in New Caledonia, has been a source of great annoyance to them, owing to
the frequent escapes of récidivistes, many hundreds of whom have landed in
Queensland and New South Wales. Australians would, however, naturally
greatly prefer that Oceana should be held by themselves, or by a confederation
of the English-speaking races, who are properly trained to the working of
free institutions, and powerful enough always to preserve peace throughout
the southern seas, rather than by several foreign powers who would introduce
old-world strifes to be fought out on the waters of the Pacific. The proposed
union of the Australasian Colonies will, it is hoped, therefore, be but a
step towards closer union in citizenship between the peoples of Great
Britain, the United States, Canada, and Australasia, and ultimately lead to
that federation for the peace of the world, foreshadowed by Albert the Good
when he choose for the Great Exhibition of 1851, the noble motto :—"God has
made of one blood all nations of the earth." The late Right Hon. W. B.
Dalley, P.C., a distinguished native Australian, once said to a number of
American New South Welshmen who met at Sydney to celebrate "the 4th
of July":—" But this is not only a day of proud memories and rejoicing, and
national, and hearty, and loving congratulations. It is a day on which we
should draw closer to each other, learn to take our places together before the
whole world, and prepare ourselves for the future. Upon the English-
speaking peoples of the world will be cast, sooner or later, the duty of
maintaining—nay, of commanding—its peace, guarding its liberties, and perpetuating its institutions. They comprise already 320 millions of the people of
the world under our own Empire, and more than 60 millions of Americans.
We have united revenues of nearly 300 millions, of which we have 210
millions, and America nearly 90 millions. We have a united commerce of
one billion one hundred and ninety millions, of which England has nearly
900 millions, and the United States 300 millions. We have between us one-
fifth of the area and one-third of the population of the world. United we
can guard the freedom and guarantee the peace of mankind." There ought
to be no wars in the twentieth century, as all international differences should
now be settled by arbitration, and a recent allocation of the Pope expresses
the hope that the Powers will confer with a view to disarming. No wars of
any consequence have occurred in Australasia, except the Maori War in New
Zealand, over a quarter of a century ago, which was ended by Imperial troops,
assisted by Colonial regiments. In 1885 a military contingent was sent by the
people of New South Wales to the Soudan, during the war in that country,
and to assist Great Britain in her endeavours to put down slavery. The cost
of sending the Soudan Contingent away approached nearly half a million
sterling, and the late Hon. W. B. Dalley for his services in this connection
(as the Acting Premier of the Colony) was made a Privy Councillor of Great
Britain, and since his death a tablet has been erected to his memory in
Westminster Abbey, by the people of England, and this first imperial memorial to a native-born Australian is placed near those of many distinguished
British and Colonial statesmen and warriors.

Although the wisdom of interfering with European politics by sending away the Australian Contingent has since been questioned by many Australians, there can be no doubt that the colonists are deeply interested in having the Suez Canal kept always open as the present great route for Colonial commerce from Europe; and the late W. B. Dalley, in probably the last letter written by him on any public question, claimed for this act of the New South Wales Government that it had done "more to elevate these Australian Colonies in the eyes of the universal world than anything which has taken place since their foundation."

The trade interests of Australia with Europe require that, not only the route through the Suez Canal should be kept open, but that outward bound vessels passing the Cape of Good Hope should be protected, as this trade is estimated to reach twenty millions sterling, although very much less than it would have amounted to had not the Red Sea route became the favourite one for vessels from Europe. Coaling stations are a necessity for the modern steamer from Europe to Australia, as even the latest war vessel, it is stated, can only carry sufficient coal for a voyage of 4,000 miles, consequently the extensive carboniferous deposits on the Pacific shores of the Australasian Colonies require to be defended, or colonial commerce could be greatly interfered with by steam privateers who would attack after the style of the notorious "Alabama." Mr. Louis Brennan, an Australian, obtained from the English Government £110,000 for a controllable torpedo invented by him, which was favourably reported on by the military authorities, and therefore ought to do good service against attacking war vessels.

The late Henry Ward Beecher once remarked, "that it was for old men to be conservatives and for young men to be democrats"; and as this proposition applies to nations as much as to individuals, the United States is found to be in many ways more conservative in its government than the Australasian Colonies. The political institutions framed by each of the colonies differ only in the constitution of the Upper Houses of Legislature, which in New South Wales, Queensland, and Western Australia are nominated by the Crown, but in Victoria, South Australia, New Zealand, and Tasmania are elected by the people. The members of the Lower House are elected by manhood suffrage, and the voter is protected by a system of ballot. Mr. Andrew Carnegie, in an article in the *Nineteenth Century Review* on the recent general elections in England and America, reckons the three branches of the American Government to be more conservative than the British Government, as "there is always in existence a Senate and a House of Representatives, and an Executive, each with fixed terms of office, who have in their hands the guidance and control of all important questions, and whose terms of office do not all expire at the same time, while the affirmative action of all three is indispensable for any action at all." He further says: "But the contrast between the Monarchy and the Republic, great as it is at present, is one which I believe is to become less and less, year after year, until the two great branches of the English-speaking race, possessed of the same language, literature, law, and religion, shall possess the advantage of similar conservative institutions. Old England and New England cannot permanently differ very much, only such light variations can remain as a slightly differing environment renders necessary and healthful to both. The democracy, after sweeping away every shred of privilege here, may be trusted to pause, and become as truly conservative in the old world as the new, for the political equality of the citizen once established makes all citizens conservative."

The English form of constitution is now in operation in Australasia and in Canada, and, as in Great Britain, the judiciary is appointed by the Government, and there is a permanent Civil Service, so that there are not the same complaints against the administration of justice and the public departments that there are in the United States, where the offices are often given to zealous partisans at each change of Government, who are also ousted before obtaining much experience of their duties, on the maxim that "to the victors belong the spoils." Besides the seven colonies in Australasia, Canada, Newfoundland, and Cape Colony have responsible institutions, and the Governor, as arbitrator, is, therefore, the only connecting link between the Home and Colonial Governments. There is, however, a much stronger bond between England, Canada, and Australia, in the sentiment of nationality contained in kindred blood, similar privileges, and equal protection, than in a commercial union, which might debar them from trading with other nations. Mr. William McMillan, M.P., President of the New South Wales Commission for the Chicago Exhibition, was a delegate to the Congress of Chambers of Commerce, recently held in London, and is reported to have spoken as follows respecting a proposed fiscal union between Great Britain and her colonies:—"Mr. William McMillan (Sydney, late Colonial Treasurer of New South Wales), in resuming the debate, expressed the opinion that the questions they were discussing had great political significance. He must condemn every opinion which had been uttered by Sir Charles Tupper, except the sentiment of union. It had been said that a differential duty of 5 per cent., as referred to by Sir Charles Tupper, was a very simple one; but the difference between 5 per cent. or 1 per cent. and freetrade was the difference of a great and immortal principle. He maintained unhesitatingly that freetrade had been the dominant factor in placing this country in its position of pre-eminence. It had been argued that Great Britain had not freetrade, but he denied the aspersion. The difference between a few simple specific duties on goods well known, easily traced, through which all smuggling was easily prevented, and 1 per cent., 2 per cent., or even 5 per cent. upon the whole of the imports was a difference not altogether of freetrade or protection, but a difference between the freedom of their ports and the horrible system of restriction. He held that the moment England gave up freetrade her commercial empire would be gone."

In 1895, the British House of Commons will celebrate its sixth-hundreth anniversary, as it was called into existence by King Edward in 1295, and the nations of the old and new worlds owe much to the work of this historic assembly, and more especially the Legislatures of Canada and Australasia, though there are still defects in both these Colonial Constitutions which require to be corrected, such as abuses attending the working of party government and the consequent delay in passing necessary legislation.

Several leading politicians in New South Wales have recently urged that, in view of the importance of the legislation still needed in Australia, it would be necessary to adopt some of the restrictions allowed in the American House of Representatives, especially with regard to the delivery of long speeches, and the length of the Session. The close observance of the forms of procedure of the British House of Commons by the Australian Legislatures, since these colonies obtained representative institutions, has also, it is thought, checked the passing of many necessary measures, since government by party naturally leads to a continuous contest between "the ins and the outs," which is often decided by an appeal to the people, for the Legislative Assembly may be dissolved at any time, instead of being elected for a stated

period, as is the case with the United States Congress. The frequent change of Ministry through the tactics of the Opposition often causes Bills submitted to Parliament to be lost, and new measures have to be considered by an incoming Cabinet, who in turn may be ousted from office, as Governments do not retain office for a stated time, as in the American Union. One of the members of the New South Wales Legislative Assembly, who is a student of the politics of England and America, has recently suggested that much time might be saved by Parliament if the procedure of the United States Congress were adopted with regard to the threshing out the details of Bills by Select Committees, who would afterwards make their recommendations for adoption by the whole House. It would be, however, unwise to make many radical changes in a political system to which Australians have been long trained.

Although the Federation of the Australasian Colonies has not yet been consummated, there has been a Federal Union of Victoria, Queensland, Western Australia, and Tasmania since 1885 for the purpose of dealing with such matters of common Australasian interest, in respect of which united action is desirable, as can be dealt with without unduly interfering with the management of the internal affairs of the several colonies by their respective Legislatures. New South Wales, South Australia, and New Zealand have not joined the Union, as it was urged that it was only similar to the Confederacy of the American States in 1771, " which had no judiciary to enforce its acts, and no executive head to represent and administer its authority."

The decisions of the present Federal Council, which meets annually in Tasmania, have no power unless they are accepted by the local Legislatures of Victoria, Queensland, Tasmania, and Western Australia, the only colonies which have as yet joined the union, although it was once stated South Australia would send representatives. At the Federation Conference in 1890 an address to the Queen was adopted by representatives from the Australasian Colonies declaring that in its opinion the best interests of the colonies, require the early formation of a union under the Crown into one Government both Legislative and Executive. The Federal Convention held in Sydney in 1891, which was the most important Conference of Australian statesmen ever called together, agreed upon a constitution to be recommended for the proposed Commonwealth of Australia, which provides for a Federal Legislature and Federal Executive Government in addition to the present Colonial Legislatures and Executives.

Australia has had no occasion to call forth a mighty military genius like Washington or Grant, since it has had no foreign foes to repel or civil strife to repress. Her legislators, have, however, initiated measures of reform copied by other countries, and some of these statesmen, such as the late Lord Sherbrooke, have occupied afterwards leading positions in the British House of Commons. The great loyalty of the Australian people has now become proverbial, but in years past many political struggles were undertaken by Wentworth and other patriotic men, nearly all passed away, to secure for the British race settled in Australia the privileges enjoyed in Great Britain, and the present generation are deeply indebted to these patriots for the free institutions at present possessed by the colonists.

Before the introduction of telegraphy, both America and Australia were comparatively isolated from the rest of the globe, but the laying of cables, which in the middle of the century was thought impossible, has brought these two countries into close communication with every other nation, and the news of the world is now cabled from London to Sydney almost as soon as it is received by the New York press. It should not be long, however, before a direct ·cable is laid between ·America and Australia, as both the 'United States, Canadian, and Australian Governments are now giving the ·subject the special consideration it deserves, and the New South Wales Government has already agreed to subsidise a line *via* New Caledonia.

None of the Australian Colonies have extended the electoral franchise to women, although, when a ratepayer, she may now vote at municipal contests, and is thus, no doubt, being prepared for full electoral rights. There is at present an agitation in New South Wales for an extension of this suffrage to females on attaining 21 years of age, and a Women's Suffrage Bill was recently submitted to the New Zealand Parliament. A measure for allowing each elector to vote in one electorate is also warmly advocated by labour representatives in New South Wales, and the Government has introduced a Bill to give " one man one vote," so that the franchise of every elector should carry the same weight and in the same way as now obtains in the United States. In only a few of the United States has the suffrage been given to women, although Lincoln, Beecher, Longfellow, and other leading Americans expressed themselves favourable ·to this extension many years ago, and this omission is more remarkable considering the otherwise great deference to the female sex paid in the United States, where she often occupies the pulpit and the platform. The great majority of teachers in the United States are also females, who are admirable conductors of mixed classes in the elementary and high schools, which happens to a less extent in the Australian Colonies, where the sexes are kept apart during instruction. Women are also eligible for election as superintendents of education, and numbers of them are employed as clerks, shorthand and type writers in Government and other offices to a much greater extent than in Australia. The fact that the female sex largely outnumber the male sex may be one of the reasons why women are not given an electoral vote in the Eastern States of America, but this objection could not be urged in Australasia, where men form by far the larger proportion of the population through their greater immigration and the excess of males born over females.

Women in America take more interest in Parliamentary elections than they are found doing in the Australian Colonies or England, as, for example, at the meetings of the Republican party held in the Wigwam at San Francisco nearly half the immense audience consists of the female sex, who are accompanied by their husband, son, or in company with other friends. Although many thousands usually assembled at these gatherings, they are conducted in a most orderly manner, and this is no doubt greatly due to the presence of ladies. Unlike the political meetings in Australia and England, similar assemblages in America are held in the party Wigwam, and the speeches and recitations are interspersed with tunes from an excellent band, whilst a good choir renders patriotic and political songs, which are highly appreciated by the audience. There is seldom any appearance of rowdyism at these meetings, and no attempt is made to interrupt the speakers, as unhappily is often the case at colonial political meetings. Youths in San Francisco are found taking great interest in the State elections, and in company with adult party associations march from their headquarters to the meeting place, bearing banners with appropriate inscriptions. There are a great many subjects taught in the public and high schools in Australasia; but little attention is given as yet even in the highest of them by lessons on civil government to prepare the future electors for the task of selecting representatives for the Legislative Assembly. In the United States considerable importance is now attached to men and women being well grounded in a knowledge of the principles underlying the government of their country. The majority of American youths and maidens, even amongst the working classes in America, can therefore render an intelligent account of the practices connected with the constitution of the United States, and readily define the powers of the State Legislature and the Federal Government. This knowledge is principally acquired in the State schools, where there are excellent special text-books used, giving the requisite information to the embryo elector and legislator. The value of this training in the principles of political government is evidenced by the satisfactory manner in which the male or female citizen of the United States can usually give an account of the procedure at elections, and of the administrative duties to be performed by the members of the Cabinet.

General Booth on his recent return to England, after a triumphant reception given him in the Australasian Colonies in 1892, remarked that they were worthy compeers of the American States ; but that what Australians needed was a " strong government !" The colonists, however, suffered too much in the early colonial days from the absolute rule of the Imperial authorities and the abuses attending Colonial Office patronage to easily relinquish the right of self-government, or to tolerate a dictatorship either in politics or religion, even from the best-meaning Governor or philanthrophist.

At the commemoration of the Jubilee of the reign of Queen Victoria, in 1887, the foundation stone of the Imperial Institute was laid at South Kensington, in the presence of an imposing assemblage, with the view of bringing the whole of the British possessions better in touch with the mother country, but during the five years since this movement began none of the schemes propounded for Imperial Federation have been adopted by the colonists, who appear to be satisfied with their condition, and to desire no change in their relations with the Home Government. The varied experience gained in New South Wales when it was a Crown Colony, renders it most unlikely that its people will readily give up any of the free institutions now enjoyed by them under responsible government, or consent to be legislated for under any proposed constitution by a Council sitting in London, where their interests would command comparatively little attention. The objections to the proposal by Adam Smith for the Imperial union of Great Britain with her colonies are not now as strong as when urged by him, owing to the inconvenience of a great distance from London having of late years been annihilated by the use of the electric cable and speedy steam communication, so that it is now as easy to reach the Antipodes as it was America not many years since ; and this rapid communication is also in strange contrast with the slowness of the means of transit at the service of Great Britain and her colonies 100 years ago. It must, however, be admitted that it is very desirable, as urged in the last century, that the colonies of the British Empire, and other like communities with the same ancestors, language, traditions, and institutions, should in some way be united by political as well as commercial and sentimental ties. The kind of alliance required has not yet been selected by the communities most interested, but a union may be hereafter effected under a constitution which will tax some future Alexander Hamilton to evolve, as the proposals already published have met with far more objections than were made to the adoption of the present constitution of the United States. A cablegram from London, published in Sydney on November 14, 1892, announces the following fresh proposals for the consideration of the colonists :—" The committee of the Imperial Federation League has

unanimously advised that when Australasia and South Africa become each
united under one Government, like that of Canada, their London representatives be appointed members of the Imperial Council, which would include a
Prime Minister and Secretaries of State for Foreign Affairs, War, Colonies,
India, Admiralty, and the Exchequer. The Council would deal with the
question of Imperial defence on the lines of the Duke of Devonshire's
Commission, and would supervise the appropriation of money contributed
for the defence of the Empire by the United Kingdom and the colonies.
The committee believes that the colonies would be willing to share in the
cost of the general defence of the Empire if they were given a share in the
control of the expenditure. A common fund, making provision for the local
defence of the colonies, would be accepted as an equivalent for a direct
contribution to the Imperial exchequer. Among the subjects conducing,
but not essential, to federation, though likely to become practicable, were the
following : The admission of colonial securities into the list of trust funds,
an Imperial guarantee in regard to local loans for purposes subservient to
Imperial ends, immigration, dry docks, strategic cables, railways, the opening
of outside administrative services of the Empire to all, the appointment of
colonial jurists on the Judicial Committee of the Privy Council, increasing
the uniformity of the statute law, and uniform Imperial postage. Special
arrangements in connection with the telegraph service would be provided
for later on. The committee expects that much could be done to improve
inter-Imperial trading relations, and is of opinion that a conference to
consider the question of Imperial defence ought to be summoned at the
earliest fitting opportunity, with a preliminary inquiry by a Royal Commission." There has been no public meeting called as yet in Australia to
consider these proposals of the Imperial Federation League.

The lines of the proposed Bill for constituting the Commonwealth of Australia, compared with the Federal system of the United States and Canada,
have been described as follows :—The principle on which the Senate is to
be elected is taken from the constitution of the United States, which provides that the Senate should be composed of two senators from each State
chosen by the Legislature thereof for six years, and that each senator shall
have one vote. Objections have been urged against giving the same representation in the Senate to Western Australia as to New South Wales, as the
latter has over fifty times more population. It has, however, been stated
that the reasons which induced the American statesmen to frame the Senate
on principles unknown to the British constitution, apply with equal force to
the traditions of the colonies as they did to those of the States. The main
principles on which the House of Representatives is to be elected are taken
from the constitution of the United States. With regard to the relation of
the Federal Parliament to the State Parliaments, the Bill adopts the principle established in the United States, where the federal powers conferred
by the constitution are strictly delegated powers, the result being that as to
matters not specified as being within the exclusive usage of Congress the
States retain all the powers vested in them by their respective constitutions.
The plan adopted in the draft Bill as to money bills is sanctioned by both
the English and American systems. On the one hand, it resembles the
English practice by saying that the Senate may reject but not amend a
money bill ; on the other hand, it partly follows the American practice in
saying that where the Senate may not amend a money bill it may return it
to the Lower House at any stage, with a request for the omission or amend-
ment of any item. The power of finally dealing with the amendments, how-

ever, rests with the Lower House. The Federal Executive Council is intended to resemble in character and functions the Privy Council of Canada. Provision is made for the appointment of a Federal Judicature, and the Supreme Court of Australia, as a final court of appeal, will take the place which is now held by the Privy Council in London.

It is believed that America and Australia will greatly help to solve some of the social problems which are agitating European countries, where " the rich are becoming richer, and the poor are becoming poorer," but it is found there is a tendency even in new lands to repeat the miseries of the old world, as it is stated that in 1891, 23,895 warrants of evictions were issued in the city of New York, and that one-twelfth of the population of the State of New York receive charity or public aid of some kind. The recent conflicts between labour and capital in the United States have greatly surpassed in extent and violence similar strikes in Australia, although the latter have proved most disastrous, and show that the happy time has not yet arrived in either country to secure that:

> The war-drum throb no longer, and the battle flag be furled,
> In the Parliament of man, the Federation of the World.

Dr. Garran, the President of the recently-formed Council of Conciliation and Arbitration, which has been appointed under the "Trades Disputes Act" of New South Wales, in his opening address, stated that " by the last mail I received a letter from the American editor of the *Review of Reviews* expressing his extreme admiration at the result of the Royal Commission on Strikes. He expressed his high appreciation of the report, and said that it contained very important suggestions of a practical nature, which would be of assistance in determining questions of a similar character arising in that part of the world : "They were struggling with the same industrial difficulties in America, and many people there were looking eagerly to Australia to see how we are working out the different problems which have to be considered."

Lord Coleridge, on the occasion of his visit to America, reminded his hosts that—" It is not the mere extent of their country, the height of their mountains, the length of their rivers, nor yet the immensity of the capabilities of the soil they tread that makes a people great"; but there can be no doubt that new countries, covering immense territory like Australasia, Canada, and the United States, afford opportunities for the exercise of enterprise and intelligence in developing their vast natural resources not to be found in European kingdoms, where the mines and the land have been worked for many ages, and are in the possession of a comparatively few people under a law of primogeniture such as that in force in Great Britain.

North America is acknowledged to be the wealthiest part of the world, so that the United States and Canada have always drawn large streams of immigration from the countries of Europe, and, therefore, now afford the highest material standard of industrial progress by which Australasia can be measured.

Municipal government is kept quite apart from party politics in Australia, and, therefore, much of the jobbery complained of with regard to the management of many of the American cities does not obtain there. It is believed that a measure about to be passed in New South Wales to make local government compulsory, will do away with any political logrolling in the Legislative Assembly for works in unincorporated districts, and otherwise relieve Ministers of work which can be more economically performed, as in the United States, by Municipal authorities elected by the ratepayers.

Although Australasia is not covered with a network of local government as is found in the United States, yet the colonies have a large number of municipalities in the more settled parts which, during 1890, expended £5,713,071 on sanitary improvements, of which £4,109,297 was collected from the ratepayers, and these amounts have been disbursed without that jobbery so prevalent in some of the cities in the United States in which irresponsible combinations known as "rings" control the administration of affairs.

The law is fairly and firmly administered throughout Australasia, both in criminal and civil cases, and the tribunals secure greater public confidence than in the United States, so that, like in Canada, there is never recourse to "Lynch" or mob law, under which a prisoner is put to death without a proper trial by the duly appointed authorities, which has often been done in the American Union owing to the great difficulty in obtaining convictions against wealthy offenders.

In Australasia the committals average 1·0 per 1,000 of population; the convictions in superior courts, 0·6; and the apprehensions, 33·8, which figures when compared with those for other decades shows a decrease of crime during the last decennial period.

The proportion of the native-born population in the number of criminals arrested in New South Wales is very much less than of colonists born in the United Kingdom, but this may perhaps be to some extent accounted for by the fact that the majority of Australians are much younger than those who have come from other countries, although there have now been three generations of colonial-born on the soil.

Both in the United States and Australia the native-born as a rule are found more law-abiding and intelligent than the great mass of immigrants from European countries; but this is no doubt greatly due to the better educational opportunities available for even the poorest child in these new lands. The Australian, however, has not as yet received at school that training in political science and constitutional history which induces so large a proportion of the American youth of both sexes to take such an intelligent interest in matters affecting the welfare of the Republic, and makes them so well posted in the mode of civil government in the United States.

The native youth in Sydney were once remarkable for their great sobriety, although, like most young people, fond of boisterous sport; but of late years there has been a more marked increase of disorderly conduct through groups of idle boys assembling in the streets, which has led to special legislation for checking "larrikinism." Much of this misconduct might be prevented if the Public High Schools were open free of an evening as in San Francisco, in which thousands of youths are found continuing their education in advanced subjects, after leaving the primary schools, and when engaged in earning a living.

The number of those signing marriage registers with marks is less in Australasia than any European country excepting Prussia, where the number is only a little less; so that Australians compare very favourably by this educational test with the most cultured people to be found in the world.

The Primary School systems of Australasia are similar to those which have proved so advantageous in the United States, where the excellence of the "little school-house" is often quoted by fervent orators, in the same way as the Public School system in New South Wales is considered by some to be perfection itself. Denominational schools in Australasia are now principally conducted by the Roman Catholic Church and not subsidised by the State, although for many years they obtained a portion of the public funds in a similar way to that obtaining now in Canada. The education imparted by the State throughout Australasia is compulsory, nearly secular and free except in New South Wales, where undenominational religious lessons are given and a small charge is made except to those who cannot afford to pay it. In the United States education even in the high schools is given free, as a maxim carried out by Americans is to prefer to pay the schoolmaster rather than the gaoler. The excellent American system of appropriating large portions of the public lands in every State as a perpetual endowment to schools and universities has unfortunately not been adopted in Australia; but the amounts expended from annual parliamentary votes for education per head of population is even larger than in either the United States or Canada. Although the systems of public instruction in operation in Australasia are excellent, it is believed that much could be learnt by Australian experts from the courses of training now pursued in many of the educational institutions of the United States, especially with regard to the best methods of agricultural, scientific, and manual training as adapted to the requirements of a new country.

There were in Australasia in 1890, 7,287 State schools, 14,586 teachers, and 426,924 scholars in average attendance; but in Canada there were 142,212 more pupils attending school than in Australasia, no doubt mainly owing to the larger population, greater number at school age, and the fact that in North America school is not generally kept all the year round as is the custom in the southern colonies, where the country children are not so largely employed in harvesting the crops as in the United States and the Dominion. In Australasia, 2,425 private schools were in operation, having 6,736 teachers, with a gross enrolment of 130,061 students, who as a rule are receiving excellent instruction in elementary and advanced subjects. Thus the total number of scholars is 832,808; but there can be no doubt that many children are not attending school owing to the compulsory clauses of the Education Acts not being enforced as rigidly as in England.

Australia, with a much smaller population than Canada, spends from public funds nearly £500,000 sterling more on primary education; but this is greatly owing to the school-houses erected being more substantial, and the teachers being principally males, and therefore better paid than is the case in the Dominion.

There are about 2,300 students in the Universities of Australasia, and at the Sydney University (founded on motion moved by Mr. W. C. Wentworth in 1849) there are 33 professors and lecturers and 647 graduates and students. At the Sydney Technical College (founded on motion moved by Mr. Edward Dowling in 1879) and its suburban and country branches, there are over 7,000 students and 131 teachers and lecturers. A large collection of the works of the students of the Sydney Technical College will be shown at the Chicago Exposition.

Canada, from its earliest days, has been noted for excellent colleges established to give higher education, but the value of the degrees given in these institutions does not surpass those of the Australian Universities whose standards of examinations have been raised from time to time since their foundations.

In Australasia there are 1,134 Public Libraries, containing 1,624,813 books, and in no part of the world are there more Free Libraries and Mechanics' Institutes in proportion to population than are to be found scattered throughout these colonies. In New South Wales alone, in 1891, there were 3,161 public and private educational institutions, 7,028 teachers, and 250,691 scholars, or, of the latter, about 22 per cent. of the population, as against 4·40 per cent. in 1836 and 13·96 in 1866, so that the number receiving instruction is being largely increased.

There is no country that expends so much on education in proportion to population as the Australasian Colonies. Like the United States, the expenditure on education surpasses that for defence purposes, and in this respect both form a marked contrast to European countries. The Australasian Colonies spent in 1891 on primary schools alone £2,244,291, or £4 7s. 11d. per child in average attendance, whilst the expenditure for defence purposes was £793,750, or at the rate of 4s. 3d. per inhabitant.

The total debt incurred by Australasia for fortifications to the end of 1890 was £2,065,517, or 10s. 10d. per head of population. As the continent of Australia has never been the scene of either foreign or civil war its experiences have been happier than even the continent of America, whose soil unfortunately from the earliest days has often been stained with the carnage of contending forces. The United States had to incur a debt during the late civil war of more than 400 million sterling, most of which she has paid off during the past quarter of a century, showing the wonderful recuperative force of the industries of that country. She now willingly pays a pension roll of £20,000,000 sterling for the benefit of the worn-out soldiers who made so many sacrifices to preserve the Union, and also gives a further noble example to the countries of Europe in taking care of the widows and orphans of those who perished in her defence. The policy of non-intervention in foreign politics has happily saved the United States from many of the cruel wars which have devasted other countries, and it is hoped that her peace policy will always succeed in the preservation of peace throughout all parts of the American continent and the adjacent islands.

The connection between the mother country and Australia has done much, not only to assist in the material development of these colonies, but also to promote education, religion, and morality among the people, as from the earliest days the great Missionary Societies of England have had numbers of their agents at work in Australasia. Many of the native populations in the Pacific Ocean have been reclaimed from cannibalism by missionaries sent by the London Missionary Society and other Protestant and Catholic religious associations, and regular fleets of vessels now carry a large trade of natural products from these islands to the Australian continent. The Fiji Islands, which were civilised principally by Wesleyan and Roman Catholic Missionaries, who have brought most all the natives under the influence of Christianity, so that they are found to behave themselves as well as the majority of Christians in other lands, instead of murdering and eating any shipwrecked crew as was done in their original savage state, and would still be done in some of the other Pacific islands where the gospel has not been preached, and where "head hunting" still prevails. The first centenary of the Baptist Missionary Society is being celebrated in the centennial year of the discovery of America, as the modern Missionary Society was founded by William Carey at Kettering in 1792, and now there are a hundred societies in Europe, the United States, and Canada, with 11,388 stations and out-stations, 4,693 male and 3,228 female missionaries, 40,083 Christian workers, and 726,883 communicants in these once heathen lands. Over 6,000 persons have volunteered in America to undertake missionary work, and there are several thousands of students and others in Great Britain who have expressed their willingness to carry the Gospel to foreign parts, so that a great awakening in heathen lands should be expected by the end of the century.

State aid to religion was abolished many years ago in nearly all the Australasian Colonies, and, although the Episcopal Church is by far the largest Protestant denomination as in England, all the sects are completely severed from the civil power. The example of America is followed in there being no national church in Australasia, without injury, it is found, to the proper promulgation of the Christian faith in both countries. The late Rev. Dr. Lang was a great champion of the voluntary system, owing to noticing its success in the United States when visiting them from Australia in 1840.

There are 3,200 ministers of religion in Australasia, and the returns of religious denominations at the late census showed that the laity of the Church of England constitutes over a third of the population. The adherents of the Roman Catholic Church rank second in numbers, or nearly double that of the Presbyterian Church, being the same relative proportion as in the United States. The Wesleyan Church in Australia which comes next in number of adherents to the Presbyterian Church, is not so numerous as in the United States, where the Methodist Episcopal Church and other branches of Wesleyans by far outnumber those contained in any other denomination. The Congregationalists, Baptist, and Lutherans number about the same in Australasia, but the two former, though very influential considering their numbers, do not furnish the same percentage of population as in America, where the Baptists are only second to the Methodists, and the Independents are nearly as many as the Episcopalians. The Episcopalians constitute about half the population of New South Wales, and relatively to population the Wesleyans are strongest in South Australia, and the Presbyterians in New Zealand. The preponderance of particular sections of religious denominations in the various colonies is due, in some measure, to the action of emigration associations on a denominational basis, by which, for example, numbers of Presbyterians were introduced into New Zealand, Wesleyans into South Australia, and Lutherans into Queensland.

It has been calculated by Mr. Coghlan that the numbers of adherents to the several religious denominations in the Australasian Colonies out of the estimated population of 3,809,895, in 1891 were as follows:—Church of England, 1,516,190, or 39·79 per cent.; Roman Catholic, 829,180, or 21·76 per cent.; Presbyterian, 495,830, or 13·01 per cent.; Wesleyan and Primitive Methodist, 414,680, or 11·57 per cent.; Congregational, 71,120, or 2·05 per cent.; Baptist, 84,340, or 2·21 per cent.; Lutheran, 75,240, or 1·97 per cent.; Unitarian, 4,230, or 0·11 per cent.; Hebrews, 14,820, or 0·40 per cent.; Salvation Army, 42,820, or 1·12 per cent.; Pagans, 49,580, or 1·30 per cent.; other Protestants, 49,770, or 1·31 per cent. Others and unspecified, 129,380, or nearly 3·40 per cent. In Canada there were, in 1881, 2,439,188 Protestants, and 1,791,982 Catholics.

Both Melbourne and Sydney are more populous than any town in the United States except New York, Philadelphia, Chicago, and Brooklyn, and the growth of the capital of Victoria is only surpassed by the principal city of Illinois, the increase to whose population is unparalleled in American history.

The Australasian colonies have been of great service to Great Britain in helping her to solve one of the greatest social problems of the present day, by providing a good living for the ever increasing over-population of the British Isles, and owing partly to this cause during the last thirty years pauperism has greatly decreased in England and Wales. Lord Derby is reported to have said: "If the current of emigration were suddenly changed we should very soon find a result in the growth of pauperism." It is, therefore, of great importance to Great Britain that Australia and Canada should absorb the surplus population to be found in the British Isles, especially as the emigrants become larger buyers of home manufactures than even the residents of England themselves. Australians would, however, warmly resist the introduction again of shipments of the outcasts of Great Britain, as Australia, like America, has suffered too much in the early days from a somewhat similar cause, and is, therefore, naturally opposed to allowing the experiment to be repeated in another form, although advocated by English philanthropists in their well meant efforts to benefit the submerged tenth at their doors.

Although there are a comparatively small number of representatives from almost every foreign nation in Australia, there have been few special immigrations, as in Canada, of communities such as Menonites, Icelanders, Russian Jews, and there are no separate villages speaking a foreign tongue similar to those found by the traveller in some of the United States, consisting of Hungarians, Slavs, Poles, Bohemians, Russians, Italians, Tyrolese, and various Asiatics. During the ninety years preceding 1880, nearly 10,000,000 foreigners made their home in the United States, and during 1890, an average of 1,000 emigrants per day was estimated to have landed at Castle Garden in New York, where there is, therefore, a more motley group from nearly every European country to be seen stepping on the shores of their new home than those who cast their lot in Australasia, and it has been proposed recently to impose a poll-tax on them equal to the extra cost of the passage to Australia. The precautions taken by the American Government to prevent paupers, insane and feeble-minded persons, or persons who are apparently likely to become a public charge, from landing, would, if carefully adopted in Australia, greatly lessen the money expenditure on charitable institutions, and reduce the percentages of deaths and insane. The United States authorities compel shipmasters to take back in their vessels any unsuitable emigrants brought from Europe, and similar action should be taken by the Australian Governments, or many undesirable persons will no doubt be shipped to the Australasian colonies in the future.

Though State-aided immigrants have had to pass medical examinations before embarking from England, there is no hindrance to individuals decrepit either in mind or body landing in New South Wales if they can obtain sufficient money to pay their passages by private vessels, and the consequence is that some social failures in England have been shipped to Australia, where their circumstances would often be deplorable were it not for the charity given them by benevolent institutions, which are as varied for the treatment of disease, and as well supported as those found in the United States or Canada.

The results of the last census show that in the United States, Canada, and Australia the attractions of city life have proved most powerful on the movements of population, and one of the greatest problems of the present day is how best to encourage settlement of producers on agricultural land. Mr. Gladstone, in a recent address, lamented the great modern tendency even in England for population to leave the country for the town, but the same fact is much more noticeable in Australia, where Melbourne (with 43·09 per cent.), Adelaide (with 41·58 per cent.), and Sydney, (with 34·11 per cent.), absorb more than one-third of the populations of the colonies of which they are the capitals. Mr. Dow, an ex-Minister of Agriculture in Victoria, stated, however, in a recent lecture in Sydney, that he was not surprised at young men not settling on the land in the present isolated condition of colonial 'farming under the liberal condition of free selection anywhere, and that the formation of irrigation colonies, so that the land could be tilled on a more scientific and social basis, would lead to better results, and prove as successful as in the United States.

The recent extension of Technical Schools and Agricultural Colleges in most of the Australasian Colonies should be the means of removing much prejudice against manual labour amongst many young men, which hitherto may have been greatly fostered by the purely literary teaching given in the primary and secondary schools. It is asserted that there are comparatively few native-born Americans found working as hands in manufactories or at domestic service, as these employments are now principally left to the foreign immigrants. A large proportion of the American farmers, however, are native-born, and it would be a good thing for Australia if as large a proportion of her sons could also be induced to engage in agricultural pursuits by observing the success attending the methods of scientific tillage carried on by their compeers on the other side of the Pacific.

In proportion to population no country has made greater advances than Australia during the last forty years ; and this progress is greatly due to the splendid enterprise and hard work of the hardy pioneers and their more favoured descendants, some of whom are now born in the third generation. Australians, like the people of most young countries, are inclined to be more extravagant both in their public and private expenditure than the members of old communities with not so much natural wealth, but this want of thrift was no doubt greatly caused by the remarkable prosperity produced in the colonies through the discovery of gold, as many persons becoming suddenly rich could not appreciate the value of money like those whose fortunes were the result of many years of hard toil. The present depression in trade will, however, teach Australians to be more provident in their habits, and to imitate many of the saving ways of the Canadians, who appear often to enjoy greater contentment than more prosperous neighbours with less simple habits.

The American is stated to be often noted for a too great devotion to business, and the Australian for a too great love of pleasure, but in order to onsure a sound mind in a sound body the pursuit of both extremes is to be deprecated. There is, however, an excuse for the native-born Australian taking so many public holidays, owing to the climate being unlike that of a greater part of North America, where the bitter cold and ice prevent that constant employment throughout the year which obtains in Australia. In the mother country, Canada, and the United States of America, the inhabitants are unable to work out doors for a considerable portion of the winter time, and therefore do not require so many proclaimed holidays as they do in Australia. If Australians took full advantage of their almost continuous fine weather there is no doubt that their physique would be greatly impaired, especially as a semi-tropical climate is more debilitating than a cold one. The colonial, however, has hitherto imitated too closely in his dress and habits the inhabitants of the British Isles, so that his clothing and food are not usually adapted to the requirements of a semi-tropical country.

The philosophical and literary institutions of Australia are named after and conducted on similar lines to those so long established in England, such as, for example, the Royal Societies, and the Mechanics' Schools of Arts, whilst Americans are not found to copy English nomenclature for their institutes, but often call their public associations after distinguished men, or in commemoration of important events in the history of their country, with a view no doubt of promoting patriotism amongst the people. An Australian in the streets of London notices on the warehouses and shops many English names with which he has been familiar from his childhood, but the mixed nationalities in the United States show their presence in the signs on numbers of the houses, denoting that the owners originally came from Germany, France, Italy, and other foreign nations. The native-born of America display a far greater enthusiasm on behalf of country than is to be found amongst Australians, who though very proud of their native land sometimes imitate Europeans in despising colonial institutions unless they are affiliated with their counterparts in the mother country. Many of the native-born in New South Wales join the Hibernian, Highland, Welsh, Cornish, and other English or Celtic Societies, but do not so readily become members of the Australian Natives Association, formed for promoting among the native-born a national spirit, encouraging thrift, literature, science, art, and securing the federation of the Australasian Colonies, and consequently works on somewhat similar lines to the Parlors of the Native Sons and Daughters of the Golden West, which take so prominent a part, in company with the Society of Pioneers, in all celebrations connected with the State of California.

Australia cannot claim to have produced popular humourists like Mark Twain, Sam Slick, Bret Harte, and Artemus Ward, but their mirthful writings are heartily enjoyed in Australia, notwithstanding the dictum of Mathew Arnold, that "American humour is a national calamity." Artemus Ward advertised the benefits of a voyage to the Antipodes by narrating that, after showing a man all over the United States as the "living skeleton," he took him on a trip to Australia, and was horrified to find that on the voyage he began to add flesh at a prodigious rate, so that when they landed at Sydney he had to show his protégé off as "the fat man."

American periodicals enjoy a large circulation in the Australian Colonies, and two of the best of them have a greater sale than any English publication of a like kind, except perhaps the *Review of Reviews* which has an Australian edition. There are no local magazines which can compete in combined interesting articles and beautiful illustrations with such periodicals as *Harper's Magazine* or the *Century Magazine* of New York. There are, however, several illustrated newspapers in Australia which will bear favourable comparison with the best American journals of a similar kind. Most of the contributions from literary men are to be found in the leading daily or weekly journals, which are edited and made up after the style of the best London newspapers, and although not so "lively" as the American journals, the local information given is fuller and the speeches of leading men reported at greater length. The American system of interviewing notabilities has been adopted in Australia, but only to a limited extent. There is also a recent tendency in some of the daily newspapers to introduce in a modified form striking head lines and rapid pictorial illustrations, like those to be found in most issues from the American press. The leading radical paper in Australasia has been for many years illustrated with clever cartoons mostly on political subjects by Mr. L. Hopkins, an American artist, who has also taken a leading part in the management of the successful Art Society of New South Wales.

During the last quarter of a century considerable attention has been paid to the study of the fine arts in Australasia, and there are now excellent picture galleries in New South Wales, Victoria, and South Australia, which contain many fine examples of the various arts of modern oil and water colour painting, sculpture, and pottery, selected mostly by able judges in the mother country. Many prosperous Australians have embellished their homes with works of art purchased from the courts in the various International Exhibitions they have visited, and from the studios of local artists, who are now making a special study in their pictures and models of the scenery, fauna, and flora of Australia. Several pictures produced by Australian artists have been chosen by the judges to occupy prominent places in the annual exhibitions of the Royal Academy in 'London and in those of the Salon in Paris, and exhibitioners sent from the Colonies have studied in both these institutions, no doubt in company with many American and Canadian students. Several American artists were obtained from New York to produce the beautiful illustrations contained in the " Picturesque Atlas of Australasia," published in Sydney by a local company. The appropriate certificate of award of the Sydney International Exhibition of 1879 was well printed by the American Bank Note Company of New York, from various designs made by colonial artists for the border, illustrating examples of the flora, fauna, and industries of New South Wales.

The domestic architecture of Australia is made suitable to a semi-tropical climate, in which verandahs are found indispensable, and, therefore, the style more closely resembles the buildings in California than in any other State of the Union; but there are many public structures in the Renaissance and other styles which would favourably compare with even the best of those erected in the great cities of America, not only as regards comfort, but also in the display of artistic decoration.

The observations of the transit of Venus taken by Captain Cook in 1768 and by the more recent expedition of colonial scientists in 1874, show that, in the opinion of experts, Australia is most favourably circumstanced for the study of astronomical science. The Government and private observatories are doing valuable work in original investigation, by mapping the stars of the Southern Hemisphere, and in compiling meteorological forecasts, which latter of late years have proved of great service in warning mariners of coming storms along the coast, as they are made on similar lines to those so successfully performed under the direction of the Observatory at Washington. Magnificent photographs of the moon, comets, southern cross, milky way, and other constellations have been taken by Mr. H. C. Russell, Government Astronomer, at the Observatory, in Sydney, and will be sent to the Chicago Exposition, so as to give some idea of the glories of the heavens in the southern hemisphere.

The wealthy men of Australia have not as yet devoted much of their wealth to the furtherance of science or education; but several of the Universities and Working Men's Colleges have received large bequests from a few noble colonists, which have enabled these institutions to perform similar educational work to that done at Harvard College, Cooper Institute, Girard College, Pratt Institute, the Stanford University, Astor Library, and the Lick Observatory, which were founded with the funds provided by rich Americans.

Most of the leading theatrical and musical " stars" of Europe now visit Australia, and often come by way of America, so that the colonists have an opportunity of hearing the best artistes. Australia has produced a prima donna who recently secured marked success singing operatic music in Europe,

E

and who is now engaged for an American tour. There have been several colonial actors and actresses who have made a name on the London stage, and a few of them have appeared in America.

Of late years many members of the British aristocracy and of the House of Commons have taken Australia as a " grand tour," and, in addition to studying colonial institutions, have found there a new wonderland of scenery in the harbours, rivers, mountain gorges, caves, volcanoes, and other natural features which vie in beauty with the magnificent views to be found in the great national parks of the United States and Canada, as will be seen by the many large photographs shown at the Chicago Exposition.

The Hon. Arthur Renwick, B.A., M.D., M.L.C., Executive Commissioner for New South Wales to the World's Columbian Exposition in Chicago, has presided, during the last thirty years, over many of the charitable and philanthropic institutions in New South Wales, such as the Sydney Infirmary, Benevolent Asylum, Deaf and Dumb and Blind Institute, Boarding-out Destitute Children's Board, and other bodies, the members of whose committees, prior to his departure, passed resolutions expressing their regret at losing his valuable honorary services, even for a short time ; but with the hope that during his travels in England and America his inquiries into the working of similar institutions would prove of much service to the poor and suffering in Australia. The London *Times* has expressed the opinion " that the legislation which Dr. Renwick proposed in 1883, curtailing parental rights, would tend to correct some of the evils existing at home and abroad."

At present in Sydney, Melbourne, Brisbane, and Adelaide there is a considerable number of unemployed, but several authorities have estimated that America has sometimes had about 1,000,000 out of work, or a much larger proportion of the population than in Australia, often it is stated through a faultiness in the distribution of labour. The tendency of working men to gravitate to the cities is becoming more marked in all countries, as owing to organisation there are more attractions found, the hours of labour are reduced, living is better, and educational facilities greater than in the country parts. The progress of rural population, however, shows the percentage to be about the same in Australia as in the United States, for during the last decade it was 27·92, against 27·39 per cent. for the previous decennial period in the United States. There is, however, a better opening for wheat farming in New South Wales than in the United States as will be seen by the following calculations of the Hon. L. Fane De Salis, especially as the Colony only produces half its present consumption of flour :—" On the picked western slopes of our elevated dividing range, comprising about one quarter of the Colony, by the use of American machinery, wheat of the best quality can be ploughed in, seeded, and bagged at 6d. per bushel. Fencing in 2,500 acres of the needed land and clearing same will cost but one-fourth of the result (at only 2s. 6d. per bushel) of the probable first crop. Two-fourths will buy the needed American machinery, and the last quarter will pay yearly rent, minor improvements, &c., thus converting at the end of the first twelvemonth into an independent employing yeoman any man of character who will, with prudence, temperance, and energy, build up a property for his family. Now, 4s. per bushel in London is the lowest value of our magnificent wheat. Of the land I am speaking of none is, or ought to be for any long time, further from railway carriage than 50 miles. According to estimates in Tumberumba railway inquiry, 5d. is the cost of moving one bushel over this distance per waggon to the railway. Mr. Eddy allows he can carry same, on such large additional business, without loss at one-eightieth of a penny per mile. Thus over the average 250 miles, 2¼d. goes to the railway and 5d. to the waggon—in all, 7½d.—while a second similar amount ought to cover all sale, freight, and shipping charges. This looks like a profit of 1s. 9d. per bushel over the (say) 2s. 3d. cost of growing and sending our wheat to market."

In New South Wales during the last half-century the wages for some of the mechanical trades rose as much as from 6s. to 12s. per day, or 100 per cent. The wages of labourers have also risen from 3s. to 8s., or 166 per cent., which has been paid for the best descriptions of unskilled labour; while the hours of work each day have been generally reduced from ten to eight, or 20 per cent. Recently these rates of wages have been lowered in many of the trades, in some cases more than 25 per cent., but late severe experiences have taught artisans not to imitate shepherds in "knocking-down their cheques." Owing to the existing depression in building and other trades, an addition to the number of artisans and unskilled labourers is not now required in Australia, and it is probable that there will be a still further reduction in the standard rate of wages fixed by the unions, owing to the supply of workers being greater than the demand of the employers, and as capitalists are not now investing much money in the erection of houses.

The wages ruling in Australasia for several years past have been higher than the average rates in most parts of the American Union, but even there the amounts paid are found to be sometimes half as large again in the Pacific States as in some of the Eastern States. As meat and clothing are cheaper in New South Wales than in the United States, the colonial work-man when employed should have more of his wages remaining in his hands than the American craftsman, even though the latter may in some cases receive a higher wage.

The wages of working men are much higher in California than in the Eastern States of America, owing to the great wealth on the Pacific coast and to the influence of trades unionism preventing the introduction of many competitors in the various trades, even from the Eastern States. The Council of the Federated Trades in San Francisco has the power to order a boycott or a contribution from unions in aid of strikes, but it has no power to call out a union in the way that was done by the Australian Labour Council during the great strike of 1890.

From 1878 to 1881 there was great slackness in the labour market in California, but since that time there has been as much general prosperity there as obtained in New South Wales during the last decade. The new constitution of California when adopted in 1879 frightened capitalists out of the State as through its confiscatory character it arrested development, by stopping mineral production, railroad extension, and house building. As a consequence of this stoppage of enterprise, there was even less demand for labour in California than there is now in New South Wales; but as the present depression throughout Australia is not due to unwise legislation, and arises from other causes, it is believed that the Colony will recover more readily from the depression than was the case even with the American State.

The value of the labour of those mainly engaged in the production or acquisition of food products and in obtaining the raw material from natural products in Australasia, in 1890, amounted to £86,411,400, or at the rate of £23 2s. 2d. per head of population, being £8 19s. 7d. per head more than in the United States, £11 14s. 7d. per head more than in Canada, and £9 11s. 2d. more than in Argentina.

The estimated average annual cost of food and beverages in New South Wales was £18 14s. 9d., in the United States £9 17s. 7d., and in Canada £8 9s. The ratio of cost of food to earning was 32·5 per cent. in the Australian colony, 25 3 in the United States, and 32·5 in Canada. The day's earnings equal to annual cost of food was 98 days in the Australian colony, 76 days in the United States, and 98 in Canada.

The American Consul at Melbourne has recently recommended Americans not to come to Australia without some capital in the present state of the labour market, and a similar warning might also be given by Australians if they were not careful to avoid laying themselves open to a charge, which has been sometimes urged, of trying to keep a good country all to themselves.

Australia is now suffering from a commercial depression; but New South Wales with an annual revenue of over £10,500,000, is even better able to weather the storm than any of the other Colonies, although the temporary depressed condition of Australasia is even now not as much as the poverty to be found as a permanent institution in European countries. The credit of Australia has been, it is feared, injured to some extent by interested parties who wish to "bear" colonial stocks in the English market, and also no doubt by want of foresight on the part of the colonists themselves, as they often acted as if seasons of prosperity would always last, and consequently did not practice that persevering industry and economy which would have tided them over those reverses which appear to come periodically even to the wealthiest communities. The present industrial crisis will lead to more settlement on the land for agricultural production and development of neglected natural resources of the greatest richness and variety. The current depression has been intensified in Australia by numbers of persons being thrown out of employment through there being fewer public works undertaken than in past years, owing to requisite funds not being obtainable except at high interest in the English market. There has been also considerable friction of late years between employers and the trade unions, which has caused social unrest, and, it is stated, has prevented investments in industrial undertakings; but this has not been the principal factor in the present depression, as alleged by some. It is believed, however, that these conflicts will teach lessons to both masters and men, and should lead to that better understanding hereafter being maintained between capital and labour which is so necessary to the best interests of both, as the money spent in strikes could be far better utilised by the workers in buying shares in the mines or other industries in which they are engaged, and so enable them on co-operative principles to have a voice in the management, and reap a larger share of the profits of the enterprises for which they labour.

The fact that the present financial crisis has been caused principally by the disturbances in the English money market, through failures of bankers who lent money to the South American Republics, shows that the pulse of monetary transactions is felt throughout the civilised world, and the financial troubles of one country is therefore often shared by others with little else in common. The present failures of land companies in Australia are, however, nothing to be compared in extent with the crisis in the United States in 1857, when the failures were for £111,000,000, as there have been but few colonial mercantile houses who have had to seek the protection of the Bankruptcy Court. In Victoria, out of those who made private composition with creditors, singular to say, the legal profession contributes the largest number, only a comparatively small number of the bankrupts being connected with trade or manufactures. The value of the wool export from the Australasian Colonies alone since 1850 would pay off all the public and private borrowings of English capital, and there is now an accumulated capital of £600,000,000 sterling in these countries.

The enormous national debts of Europe for military and naval establishments impose heavy loads on the people, and induce an amount of poverty and wretchedness which is not to be found from similar causes either in America or Australia. At the present time there are many persons out of work in several of the Australian Colonies; but as there have been good seasons and splendid crops from the agricultural and pastoral industries, and with the restoration of financial confidence and an easier money market ample employment should ere long be found. There is, however, a tendency to pay a lower rate of wages to artisans than that now ruling, which has been fixed higher than the average rates in the United States, taking into account the cost of living, and the more days in each year in which outdoor work can be done.

Owing to the sale of the Government lands in the United States through its large and rapidly increasing population, there appears to be a greater difficulty in obtaining good farms than formerly, and by the end of the present century it is estimated by Mr. C. Wood Davis, an American writer, that the selector will have to go elsewhere. He says: "The uncultivable character of the land of plain and mountain districts, and the rapid diminution of the unoccupied arable lands of the United States, have been clearly shown by the events following the opening to settlement of the limited and not over-fertile Oklahoma country. When men had failed to find satisfactory locations in California, Oregon, and Washington, they retraced their steps, hoping to secure land on which to found a home, only to find in advance of them an army of would-be settlers large enough to occupy a territory ten times the size of Oklahoma." Large areas in Australia are leased by the Crown for sheep and cattle farming, which, in the natural growth of the country, should now be utilised for tilling. A great want at present in Australia is a larger settlement of population on the land, which would also give greater development to manufacturing industries in the cities.

In Australia during the present century farms have grown into villages, and these again have developed into towns, to such an extent that along the sea coast and river basins and on the inland plains many centres of population are found. Two colonial cities contain more people than Bristol and other prosperous towns in Great Britain, which were founded six centuries ago, or in municipal districts in America incorporated twice as long as the Australian towns. Fifty years ago there were only 5,000 persons in Melbourne, now it has half a million inhabitants.

Since the discovery of gold within its borders Australia has proved a land of promise to crowds of labourers from Europe, so that many of the wealthiest colonists have stated that when they arrived in Australia they had but a small sum in their pockets, but by steady perseverance and systematic saving they had managed to accumulate a handsome competence.

The great social problems now agitating the world, especially in regard to the relations of labour and capital, are discussed, not only in trades union meeting places on week nights, but also by speakers at out-door meetings on Sundays in the Sydney Domain almost in similar terms to those used on the San Francisco sand block. The working classes in New South Wales at the general election in 1891 returned thirty-five members to the Legislative Assembly, and formed the first great labour party in politics, and, as the other two parties were almost equal, the new comers held the balancing power. There has been no charge of corrupt practices against any class of politicians in Australasia such as those alleged against political "bosses" in several large towns in the United States, or other "paid advocates of party measures." Nearly all the leading politicians in New South Wales during the last quarter of a century possessed but little wealth, so that they could not have taken advantage of their position to acquire riches for themselves and their friends. A recent English writer names as the darker tendencies of American democracy such evils as plutocracy, poverty, political corruption, race problem, and labour difficulties, but as yet they are not felt to the same extent in Australia as in America, where there is, however, fifteen times more population to foster these evils.

The Great English Republic of the United States has had a century of experience in which it has shown itself "strong, popular, united, and enduring," and its experiences are being noted by those nations who are marching towards democracy, but there can be no doubt that America and Australia will have their rise and fall like many nations in ancient and modern times, and this fact should be realised by their statesmen so as to be prepared for the contingency, even though it is far off. Thomas Carlyle said of America:—"You may boast of your democracy as much as you please, but it is the vast quantity of land and your sparse population which give you your great prosperity." In a somewhat similar strain Lord Macaulay remarked in 1857:—"Your fate I believe to be certain, though it is deferred by a physical cause. As long as you have a boundless extent of fertile and unoccupied land, your labouring population will be far more at ease than the labouring population of the old world, but the time will come when New England will be as thickly peopled as old England, when wages will be as low and will fluctuate as much with you as with us. You will have your Manchesters and Birminghams, and in those Manchesters and Birminghams hundreds of thousands of artisans will be fairly brought to the test. Through such seasons the United States will have to pass in the course of the next century if not in this." In the event of the predictions of the Chelsea seer and the great historian being fulfilled, and a surplus population unable to find remunerative employment in the United States, there are thousands of miles of uninhabited land in Australasia, abounding in natural resources, to which intelligent farmers and miners from the other side of the Pacific may come and find a happy home in a healthy climate, provided that they have some capital to carry them on until their crops could be sold or their mines developed, and that they are not afraid of the hard work necessary for settlement in a new country.

The Australian aborigine is of a different race from the Aryans, Mongols, and Negroes, the Papuan of New Guinea or the extinct Tasmanian, and he has even been classed by Professor Huxley with the brown people, such as the earlier inhabitants of India, Egypt, and Nubia, and recently by a Canadian anthropologist as having come from Africa, whilst the late Rev. Dr. Lang believed him to be one of the original occupiers of the South American continent. He is, however, of different species to the present North American Indian, whose copper colour evidences more traces of a Chinese or Japanese descent. Dr. Carroll, of Sydney, states that anthropologic facts demonstrate that there were at least three black and one yellowish brown races combined represented in the Australian tribes, and he believes that in the old geological deposits of Australia could be found the remains of the primitive races often spoken of as the missing link or the rudest man.

Christian missionaries have performed a noble work in civilising the natives of many groups of islands in the South Seas, such as those in Fiji, the Loyalty Islands, and the New Hebrides, but, notwithstanding the expressed wishes of the English Government in instructions to early Governors sufficient attention has not been paid by the Colonial Governments and the various churches to the Australian aborigines on the mainland, who are now fast dying out through readily copying the vices instead of the virtues of the white man, as they are not near so well cared for as the Canadian Indians who are consequently not decreasing in numbers.

Great Britain rules over people belonging to all the chief racial divisions in the world, and a great responsibility cannot but rest upon her rulers with regard to the treatment of the coloured races in her dependencies, especially those whose countries she has taken. The American Indian has had his wild buffalo exterminated by the progress of settlement, so that there are but few remaining of the bison of the plains. The Australian aborigine can only now hunt the kangaroo in the far interior of the continent; so that a recent American writer proposes to acclimatise this marsupial in the United States " on account of their economic value in fur and boot wear."

The Maori will in time become as extinct as his predecessor the hunter of the Moa, or the remains of that gigantic bird itself, as there are now only 44,000 native Maories in New Zealand, notwithstanding that they have been better treated than the aborigines on the mainland, as they have had their land purchased from them, and not taken without compensation, as has been the invariable practice on the Australian continent, although half-a-century ago Lord John Russell recommended that 10 per cent. of the proceeds of land sales should be set apart as an endowment for the aborigines by the Colonial Governments. The Red Man in the United States, notwithstanding the treaties made from the days of Penn downwards, has had to quit many of his reserves through the onward march of the white population, and his treatment has been almost as bad as that of the Australian aborigine, who, however, has had but comparatively small reserves to be ousted from, as he was too inoffensive to assert his rights in a similar way to the American tribes. The remnants of both races should now receive more protection from the people who have taken their lands from them, or any attempts at reparation will soon be found too late to benefit them.

The Australian aborigine has been greatly underrated by most writers, who generally class him only next to the brute creation. In some respects he is, however, believed to be superior to the American Indian, as Mr. Bonwick, a well-known Australian writer, told the Royal Colonial Institute in 1890, as the result of his study of early records, that before decay set in, the aboriginal had considerable intelligence and was an admirable mesmerist. The Australian blackfellow has some knowledge of astronomy and mythology, he has displayed considerable inventive power in the construction of the boomerang and a throwing lever for spear casting, and he is found to be a superlative tracker in the wild bush.

The Spanish Colonies founded in South America in the early days are all now independent republics, as the result of the methods of empire pursued by Spain, thought far more for the good of the old country than that of the new possessions. A similar policy with regard to the interests of the colonists appears to have actuated the British Government after founding New South Wales, which for many years was only a penal settlement under military rule, and the unfortunate aborigines were brought mainly into contact with those who could do little to elevate even a barbarous race.

The kind conduct of Queen Isabella and the Spanish missionaries in South America was a pleasant contrast to that of Pizarro, Cortes, and other military adventurers, who appear to have often acted on the maxim that "the only good Indian was a dead one." In like manner the noble work performed by the English and American missionaries in Polynesia cannot but be regarded as some atonement for the treatment of the native races originally inhabiting Australia and America, all of whom may become extinct in both countries before the end of the next century unless more care is taken of them for the future.

There are many groups of islands in Polynesia which have been evangelised by Christian missionaries, such as Samoa, Niue or Savage Island, Aneityum, Tana, Erramanga (where the martyr John Williams was massacred), Maré, Lifu, and Uvea of the Loyalty Islands; the Tokelau, the Ellice and Gilbert Groups, and New Guinea. In Samoa, where the soldiers of La Perouse and the natives met in deadly conflict at the end of last century, the great change for the better in the disposition of the Samoans was evinced in the circumstances attending the great hurricane a few years ago in the harbour at Apia when several American and German war vessels were wrecked, and H.M.S. "Calliope," by the brave action of the captain, was the only ship that escaped to sea. At this time Germany was at war with Mataafa, and sent vessels to crush the rebellion, but when the German sailors and soldiers were overwhelmed in the billows at great personal risk the natives nobly rescued their proclaimed enemies from a watery grave.

Although the Australian aborigine has not received the same paternal attention as the Canadian Indian, there has been no destruction of life comparable to that during the Spanish conquest of Central America, when it is believed that 10,000,000 from the civilised tribes in Peru and Mexico were destroyed by the invaders. It is, however, remarkable that, notwithstanding this great slaughter, the Spanish and Indian races in South America have since largely intermarried, and that the native races are not so likely to become extinct as in Australasia and North America, where they have been better treated by their conquerors.

It is estimated that there are 200,000 aborigines on the Australian continent, and 41,523 Maories in New Zealand; so that the total population of the Australasian Colonies, counting these native races numbered at the end of 1891 about 4,141,170 persons, while the population of Canada numbered 4,829,411, or 688,241 more, including 108,547 Indians.

The Maories appear to be decreasing, being in 1881, 44,097; and in 1891 41,523 exclusive of 2,119 half-castes. When the colonists first landed in New Zealand the number of Maories was 120,000; but this race is sharing the fate of all the other tribes, who are gradually disappearing on the Australian mainland and in the adjacent islands.

The colonists are now being agitated over the question as to the desirability or otherwise of continuing the introduction as labourers into the Australian continent of Kanakas from the South Sea Islands and coolies from India, so that the large experiences of Africans and Asiatics gained in the United States, the West Indies, and the Sandwich Islands are invaluable, and often cited in the discussion. The Polynesian labour traffic with Australia in years past was attended with many abuses, which had to be often checked by the war-vessels on the Australian station, but it is stated that these atrocities will be prevented under the provisions of a recent Act for employing Kanakas passed by the Queensland Parliament. It is the desire of Australians that no semblance of slavery should be tolerated on their shores, or that a conflict similar to that of the American Civil War should ever be fought out in Australia, and the importation of coloured labour is therefore deprecated by the great majority of colonists. It is alleged, in a cable message, that the natives taken from the Gilbert Islands to Guatemala in Central America are now virtually kept in a state of slavery on the coffee plantations, although the English Government has recently proclaimed a protectorate over this group, and the inhabitants are clamouring for a British Resident to carry out a new code of laws enacted by the Commander of H.M.S. Royalist.

The coloured labour question on the Australian continent bids fair to be hereafter almost as engrossing to the colonists as the negro question in the United States, especially as China with its 400 millions of population is a very near neighbour to Australia, the two countries being only separated by narrow seas. There will no doubt hereafter be a determined opposition made against the introduction of Asiatics on the part of the white labourers in Australia, whose means of living would be affected by coloured competitors from China, India, and the South Sea Islands working for wages on which an European could not possibly exist.

Pearl-shell fishing, principally by black divers, off the coast of Queensland, has been successfully carried on with capital invested from Sydney, and large quantities of shells are exported for use in European and American manufactories to make shirt-studs, buttons, and other useful and ornamental articles. Recently pearls were brought up by the divers valued at several thousands sterling.

Although there is a poll-tax on Chinese, there is none on Japanese immigrants, but there are comparatively few of the latter in Australia, so that there has been no necessity for any exclusion of Japanese labourers similar to what has recently taken place in America. The Japanese Emigration Company at the beginning of 1891 imported 600 Japanese to work in the nickel mines of New Caledonia, and agents recently visited Fiji, with a view to their introduction into these islands. The planters now employ Indian coolies who are not popular with Fijians owing to their fondness for litigation, but they would not hereafter prove so dangerous as the intelligent Japanese to the permanent occupation of Fiji by the white races. The proximity of China, Japan, and India to Australia renders it easily accessible to many millions of the Asiatic races, and in this nearness to the hives of the coloured races is one of the great dangers to preserving the present homogeneity of the Anglo-Australian race. Notwithstanding the edict against Chinese coming to the United States, many find their way across the Pacific to British Columbia, and after payment of a poll-tax of £10 to the Canadian Government cross into the United States; and a similar condition of affairs is commencing on the Australian mainland. At the present time there are several thousands of Chinese introduced into the Northern Territory of South Australia, who are desirous of making their way into the more Southern Colonies, and if not prevented these would only be forerunners of hordes of Mongolians who would in time outnumber the white races. The results of the recent terrible civil war in the United States, which cost £400,000,000 and half a million of lives, has taught Australians the undesirability of importing foreign coloured labourers, who once in a country make it their permanent home, and cannot intermarry like the white races, or without much friction be admitted to equal political rights with Europeans. Similar arguments to those once used for the retention of slavery by the American cotton planter are now being urged on behalf of coloured labour for the sugar industry in Queensland, which it is asserted cannot be profitably carried on except with the assistance of Kanakas, although similar work on the Northern Rivers in New South Wales is done by white labourers receiving the ordinary wages. Although under strict Government supervision past abuses may not be repeated, yet the introduction of large numbers of the coloured races into Australia is not only strongly opposed by the British and Foreign Anti-Slavery Society from their standpoint, but also by the great majority of the colonists throughout the continent, and the Australian Natives Associations in New South Wales, Victoria, South Australia, and Western Australia have passed resolutions, in view of the experiences of the importation of Africans into the United States : "that in their opinion the introduction into any part of this continent of an inferior and servile race, who cannot be permitted to participate in the government of the country, is inconsistent with Australia's existence as a free community, and fraught with danger to the best interests of its people."

Only 5 Americans were naturalised in New South Wales during the last ten years. During 1890, 1,067 persons were naturalised in Australasia, of whom 475 were Germans and other German-speaking nations, 402 Scandinavians, 9 Chinese, and 181 other nationalities. The number of Chinese in Australasia at the last census was 40,943, of whom 14,156 were in New South Wales, notwithstanding that a poll-tax of £100 was imposed and all vessels are restricted to one Chinaman for every 300 tons, which has greatly reduced this class of immigrants, except in Western Australia where the poll-tax is £10, and in the Northern Territory where no tax is charged.

Chinamen are generally employed in Australia as market gardeners and vegetable hawkers in townships, gold-diggers on otherwise deserted mining fields, cabinet-makers in the principal cities, and cooks at country hotels. There are also numbers of Chinese to be found keeping shops for imported manufacturing products in Lower George-street, Sydney, and in Little Bourke-street, Melbourne ; but the Chinese quarters in these cities are not to be compared either in extent or moral depravity to the one which disfigures San Francisco.

The working classes in New South Wales are as strongly opposed to the introduction of large numbers of Chinamen as the artisans and women in California, who find them entering into competition with them far more than what is the case in Australia, such as in making all kinds of clothing, boots, and cigars, also for laundry work in which numbers are employed to do most of the washing and ironing of the Europeans.

It has been recently asserted that Levantines who are styled "Syrians," will prove a more undesirable class than even the Chinese, as numbers of these traders—with Indians who have of late years come from Bombay—make their living at hawking fancy articles in Australia at which they excel in persistence even the Chinaman, but, unlike him, they do little towards increasing the production from the soil, and are often impudent to unprotected white women in the country districts. Chinamen in Australia, though hard-working, are very fond of gambling, notwithstanding their desire to acquire enough money to keep them when they return to their own country, and their dens are also often found frequented by many European gamblers when the police make an occasional raid to catch them, and have otherwise a demoralising effect on the community. Notwithstanding the stoppage of Chinese immigration there are more than five times as many Chinese in California as in New South Wales, where the imposition of a poll-tax of £100 per head of late years has had a restrictive effect upon their arrival in the Colony, but it is feared has only temporarily checked the advance guard of a great army preparing for speedy marches to Australasia and America.

The populations which have grown up on both sides of the Pacific are unique in their character, and, although the Australian people are not of such a cosmopolitan character as the Californian, there is to be found in both centres many of the faults usually attending new communities. The lessons taught by social reverses will no doubt have a restraining effect on the future of both the British Colony and the American State, as the discoveries of great mineral wealth and the possession of beautiful climates have had a tendency to spoil the people of both countries for that patient industry which prepares for bad seasons as well as for good times.

The employment of Chinese in San Francisco at lower wages than payable to Europeans has led from the earliest times to much riot and bloodshed, so that "capital was driven away, real estate depreciated in value, and there was a general depression in business." The Chinese are found more to conform to English habits in Australia than the Mongolian elements have done in California, as they are not found wearing their national dress in Sydney to the same extent as in San Francisco, where even their hair made into a pigtail is allowed to fall down the back without any fear of being pulled as it is feared it often would be in the Australian colony. In both countries it appears to be the desire of the Chinese to get rich as soon as possible, in order to live retired in China, so that not many rich Mongolians remain in Australia. The body of a Chinese merchant recently dead, who once lived in America, reputed to be worth £60,000 to £70,000, was recently shipped from Sydney to Canton, and the funeral to the steamer cost £1,000, and was stated to be the longest procession of the kind in Australia.

Both in America and Australia the European born are found to furnish a larger proportion of paupers and criminals than the native element, no doubt because the immigrants are of the poorer half of society in the countries from which they come, and have not had many educational advantages in their youth. It is stated that the immigrants into the United States during the past century from Germany were about 1,000,000 more than those from Ireland, and 2,000,000 more than those from England. In Australia the Germans, though a comparatively small proportion of the population, have been a very useful one. The trade with Germany of New South Wales alone increased in volume during the last decennial period to about a million sterling, and there is now a much larger export of wool to German ports, owing to manufacturers purchasing their supplies in Sydney instead of in London as heretofore, and receiving them direct by a line of German cargo boats.

The number of Chinese in Australia is 40,943, less than half the number in the United States; but the proportion to the general population is of course much greater than in America. Chinamen have obtained a better position on the Pacific coast of America than their countrymen have in Australia, where they are tolerated for their usefulness, but disliked on account of being undesirable competitors with the European races.

In addition to the Act of 1882 suspending Chinese immigration, the laws of the United States prohibit the Coolie trade, and exclude all persons who shall contract for labour in the United States before arrival therein. Many of the Chinese in California and in British Columbia, as well as in Australia, find employment in working the gold-fields abandoned by Europeans; but the most remunerative employment found by Chinese in Australia is growing vegetables. There are not so many Chinamen engaged in Sydney in mechanical trades, with the exception of cabinet-making, as in San Francisco, where large numbers are found working even in the cigar, clothing and boot trades.

In San Francisco and in Sydney there are recognised secret societies among the Chinese, but the power of the "high-binder" has not been exerted to the same extent in Australia as in California, and consequently immorality and other crimes, although too much prevalent, are not nearly so rife as in the Chinatown of San Francisco, where murders of Chinamen are committed which cannot be detected by the police, owing to the power of these organisations.

The first settlement in Australia was only made 100 years ago, and the present condition and future prospects of the colonies will bear favourable comparison with communities which were founded three centuries ago and are placed very much nearer the great hives of European industry and commerce. Australia contains some of the finest forests, pastures, and fisheries in the world. It has a large output of the precious metals, great and extensive deposits of the most useful minerals, and it produces the best wheat, wine, corn, and fruits. What is principally required is capital and population to develop these great natural resources, as there is no country in the world affording a better field for investment. The present large exports of wool, gold, silver, tin, copper, coal, frozen meat, horses, butter, sugar, and many other valuable products are capable of being very greatly increased. If the large accumulations of money in Europe and America were invested by capitalists in developing the great resources of Australia they would secure the safest and most remunerative returns. The principal industries in Australia are the pastoral, mining, and agricultural, as manufactures have not received the same attention as in the Eastern States of America owing to their being less profitable than the growing of raw material for manufacture in Europe and America. The Australasian Colonies have, however, during the last ten years surpassed the Pacific States of America and the Pacific Provinces of Canada in manufacturing industries, although Chinese labour is engaged in more trades and other industries in California, Oregon, and British Columbia than in Australasia.

In the year 1891 the value of horses, cattle, and sheep, together with improvements and plant on the runs of New South Wales, amounted to £78,756,000, and the value of the annual returns from stock to £13,359,800. The system of absenteeism once practised by the Australian squatter has given way to the desire to purchase his run as a freehold estate, and to encircle it with all the surroundings of a comfortable home, in which his family can always reside. The pastoral resources of New South Wales are far superior to those of California, or indeed of any country in the world, owing to the favourable climate for all kinds of stock. The millions of acres found within the borders of the Colony with excellent natural grasses and fodder plants make it otherwise eminently adapted for grazing purposes. Mr. Fred. Turner, F.R.H.S., Botanist to the Department of Agriculture, says, respecting the grasses of New South Wales: "That we have far more valuable native grasses in this country than any yet introduced I have abundant proof, having experimented on upwards of 100 species of European, Asiatic, African, American, and Australian grasses to test their true qualities by comparison. In these trials the bulk of the Australian grasses yielded more forage and withstood the drought much better than did the exotics."

The present depression in Australia is nothing like so bad as the monetary crisis in New South Wales fifty years ago, when live stock were so unsaleable that the animals had to be boiled down for their tallow, and when sheep were sold at from 6d. to 1s. per head, until it was found that they would produce 5s. for their fat when exported to England. The favourable seasons at present visiting the Colony will no doubt give work to large numbers of shearers and labourers who have had to congregate in the metropolis, owing to there not being many works in progress during the year 1892. Sheep and cattle runs are now enclosed with wire, so that one boundary rider has taken the place of several shepherds. In the United States it is usually found necessary to place the sheep under cover during winter months, but this precaution is not required in Australia. The annual shearing is done by men who usually travel from station to station, and are paid at the rate of £1 per 100 sheep. A sheep-shearing machine invented by a squatter in New South Wales, who is a brother of General Lord Garnet Wolseley, the commander of the Red River Expedition, has proved successful, and this, with other machines since perfected, is now used on many of the stations, and would be found most useful for the same purpose in the United States and Canada. The great drawback hitherto in starting new industries in Australia has been the want of requisite labour; but the recent difficulty in raising loans in England has prevented the carrying out of many works, so that there would now be a good opportunity for the investment of American capital in branch manufactories, as operatives could be easily procured at lower rates than are current in some of the American States.

Although in the history of both New South Wales and California there have been seasons of financial depression, caused by speculation and overproduction in some industries and the fall in mining stock, yet the great natural wealth and resources of both countries enabled them easily to sustain losses that would be felt a great deal more in other lands. For example of late years in New South Wales there has been great speculation by land companies in real estate, which led to inflated prices in many of the properties, but the results have not been anything like so diastrous as those from the land boom in Southern California in 1886, where "numbers of towns were laid out on desolate plains." The millions of eastern capital invested on the Pacific slope of America suffered much loss through this excessive inflation in landed property, and similar results have happened to capitalists in the Australian colonies; but there is no doubt that healthier conditions will arise from the lessons gained by investors often brought about from an undue desire for excessive profits in both countries.

Mulhall, the eminent statistician, credits the people of New South Wales with surplus earnings of £9 13s. 9d. per head per annum, against £4 per head for the people of the United Kingdom, and £6 per head for the people of the United States. The deposits in the banks of Australasia amounted in 1890 to £128,889,050, and were twice as' much as those in similar institutions in New York, the empire city of the United States, and the amounts for New South Wales alone were £40,390,159, or over £8,000,000 more than for similar institutions in Chicago and Philadelphia combined (£32,083,935).

While the colonial assets of Australasian banks now reach £172,000,000, the total deposits amount to £154,032,304, of which £110,689,931 were held in the colonies, leaving £43,353,306 approximately in Great Britain. In the last twelve months there was an increase of £3,600,000 in the Australian deposits. Notwithstanding the recent unexampled monetary disturbance the profit and loss accounts of thirty-one banking, land, and investment companies other than banks of issue which received deposits in New South Wales, are not of such a character as to cause utter disquietude to their creditors, as the total liabilities to the public amount to £5,362,320, and the assets are estimated at £9,258,628, much of which will be realised by the liquidators. If a general supervision of the Australian banking system were introduced, as is now adopted with regard to the Bank of England, and also the system of inspection pursued in the United States and provided for in the recent banking legislation in Canada, there is no doubt many benefits would be derivable therefrom to all parties concerned, and the Government of New South Wales is now taking steps in this direction.

The savings of the people deposited in the Australian banks evidence that there must have been great prosperity in past years compared with that in other countries, as the style of living amongst the working classes is costlier than even amongst artisans in America.

Outside of the regular long established and wealthy banking institutions of Australia there have sprung up of late years land and loan societies or other mortgage institutions, giving larger rates of interest to depositors than the regular banks, and, as a consequence, some of these societies have recently collapsed, as many similar institutions from like causes also did some years ago in California. The building and loan societies had deposits in New South Wales in 1891 amounting to £2,355,747, and many of the building societies have enabled thousands to obtain houses during the past quarter of a century. There is no national bank in Australia like the Bank of England or the monetary institutions specially recognised by the Government in the United States, but the regular banking institutions, whose operations are principally confined to the colonies, owing to profitable investments by borrowers, can afford every year to give large dividends to their shareholders, and are possessed of considerable reserve funds available for use. The Commercial Bank of Sydney has given dividends amounting to 25 per cent. to its shareholders for the past quarter of a century, besides setting apart large sums for reserves. The banking capital of New South Wales is greater than that of California, as in 1890 there were nearly £3,000,000 more deposits in the banks of the Colony, and in 1891 these deposits amounted to £43,357,352, or £37 4s. 2d. per inhabitant. Out of the total deposits in the regular Australian banks, amounting to £151,000,000, only £39,000,000 has been furnished by British capitalists, so that the colonists display great confidence in depositing their savings in these monetary institutions. The Union Bank of Australasia has recently held its annual meeting in London, at which it was stated by the Chairman that "it had not suffered any direct losses from the failures of the various building societies and other financial institutions," and consequently paid a dividend of 12 per cent. per annum, and carried forward a sum of £12,000 to next half-year. The Bank of New South Wales has recently declared its usual dividend of 17½ per cent. per annum. In Australasia the amount of private wealth has been estimated to have amounted in 1813 to £1,000,000 ; in 1838 to £26,000,000; in 1863 to £181,000,000 ; and in 1890 to £1,169,000,000, which shows the wonderful accumulation made by the colonists during late years. The average deposits in savings banks per depositor is £73 16s. 7d. for the United States, £25 4s. 7d. for Australasia, and £42 7s. 6d. for Canada. The amount of deposits in the savings bank was £17,873,888 in Australasia, against £4,602,284 in Canada, so that the amount is four times as large in the Southern Colonies. The average deposits per inhabitant was £4 11s. 9d. in Australasia, £4 15s. 9d. in the United States, and 17s. 8d. in Canada.

The capital and deposits in all banks amounted in 1890 per inhabitant to £37 for Australasia, £8 for Canada, and £16 for the United States.

The amount of deposits per inhabitant in the banks of Australasia was, therefore, more than twice that of the United States, and more than four times that in Canada, notwithstanding that these three countries are all gold-producing, and have had a rapid and continuous development of wealth. The principal banking establishments in Australasia have their centre and route in the country itself, and of the paid up capital of £17,500,084 returned only £7,657,156 was for banks whose head offices are in England.

The average number of life insurance policies per 1,000 of population was sixty-five in Australasia, against twenty-five each in Canada and the United States, and the average amount of insurance per inhabitant was over twice as much as in British North America, and nearly twice as much as in the United States. In New Zealand there is a successful Government department for life insurance, and there are many branches of English and American Friendly Societies in all the Australasian Colonies.

There are no continuous railway lines across the continent of Australia such as the Canadian Pacific in North America; but along the shores of the South Pacific and Southern Oceans in New South Wales, Victoria, Queensland, and South Australia there are main trunk roads reaching from Brisbane to Adelaide, a journey of over 1,500 miles which can be travelled in Pulman vestibule cars. There are also branch lines which radiate to centres of settlement in the far interior, and the convenience of the farmers is naturally more studied under State supervision than by the private railroad companies in America.

It is absolutely necessary in order to ensure success in manufactures that the processes used should be the best, and have the most modern machinery, so that the appliances used in several lines by Americans ought to be as successful in producing cheap and good articles in Australia as they have been in the United States. One of the results hoped for from the Chicago Exposition is the introduction into Australia of the best labour-saving machinery invented in the United States to deal with raw materials. A great part of Australia is still passing through the first stage of settlement being employed in the pastoral industry, but greater attention is commencing to be given to growing of agricultural products. As Australia, however, contains within its borders the capacity of raising almost everything that its population requires, there can be no doubt that in due time nearly all the articles needed by the people will be made at home.

Until recently New South Wales has followed the example of the mother country in the policy of free trade, by only imposing customs duties for revenue purposes, but last year protective charges on some imported goods, like those in force in all the other Australian Colonies, and on similar lines to those of the United States and Canada, were adopted by the Legislature. It yet remains to be seen whether these protective duties will enable the people of New South Wales to build up great manufacturing establishments, instead of relying for support on the growing of raw products, which many believe to be the most profitable to the community at present. The diverse customs tariffs of the several Australasian Colonies have been productive of much friction, especially on the border line, where even live stock crossing from one colony to another are taxed, so that there is a consensus of opinion in favour of intercolonial freetrade. It is proposed therefore that when federated freetrade shall obtain between all the Australasian colonies, as is the case throughout the United States, and also in the provinces of the Dominion of Canada.

A difficulty felt by the States of the Union for several years after their separation from England in having diverse customs tariffs, is now repeated in the experience of the Australian colonies. The collection of inland border duties between the different colonies especially is found to be as difficult as the exaction of a similar impost was between the various States of America. The United States has now made reciprocity treaties with most of the South American Settlements and the British West Indies. Whether the policy of Canada and Australasia in charging the same customs duties on goods imported from the mother country as on those from foreign countries will be continued, or a system of reciprocity instituted in all parts of the British Empire, has yet to be determined. There is, however, a strong feeling prevailing among · a large portion of Australians for the further encouragement of local industry, and the adoption of protective policies by all the Australasian colonies seems to point in that direction.

In the United States there are great complaints against the wealthy private trusts monopolising many industrial undertakings, and similar charges, although not nearly to the same extent, have been uttered in England, such as the following from Mr. John Burns, a member of the London County Council, who has pointed out " that through the great metropolis permitting private companies to have charge of its water supply, gas, trams, and other industrial and municipal works, which other corporations in the United Kingdom have undertaken themselves, there are no remunerative assets for the payment of the debt incurred." A similar outcry might have arisen in Australasia if the Governments had granted the same monopolies in the construction of public works, as a number of wealthy trusts would have been formed, which would have reaped the profit on these improvements, instead of, as now, the general public receiving the benefit.

In the Legislative Assembly of New South Wales the Hon. John See, Colonial Treasurer, said, when making one of his recent financial statements with regard to the public accounts of the Colony : " Our reproductive works are all very valuable assets, and are more than sufficient to repay all that we have borrowed; but, at the same time, it is the duty of Government and of Parliament to maintain the credit of the country as much as possible, and to show our creditors that while we are prepared to meet all our just obligations, we intend to carry out minor public works for the improvement of our estates with money raised by ourselves, which will yield a return equal to the interest which we have to pay." More recently Mr. See said : " During the last three and a half years, no less than £12,000,000 had been spent on loan works. They certainly had magnificent assets in their railways and water and sewerage schemes. They had a vast future, as the intrepidity and industry of the Australian people were undoubted. In no country in the world could they find 4,000,000 of people who had accomplished more in the same time than the 4,000,000 who inhabited Australia." The general and local Government public debt of Australasia, excluding capital invested in railways, in relation to private wealth and population, amounted per inhabitant in the seven colonies to £17 18s. 8d., against £24 14s. 8d. for the United Kingdom. The Government Statistician for Tasmania has reckoned that the railways of Australasia in 1890, not only accomplished the great end for which they were introduced, but by cheaper modes of transit alone showed a clear balance and gain equal to £17,000,000, after allowing for interest on debt ; and representing a clear capital gain of £425,000,000 over and above the whole of the £107,000,000 of capital invested in railways, and that its gain in that respect represents at least threefold the amount of the present public debt.

Sir Edward Braddon, in a paper read before the London Society of Arts, showed the progress which had been made by the Australasian Colonies during forty years by the following table, giving the figures for the years 1850 and 1890 respectively :—

	1850.	1890.
Debt	£57,917	£184,912,804
Population	648,133	3,532,050
Wool Exports	£2,836,514	£23,734,332
Total Exports	£4,763,594	£70,901,685
Total Imports	£4,619,930	£68,495,581
Horses...	183,892	1,613,585
Cattle	2,302,327	10,346,661
Sheep	22,186,833	114,141,893
Shipping (inwards and .outwards)—tons	1,209,515	15,395,186
Bank Deposits (say)	£6,000,000	£110,855,571
Do Savings (approximate)...	£1,500,000	£17,312,795
Minerals exported	......	£14,122,117
Revenue	£1,201,068	£29,306,217
Railways (miles)	......	11,600

The external trade of Australasia, apart from borrowing, gives an average of about £16 per head, as against for imports and exports £5 13s. 8d. for the United States and £9 6s. 2d. for Canada. The Australasian Colonies, owing to their insular position, appear like Great Britain destined to carry on a large sea-board commerce with other countries, as already the trade per head is about three times that of the United States and nearly twice that of Canada.

Australasia now shows a larger ratio of trade compared with population than any other country. The depreciation of late years in the value of wool has lessened the value of trade per inhabitant, although the volume of merchandise was much greater. The percentage of steam tonnage was much higher in Australasia than in the United States, and the average daily movements of tonnage in 1890 was 42,582, against 24,583 in 1881. The percentage of tonnage in ballast was in Australasia only 3·5, while in the United States it was 11·2 per cent.

Both North America and Australia are indebted for much of their development to the loans from British capitalists, who, however, received from these countries much higher rates of interest for the money than could have been obtained in Europe with a similar security. Many of the works in the United States have been purchased by British syndicates, and immense tracts of land have also foreign owners or mortgagees, who see that investments in new countries are generally safer and more reproductive than those in the old countries of Europe, where the lands and mines do not yield such good results.

British investors have in the past lent considerable sums of money to the Central and South American Republics on exorbitant terms, but the results of some of these speculations have shown that there is more profitable investment for money to be found in the settlements of British origin than can be obtained in countries whose people have not been trained in the working of free institutions, and therefore often liable to revolutions involving destruction of life and property, which would sometimes prevent them meeting even the interest on the loans. English capital has been recently largely invested in the Asiatic provinces of the Ottoman Empire, in India, and in South Africa.

The public debt of the United States is now less than that of Australasia ; but owing to the American Government not being a paternal one, and leaving the construction of the great majority of public works to the enterprise of

F

her people, there has not been the same call on it as in Australia for
loan moneys to construct railways, build docks, improve harbours, establish
water-works, open up roads, and construct bridges.

The United States in 1890 had a population of 62,622,250 ; a revenue of
£83,975,000 ; an expenditure of £69,763,948; and a public debt of
£194,631,000, which was reduced on 30th April, 1891, to £169,703,118, and
this public debt could be paid off by accumulated revenue in little over two
years.   The public debt of England in 1890-91, at the close of the financial
year, was £618,681,581, and, as in America, there are comparatively few
revenue-producing public works which could be realised upon to pay it off.
The total annual charges for the English national debt was £25,207,000.   The
amount of revenue in England is £89,489,112, or over £5,000,000 sterling
more than in the United States.   The accumulated revenue of Great
Britain would pay off the public debt in seven years, and the accumulated
revenue of Australasia would pay off her public debt in six years, so that
looked at in this light the Governments of these colonies are in a better
financial condition than that of the mother country.

Although the rate of railway development in both Australia and America
exceeds the ratio of both population and revenue, this is in itself an index of
increasing wealth, as the back blocks in the interior of both countries are by
this means rendered accessible for the employment of capital and emigrants.

The railways in Australia have employed only European labour, while in
America many of the railways have engaged numbers of Asiatics in their
construction.   In British Columbia, Chinamen not only do the work of railway fettlers, but also are employed in many of the trades.

Up to 1880 the United States Government have given land grants for
the construction of railroads to private trusts amounting to 110,000,000 acres,
as alternate sections along the railway lines, including 23,000,000 acres and
a money subsidy of £10,970,000 to the Union Pacific Railroad Company.
In Canada there was handed over money and land amounting altogether to
the value of £76,189,244 to the Canadian Pacific Railroad and other railway
companies, as will be seen by the following figures compiled from the Canadian
Year Book : Government aid has been given to railways in bonuses to private
companies to the amount of £29,113,685, which sum represents a considerable portion of the public debt, and exclusive of outstanding loans to them
of £4,416,940, and contributions from the provincial government of
£5,218,497, and from various municipalities to the extent of £2,856,171.
Subsidies of land have been granted to railway companies by the Dominion
Government amounting to 46,499,433 acres, now valued at £34,583,951,
besides 7,990,500 acres from the Government of Quebec, and several land
grants from some other provinces.

Owing to the extent of territory and variety of resources on the Continent of Australia, it is well adapted to produce everything required for
the sustenance and comfort of its inhabitants, who are consequently not like
some European States, greatly dependent on the supplies of raw materials
from other countries.   The struggle in these new lands for existence is not
so fierce as in Europe, and the thrifty are consequently enabled to provide
for sickness and old age, not only in purchasing real property, but also in
placing money at interest in the banks.

The total capital and deposits in Australasian chartered and savings banks
in 1891 amounted to £155,873,888, and £33 16s. 3d. the amount of deposit,

reckoned per inhabitant is much larger than that found in other countries, the nearest value to it being £24 in the United Kingdom, and £16 in the United States.

The Australasian Colonies had, at the end of 1892, a public debt amounting to £192,565,327, nearly four times that of Canada. This sum, unlike the national debts for wars in other countries, was principally contracted for services, such as railways, tramways, electric telegraphs, water supply, sewerage, roads and bridges, harbours, rivers, lighthouses, docks, school buildings, defences, and other public works, of which many are of a remunerative character. The total public debt is only equal to 6·09 year's revenue now received by their governments from taxation and sale of public lands.

Railways have been constructed which do not directly pay in other countries besides Australia, such as those in Canada, South Africa, India, Russia, and South America, but the lines are otherwise productive of much good, and are therefore desired by those who pay for and use them.

The railways alone in New South Wales are valued at about £45,000,000, which is £13,000,000 more than the amount borrowed for their construction. In addition to this realisable asset there is a sum of about £12,000,000 due by the conditional purchasers of Crown Lands, and about 154,000,000 acres of the public estate are still unalienated, the rents from which amounted in 1889 to nearly £900,000, and the freehold value of which is almost incalculable.

The major portion of the public debts of each of the Australasian Colonies was contracted for the purpose of railway construction, but smaller amounts were borrowed for water supply, emigration, electric telegraphs, harbour and defence works, roads and bridges, school-houses, and other public works. Although no doubt the amount borrowed by the Australasian Colonies is large, yet when contrasted with the annual receipts it will be seen that the multiple of revenue compared with the debt is more favourable than in other countries.

The Sierra Nevada on the Pacific Slope much resembles in height and conformation the Blue Mountain range along the coast of New South Wales. The Blue Mountains are crossed by the railway from Sydney in the same direct way as the Sierra Nevada are crossed by the lines from the Eastern to the Western States of America. Not so good an opportunity is, however, afforded to the excursionist on the Blue Mountains to survey from the railway train the world-famed gullies of New South Wales, such as those at Wentworth Falls and Govett's Leap, as is given on the observation cars of the grand passes at the foot of the mountains on the Rio Grande route, or when traversing the plains around the base of Mount Shasta in Northern California, or whilst crossing the Rockies on the Canadian Pacific Railway.

The permanent-way of the railways in Australasia is reported to be most substantial, as the Government engineers value their positions too much to specify other than the best description of work. The average number of persons killed per million travelling on the railroad was 0·86 in Canada, and 0·32 in New South Wales. The proportion of accidents is also less in New South Wales than in the United States, as there is not as much danger to the railway traveller in Australia as there is in America from blizzards on the prairies, or snow-storms on the mountains, which may occur on the main routes through the United States and Canada. There are triumphs of railway engineering to be found in Australia, such as the Zigzag at Lithgow Valley, and on the track of the Cairns-Herberton Railway, which perhaps are only surpassed by the windings on Marshall's Pass in Colorado, or the Great St. Gothard tunnel in Switzerland, and some of the works constructed for crossing the Rocky Mountains on the Canadian Pacific. Such comfortable buildings, extensive platforms, and obliging porters as are provided at the suburban railway stations in New South Wales are not to be found on the American lines, but more conveniences are generally given in the ordinary travelling-cars than in the colonial first and second-class carriages, except in the Pulman vestibule cars. There is also a better system adopted of checking baggage on the American lines, as the traveller need not see his luggage from the time it leaves his home until delivered by the express agent at the proper destination.

In the middle of 1892 there were in course of construction in New South Wales 266 miles of railway and 7 miles of tramway. There are 2,182 miles of railway open for traffic and 42 miles of tramways. All the tramways have been constructed within the last fifteen years, and are worked by steam, but there is a small cable system in North Sydney similar to those in San Francisco, and an experiment was made with the over-head electric wires near Sydney, but these wires have since been removed owing to the cost of working being found much greater than that of steam. In 1892 the railway revenue was £3,107,296, and the working expenses £1,914,252, giving a net revenue of £1,193,044, and interest of 3·581 per cent. (which is almost equal to the price of colonial securities on the English Exchange) on £33,312,608, the capital invested. The total cost of tramways constructed was £1,128,605, and the interest paid on capital was 5·54 per cent. The cost of works in progress in 1892 was £3,582,429. The total number of men, including those employed by contractors, directly paid from the Department of Public Works was 20,000. As each of these men probably had four or five people depending on them, the number of people directly dependent on the department for support would be about 100,000. The number of miles for roads and bridges was 31,000, and there are 62½ miles of sewers completed. The amount spent on these public works in 1889 was £2,015,489; in 1890, £2,139,724 ; and in 1891, about £3,472,777. The amount of road votes in 1889 was £827,341 ; in 1890, £665,000 ; in 1891, £835,484 ; and in 1892, £942,939.

The cost of railway construction per mile open for traffic in Canada was £12,182, and in New South Wales £14,559. The area per mile of railway lines was 137 in New South Wales, 270 in Canada, and 19 in the United States. In New South Wales there was one mile of line for every 520 persons, and in the United States one mile to every 315 persons, on the basis of the increase in population during the last ten years. In order that railway construction should keep pace with population in New South Wales there ought to be made 1,050 miles of new lines in the next ten years, or an average of increase of 105 miles per annum.

If the revenue of the United Kingdom per head of population was as great as that of Australia, it would be three times as large as it is at present. The national debt of Australia does not now represent only so much war material destroyed as in Europe and the United States, but a safe investment of money to make improvements on a grand property increasing in value every year. The proportion of loan expenditure devoted to revenue-yielding works averaged 71·3 for the Australasian colonies, and 85·3 for New South Wales.

Great Britain has financial interests in the rest of the world amounting to £2,000,000,000 sterling, of which it has been estimated over £1,000,000,000 is lent in the British Empire. The borrowings of the Australasian Governments, amounting to about £200,000,000, have been exceeded in amount by India, where £350,000,000 has been sunk in enterprises on official or quasi-official guarantee; and a further vast amount of British capital is employed by purely private British enterprise in various industries. Canada has borrowed from British capitalists about £100,000,000, being £50,000,000 for public purposes, and the other half for private undertakings, and her last loan was floated at 3 per cent., principally owing to a guarantee by the Imperial Government, which is not given to other colonial borrowings. Some of the South American Republics have obtained large loans from the investors of Great Britain, but at high interest, and these republics owe now £200,000,000, about two-thirds of which has been subscribed by English capitalists.

The percentage of interest on public debt to total expenditure was in Australasia 24 per cent.; in Canada, 26·1 per cent.; and in the United States, 9 per cent. The expenditure of Australasia in 1890-91, for services, was £31,035,390, or £8 3s. 2d. per head of population; and the amounts disbursed were, for the following services:—Railways and tramways, £6,990,905; public instruction, £2,386,607; post and telegraphs, £2,325,625; interest &c., on debt, £7,460,260; and other services, £11,871,993. The total expenditure from loans up to the year 1890-1891, amounted to £182,994,070, for the following purposes:—Railways, £116,288,591; water supply and sewerage, £16,396,082; electric telegraphs, £3,368,173; and other works and services, £46,941,224.

About six years' annual revenue of the Australasian colonies would pay off all their debts. It would take nearly six years' revenue to pay off the debt of the Dominion of Canada; and a little more than two years' revenue to pay off the debt of the United States.

The multiple of revenue to public debt in 1890 in Canada was 5·96 per cent.; in the United States, 3·84; in Australasia, 6·15; in the Argentine Confederation, 4·81; in Brazil, 6·80; in Mexico, 3·0; and in Peru, 40·19. The indebtedness per head in Canada is only one-fourth that in Australasia, which is more than two and a half times as large as that in the United Kingdom.

The public debt per head in 1890 of the United States was £5 3s. 6d.; of Canada, £9 11s. 8½d.; and of Australasia, £46 5s. 1d.; but it should ever be remembered that the Governments in the southern colonies own the railways, telegraphs, and other revenue-producing public works, and are therefore solving a problem, the theory of which has recently received great attention in all parts of the world, owing to the writings of Mr. Edward Bellamy, an American author, "in which he recommends a plan of national industrial co-operation, the policy of which is the successive nationalising or municipalising of public services and branches of industry, and the simultaneous organisation of the employees upon a basis of guaranteed rights, as branches of the Civil Service of the country." Mr. Bellamy proposes that as the constitution of the United States makes it the duty of Congress to establish and conduct a post office, the Government should keep pace with the world's progress by nationalising the telegraph, telephone, parcel express, and railroad services, coal-mines, and also the municipalising of local public works, such as transit, lighting, heating, and water supply. This writer has recently pointed out that the practical objections to the feasibility of Government management are not only answered by its success in Germany and other European States, but also by the first steps towards nationalism taken in Australia, "where the form of government is popular, where its methods are partisan like those in the United States, and where the people are quite as jealous of officialism as are Americans." The Governments of the Australian colonies have undertaken the work of providing for the wants of the people in many more ways than the rulers in the United States or Canada, as otherwise Australia would not have been so quickly opened up for settlement by private enterprise; but recent experiences in borrowing for railways and other public works will, no doubt, lead to private capital being largely employed in future for constructing branch railways, tramways, bridges, and similar undertakings, probably on the land-grant system as in America. The alleged too great dependence of Australians on the Government is pointed out by critics as one of the weakest spots in the policy of Australia, and there would now be a difficulty in floating further loans in Great Britain even for the most reproductive works, though the railways are managed by Commissioners, as in New South Wales, on business principles, and not in any way as a part of the political machine. It has been recently resolved to authorise for railway extension a local borrowing of three millions sterling, which at once advanced New South Wales stocks by ½ per cent. in the London market.

Owing to the Governments of the Australian colonies undertaking services which in other countries are performed by civic bodies or private persons, the cost of administration appears excessive, as the total disbursements in proportion to population is very large. In New South Wales the Government found work for from 40,000 to 45,000 persons through the State, besides its ordinary administrative functions, in carrying on many industrial works. Deducting, for example, from the expenditure of New South Wales the amounts spent on railways, water, sewerage, and harbour services, the amount per inhabitant would be reduced about one-half, or £1 18s. less than the cost of government in the United Kingdom; while even this difference can be accounted for by the expenses incurred for police protection, country roads, poor relief, education, and many other services which in the Colony are borne by the State, whilst in the mother country and America they are defrayed from special rates levied by the municipal authorities. In New South Wales the total number of persons directly paid by the State was over 27,000, including the ordinary civil servants, police, defence force, teachers, railway employees and others. Besides this, there were usually 800 men employed in maintaining roads and repairing buildings, &c.; and in some years there were 12,000 persons employed indirectly through contractors. In 1891 the loan money spent on public works amounted to £4,835,100; but in 1892 it fell to £3,000,000, and the Government has expressed its determination to reduce the borrowing in future to £1,000,000 or £1,500,000 per year.

Australasia may be said to have led the world in experiments in State socialism, as nearly all the railways, tramways, telegraphs, water supply, and other revenue producing works, are owned by the Government or the municipal authorities, and in this respect those colonies have a policy quite different to that of the United States, which have always thrown on private enterprise the onus of providing for public wants with regard to internal transit, with the exception of carriage by the Post Office, which has to be performed under the provisions of the American Constitution. Recently critics have censured the Australian Governments for acting in a paternal manner by incurring a large public debt for the construction of railways, telegraphs, post offices, docks, harbours, reservoirs, and other services, although these undertakings are no doubt mainly of a reproductive character, besides enabling people to settle on the lands, who would not so readily go into the interior but for these conveniences, and so make the cities more congested than they are. Some leading politicians, although opposed to State socialism, are favourable even to the formation of irrigation colonies by the State, so as to secure in New South Wales a settlement of the unemployed on the land, and a consequent greater development of the agricultural industries. A conference of the Australian Socialist League is now discussing a political programme in Sydney for its future operations which are declared to be confined simply to using moral suasion through an "Australasian Democratic Federation" formed for the purpose. The capital invested in the railways of the world is estimated at £6,000,000,000, and the total national debts of the world at £6,400,000,000, but the latter amount has been unfortunately principally spent by European nations in wars of destruction, and not, as in Australasia, principally on permanent works, returning some interest on the money borrowed. In England, the United States, and Canada the railways do not belong to the State, and, therefore, are not available, as in Australasia for payment of the public debts. Being private lines, they are forced to compete with parallel tracks, and a great loss of power often results from competition of rival companies in places where one line would answer all the local requirements. The Governments of Western Australia and Queensland, owing to the difficulty of obtaining loans in the English market at a moderate rate, are now, however, submitting proposals for constructing railways by means of grants of land to private companies in the same way as has been the custom in the United States and Canada, but this new policy will probably become hereafter as unpopular in Australia as the operations of the railroad kings and rings have proved in many parts of America.

Notwithstanding the financial crisis throughout the greater part of the world the deposits in the principal Australian banks have not been much affected, and the London *Daily News* shows that these institutions are very strong in the matter of cash and have otherwise safe assets as investments. The large introduction of English capital into Australia during the last decennial period has saved her people many years of toilsome work, and enabled them better to keep pace with the competition of the inhabitants of countries whose industries had been firmly established by the growth of ages ; but some economists now think that the time has arrived for Australians not to depend so much on London money brokers.

Australian progress has been at a rate which would have surprised the people of the American colonies when they had arrived at the same age, and a comparison of the condition of both countries during the first 100 years of settlement would show a much greater development of resources in the southern colonies, owing to the manifold advantages no doubt existing in the present century and the greater mineral wealth contained in Australasia. The higher rate of interest obtainable in the Australian colonies by British investors caused them readily to lend the various colonial Governments money for the construction of railways, than which there could be found no safer investment in the world, as, besides the intrinsic value of the works themselves, they greatly improved the value of the Crown lands through which they passed. If the railways had been constructed by private speculators as in America, the Australian colonies would not have been able to give such security on the improved public estate caused by these extensions, and the profits from the lines and sale of the land grants would only make a race of millionaires similar to those in America. Both in the United States and Canada millions of money and immense tracts of land along the line were granted to private railway companies as subsidies, to enable them to carry out their undertakings; but in Australia the railroads and the adjoining lands are retained as the property of the State, so that when the line is opened the Crown lands can be sold at an increased value. The construction by the Colonial Governments of railways, bridges, roads, telegraphs, and many other public works, has now so opened up the interior of Australia as to remove the greatest obstacle to easy settlement of population on the soil, and will no doubt lead to greater expansion of natural industry, as these necessities for colonisation will not have now to be undertaken by private enterprise as in North America. There is plenty of room by energy for Australians to increase the quantity of products sold to other countries, especially as the seasons of Europe and the Eastern States of America are opposite to those of Australia, which will enable the latter to supply fruits and dairy produce when they cannot be obtained from elsewhere.

Mulhall makes the income per inhabitant to be in Australia, £40 4s.; in the United States, £39; and in Canada, £26. The Government Statistician of New South Wales has estimated the private income of the residents in that Colony during 1890 at £57 per head. Mr. Edward Pulsford, another computer, has reckoned that out of this amount £45 is the product of Australian industries, and £7 10s. the result of the expenditure of new capital, so that even excluding loan money the wealth per head of population is £5 more than in the United States, and £19 more than in Canada.

The first railways were opened in the United States in 1839, in Canada in 1836, and in Australia in 1854, so that North America had a long start of the southern continent in making railroads, as it could obtain its rolling stock and navvies from shorter distances than the Southern Colonies.

The revenue per head and expenditure per head in Australasia is more than five times greater than in Canada. If Australians are more extravagant than the Canadians, the collections are not far short of the payments for the ordinary Civil Service, although there is no civilised country known in which taxation per head of population is lighter than in Australasia.

To give facilities for intercourse with all parts of the world, Great Britain and the United States have given State subventions to steamship, postal, and cable lines, which do not return direct interest for the expenditure, as even the ordinary English telegraph system had a deficit of £190,000 for the year 1891. The Australasian Governments have also given liberal subsidies to mail steamers and cable lines, so as to have the news from Europe and America as quickly as possible.

Mainly in consequence of Mr. Goschen's conversion scheme, and the Baring Bros. disaster, the fluctuations in value of the first-class securities of the world have been abnormal, as will be seen by the following review of the present financial position by the Commercial Editor of the *Sydney Morning Herald*, who has given much study to the floating of colonial loans :—

In the first instance, the effect of the conversion was to raise all classes of securities, except the bonds of American railway companies, and even several of these rose in value. The stocks of India, the Cape, and Canada advanced in the greatest degree, those of the railways being next. Victorian and New South Wales securities were in the most satisfactory position of the colonial issues. When the first effects of the conversion scheme were over, the market for all stocks settled down to a lower range of values. No doubt the rush for stocks had exhausted supplies of surplus capital. The Baring crisis accentuated this position, and there was then a further reduction in nearly all classes of stocks. But since then there has been a substantial recovery.

The dulness of the London share market, which has been brought about by many causes entirely foreign to Australia, prevent any scheme of conversion of the public debts until the financial clouds cease to obscure the vision of the English money-lender, or until the debts of the various colonies are consolidated when they become federated, which in the opinion of financial critics should be done as soon as possible.

Mr. R. M. Johnston, Statistician and Registrar-General to the Government of Tasmania, in an article in the *Nineteenth Century*, says :—" If the £189,000,000 of Australian indebtedness, general and local government (95 per cent of which at least is represented by railways, tramways, and other public works, which enormously enhance the value of the public and private estate), be deemed excessive, what shall we say of the capital of the United Kingdom amounting to £1,825,000,000 in 1889 sunk in its public debt (general and local) and in its railways, and of the whole of which only 62 per cent. or thereabouts can be said to be represented by public works or undertakings, which in a commercial sense are either reproductive or calculated to enhance the value of its public or private estate? It is altogether misleading to ignore the fact that the £121,000,000 of capital invested in railways in Australasia by the Governments is just as much or as little of the nature of a true public debt as the £890,000,000 so invested by private companies in the United Kingdom. * * * * In relation to absolute indebtedness, or in relation to private wealth, or to population, Australasia's financial condition is greatly superior to that of the wealthiest country in Europe at the present moment, while as regards the future its potential resources and capacity for expansion are immeasurably greater, and if on the score of indebtedness Australasian finances are still deemed to be insecure, then by a similar process of reasoning the financial condition of the richest country of Europe can be proved to be hopelessly bankrupt. * * * * It can be shown by reference to all countries that the capital invested in railway construction, the major item in Australian indebtedness, has ever advanced at a much higher ratio than either population or public revenue, and more especially so at the earlier stages of railway development."

The Hon. John See (Colonial Treasurer) recently made the following statement respecting the financial condition of New South Wales, when bringing in a bill to consolidate the debt of the Colony, as recommended by Sir George Dibbs on his return from London :—" The public debt on the 19th October, 1892, amounted to £55,174,433, which included the million pounds' worth of Treasury bills and the £150,000 they received from the Savings Bank. The people who lent them money in the old country need not have the slightest alarm that they would not be paid in full, and the public need have no fear of the country's honourable intentions and ability to discharge the interest and principal of the money spent on railways and public works, whether of a reproductive or non-reproductive character, but as a rule the money had been judiciously and wisely expended. The railways, tramways, telegraphs, waterworks, sewerage, and other revenue-yielding works were valued at £44,958,000; and public works and buildings not yielding revenue or only indirectly yielding revenue, such as post-offices, roads, bridges, and other civilising requirements, £20,313,000. Everyone would admit that they were valuable assets, and had promoted settlement, facilitated the occupation of the country, and were as necessary to the well-being of the people as railways and waterworks. The value of the unsold Crown lands and the balances due on lands sold conditionally was £107,624,000, making the total value of public property or estate £172,895,000, against a liability of £55,000,000. The average rate of interest payable on the public debt at the beginning of 1892 was 3·811 per cent., a little over 3¾ per cent., and the net earnings returned by the various services in 1891 amounted to £1,433,010, or 2·810 per cent., a little over 2½ per cent. on the existing debt. The deficiency, therefore, to be made good from other sources to pay the total interest on the public debt was about 1 per cent. The railway, tramway, water supply, and sewerage services were the only ones at present yielding net revenue. The net earnings of the railways and tramways for the year ended 30th June, 1892, were 3·58 and 5·28 per cent. respectively, or, taking the services together, the return on capital expenditure was equal to 3·66 per cent. The rate of interest payable on the outstanding loans for railways and tramways was 3·94 per cent. The metropolitan water supply and sewerage services returned during 1891 net earnings equivalent to 3·85 and 3·86 per cent. respectively on the capital debt. After all expenses had been met as to maintenance, management, depreciation, and interest, there remained a credit balance from those two items of £21,073, a very satisfactory result indeed. The loans expended on the service from 1853 to the close of 1891 in directly productive works were as follows:—Railways, £34,090,000; tramways, £1,491,000; water supply, £3,867,000; sewerage, £1,701,000; electric telegraph, £775,000; docks and wharves, £1,700,000; giving a total of £43,627,789. On harbours and rivers there had been expended £1,310,154. Although they were not reckoned reproductive, the works were of a very valuable character, and enabled vessels from all parts of the world to trade with Newcastle, as well as providing facilities for trade with many northern rivers, which, unless this expenditure had been incurred, would have left them in the state that they were in when Captain Cook came to the Colony— practically useless for the settlement of the people. On roads and bridges the expenditure had been £701,282; immigration, £569,930; fortifications and military works, £1,018,679; on other public works, £1,934,673; giving a total of £49,162,507. That might be considered the assets of the public works he had mentioned. The present value of the public estate, including the amount owing on conditional purchase, was £108,584,000; the value of public buildings, £8,239,900; value of roads and bridges, £12,400,000."

Australians have a great advantage over residents in European countries in the immense reserve stock of public land which can be sold in payment of debts contracted, irrespective of the value of the railways, tramways, telegraphs, water and sewerage services, and other reproductive works which have greatly enhanced the value of property in districts in which they have been constructed.

The mother country assisted New Zealand with troops during the Maori war, and prior to Responsible Government regiments of soldiers were stationed in Australasia, but the duties performed were happily more of a civil than a military character, so that the colonists felt a pride in the uniform worn as the outward semblance of connection with England, and expressed much regret on the recall of the troops by the British Government. The formation of local forces has fostered a more reliant spirit for defence among Australians, so that the British soldier is not likely again to be required in Australia.

. Canada has a border line of 3,000 miles between her and the United States, and in this respect her situation for defence is not so favourable as that of an island like Australia, which never has had to repel raids across the imaginary border line like those which in times past called forth the bravery of the Canadian loyalists, and which has led to the British troops being still stationed at Quebec. The local forces in Australasia numbered 33,848 against 37,613·in Canada, whose troops are all on the permanent staff or partially-paid. Major-General Sir Bevan Edwards, in an address delivered before the Royal Colonial Institute, after a careful study of Australian defence, said respecting the great naval stations of Great Britain, which command the principal trade routes: "Australia as being the most remote of all portions of the Empire, and having the largest trade routes, would gain more in war from the existence of these stations than any other group of colonies. The idea that local defence will suffice for the needs of a commercial country, and that the interests of Australia end with her territorial waters, is utterly false. The real defence of the Australian Colonies and their trade will be secured by fleets thousands of miles from their shores." The total debt incurred by Australasia for defence purposes amounted to £2,065,517, or 10s. 10d. per inhabitant. During 1890, £793,750 or 4s. 3d. per inhabitant was spent on defences. These amounts were expended principally for the protection of the coast line, and not for internal defence, as there are no interior boundary lines to be guarded as with the United States and Canada. Happily no civil war or riots of any magnitude have taken place in Australia in which the military has had to be brought into collision with the people, with the exception of the insurrection of the diggers in Ballarat against taxation by a gold license without representation, led by the late Mr. Peter Lalor, afterwards elected Speaker of the Victorian Legislative Assembly, in 1854, and the riots at Lambing Flat, in opposition to Chinese mining on the gold-fields, in 1861.

The enormous national debts of Europe for military and naval establishments impose heavy loads on the people, and induce an amount of poverty and wretchedness which are not to be found either in America or Australia. At the present time there are no doubt large numbers of persons out of employment in some of the Australian colonies, but the percentage to population is less than is usually to be found in the United States. As there have been recently good seasons and crops from the agricultural and pastoral industries, the returns from this production, with the restoration of financial confidence and an easier money market, should bring back something like the normal state of prosperity to Australasia, as there is not sufficient reason for the present depression when the situation is properly considered.

That the Australian colonies will rapidly recover from the present financial depression is evidenced by the fact that a few years since, to meet the adverse times, the people of New Zealand set themselves zealously to work to develop the splendid resources of their country, and in 1889, 1890, and 1891 exported annually nearly £3,000,000 worth of commodities above their previous average, although they received no help from the investment of British capital, from which they were debarred through their previous over-borrowings.

/At the time of the gold discoveries in 1851 the Australian colonies had only about half the population of the British North American colonies ten years previously, but during the last forty years Australasia has increased in population far more rapidly than Canada. Australasia has now only the same number of inhabitants as the population of New England fifty years ago, so that the work accomplished in building cities, towns, and villages throughout a new and extensive territory appears even more remarkable than the highly successful colonisation of North America.

The value of the principal minerals won in the Australasian Colonies up to the end of 1890 is estimated at £427,776,035 as follows,—gold, £342,031,743; silver and silver lead, £8,524,232; copper, £25,421,111; tin, £14,760,086; coal, £28,736,373; kerosene shale, £1,338,552; and other minerals, £6,963,938. The extensive collection of fossils and minerals shown at the Chicago Exposition by the Department of Mines of New South Wales will afford some idea of the magnificent metalliferous deposits in Australasia.

In the year 1890 the value of minerals raised in Australasia was £12,262,934, being more than four times that of Canada. The coal-fields of Australasia gave an output to the value of £1,824,216 against £516,236 worth for Canada.

Canada has had the privilege of coining at her Mint silver as well as gold, in addition to the issue of Dominion notes up to five dollars. As the coinage is on the decimal system, similar in denomination to that of the United States, there could be an interchange of moneys by allowing the coins to pass current in both countries. With the exception of gold all the coins used in Australasia are struck at the London Mint, and Canadian moneys could not pass current in Australia in the same way as they do in the United States, whose gold eagle is a legal tender in the Dominion.

The amount of the gold coin in Australia is more than six times as much as in Canada, and the amount of silver coin is also greater, but silver is not allowed to be coined at the Sydney or Melbourne Mints, although requests for that privilege are now being considered by the Imperial Government.

The mining industry in Australia is only second to the pastoral one, but the search for gold has slackened both in America and Australia in favour of prospecting for other metals. This is remarkable considering that the value of gold throughout the world has never decreased, and there is an increasing demand for it for coinage purposes, whilst there has been a gradual decline in the value of every other product, whether a natural yield or the result of manufacture. For the gold-mining interests of the Australasian colonies to prosper they only need to receive proper scientific attention and honest treatment from the capitalist, as mines have sometimes been bought only for speculative purposes instead of being purchased as a permanent investment, and steadily worked like a sheep run, a farm, or an orchard. There is a wide distribution of auriferous rocks throughout New South Wales, and if the experience of Californian mining experts could be secured for their working the extending requirements of the world for gold could be met. Of late years there has been something like a revival in gold-mining in some of the colonies, and the Mount Morgan mine in Queensland has already paid over £2,750,000 in dividends, and is now designated "one of the wonders of the world." Altogether Victoria has produced gold to the value of £227,482,000, and still leads in the value of production, although the annual output of Queensland is now nearly as much, and all the other colonies have within their borders a considerable gold-mining industry. Australasia has produced gold to the value of £342,031,743, against a yield of £270,844,444 for California, which is the great gold-mining state in America.

The modern system of gold-mining, both in the United States and Australasia, is greatly changed as it now requires a large amount of both skill and capital to work the alluvial and rock deposits, and methods quite different from the cradle and tin dish of the early gold-miners are now adopted. On the discovery of gold in California and Australia it was feared that there would be a hurtful over-production of that precious metal, and it would be so cheapened as to lose nearly one-half of its purchasing powers, but this alarm was unnecessary as population and trade grew at a rate nearly co-equal with the increment of gold. A similar question is now being raised with regard to the large quantity of silver mined, as the world's out-put shows a great increase while the yield of gold has been more steady, and the matter is being considered at an Intercolonial Monetary Conference held in Berlin, at which Australia and America are represented. The mining of gold and silver in Australasia has not increased in the same ratio as the out-put of coal, copper, lead, tin, petroleum, and other useful minerals, or as production in agriculture and sheep and cattle farming, but there are many valuable deposits of the precious metals in all the Colonies yet remaining to be worked. There has been no great artificial stimulus given to silver mining in New South Wales like the annual purchase, since 1876, of large quantities of silver by the United States Government so as to endeavour to arrest the continuous steady decline in the value of that metal. The most valuable silver mine in Australia was discovered at Broken Hill by a boundary-rider on a pastoral run or ranche in 1883. At Broken Hill the mines have a complete smelting plant on the latest and most approved principles, and before the recent strike there were 2,500 men employed, being only 500 less than those in the celebrated Comstock mine in California. The Broken Hill mines have paid dividends to the amount of £3,304,000, and bonuses amounting to £592,000, besides the nominal value of shares sold to other companies amounting to £1,744,000, or a total return from the mines of £5,640,000.

The value of silver produced in 1890 in Australia was £2,869,530. The production of silver in New South Wales last year exceeded the largest annual production of gold in the palmiest days of the diggings, and was about one-fourth of that won in the United States.

The yield of minerals in the Broken Hill and Silverton district in 1890 was valued at £2,785,398, and the machinery employed at £406,885. Mr. E. F. Miller, assayer at the Sydney Mint, patented an economic process for the separation of silver from gold whilst in a molten state by chlorine gas, which has also been successfully used in the Royal Mint in London in toughening extremely brittle gold in a comparatively short time and in a more economical manner than by the corrosive sublimate method of treatment. The manager of the principal silver-mine at Broken Hill was formerly manager of the group of the Nevada-Comstock mines.

The argentiferous lead ores from the valley of the Broken Hill district extend over 2,500 square miles of country, and the largest lode measures from 10 feet to 200 feet in width. The Broken Hill Proprietary Company, from the commencement of mining operations in 1885 to the end of November, 1891, treated 803,509 tons of silver and silver-lead ore, producing 30,707,500 ounces of silver and 125,102 tons of lead, valued in the London market at £7,059,175.

Although there has recently been a fall in the price of shares in the silver-mines at Broken Hill it is not so great as the drop which took place in 1878 in the scrip of the famous Comstock lode in California.

There has been a tendency to a considerable development in silver coinage during the past ten years, owing to the large increase in the production of silver in the world, and especially in the United States and New South Wales, the former of which produced in 1891 4,000,000 fine ounces, and the latter over 5,000,000 fine ounces more than in 1890.

Cinnabar has been found scattered through a tertiary drift near Rylstone, on the Cudgegong River. The total quicksilver product in California is very large, and the obtaining of a similar native supply would be very beneficial to Australia.

The total production of copper in Australia, to the 31st December, 1890, amounted in value to £25,431,111, of which £318,952 was won in 1890. In 1888, Australia produced 7,450 tons, the United States 101,054 tons, and Canada, 2,250 tons. If the copper-mines could be worked more cheaply by contract a larger output could be made, and the necessity for shutting down furnaces, which has taken place in both America and Australia through the low price of the metal, obviated, and the manipulations of speculative syndicates partly prevented.

About 4,296,320 acres in New South Wales are known to be of cupriferous formation. The leading mine is the great Cobar Mine. The ore consists of carbonates, metallic copper in films, red oxide, and grey and yellow sulphide.

The copper mines of Australia are stated by the leading metallurgists to produce metal equal to the best copper of the United States; the value of the production of New South Wales to the end of 1890 was £3,362,728. Owing to the price of copper falling from £172 per ton in 1872 to £47 per ton in 1892, principally through the vast increase in the output of the United States, many of the mines have not been worked, so that only £119,195 worth was produced in New South Wales in 1891.

The total value of tin raised in Australasia to the end of 1890, was £14,760,086, of which £569,264 was produced in 1890. A large quantity of Australian tin, in ingots, has been shipped to the United States, where but very little of the metal is mined, although much required in the development of the tin-plate industries started since the passing of the McKinley tariff. About £400,000 of tin is shipped every year from Mount Bischoff, in Tasmania.

Evidence of the progressive development of the mineral resources of New South Wales is found in the discovery, only twenty years since, of valuable stanniferous deposits. The amount of the tin ore received since that time has a value of £5,541,700, and a great quantity of the ingots have been shipped to America for use in her manufactories. In New South Wales there are not only alluvial deposits of tin ore but also many valuable lodes which, however, have not yet been worked to any extent owing to lack of capital or skill. Alluvial deposits were first discovered in the beds of existing creeks, but more recently ore has been largely found in the beds of old rivers or creeks, in some cases covered by basalt. There appears to be no mining of this useful mineral in California, although the ore is found there.

Last year New South Wales alone imported tin plate from the United Kingdom of the value of £46,850, as it is not manufactured in the Colony. Upwards of fifty tin-bearing lodes have been opened in the New England district in New South Wales, and in several places the American diamond-drill has been successfully employed. One of the most important uses to which iron is applied is the manufacture of tin plates, an industry which has not yet been introduced into Australia.

About 75,000 diamonds have been obtained from the mines in New South Wales to the end of 1887, the largest being 5⅜ carat or 16·2 grains, but no systematic operations to any extent in search of them have been carried on. These diamonds are stated by experts to be in their physical characters more nearly allied to those of Brazil than to those of any other country, and are largely sold in London as the product of that South American state. The Australian diamond is harder to polish than the African stone, but when polished would be of greater brilliancy and refracting power ; although these stones cannot vie in size or quantity with Cape stones, in brilliancy and fire when cut they are equal to them. The late Government Geologist said that he was fully convinced that diamond-mining will be found an important industry in the Colony, and would have been developed earlier but for the want of water. The Australian diamond is very suitable on account of its hardness for rock-drilling, mill-dressing, and for turning all hard metals and stones, and the small ones as natural stones, for glass-cutting, china-drilling, &c.

Thousands of diamonds and other precious stones have been found in the drifts of New South Wales, but through want of crystallographical knowledge many ludicrous mistakes with respect to these valuable gems have been made by prospectors. Mr. E. W. Streeter, the well-known London jeweller, stated recently that Australia was the possible matrix of abundance of valuable gems, and other British dealers believe that diamonds, emeralds, and rubies of large size would be found if the work of prospecting were undertaken by experienced individuals.

The quantity of coal extracted in the Australasian colonies in 1890 amounted to 4,103,114 tons, of the value of £1,824,216, of which over 70 per cent. was raised in New South Wales.

The output of coal in New South Wales in 1891 was 4,037,929 tons of the value of £1,742,796 ; of which 365,623 tons of the value of £200,851, were sent to the United States.

As in California there are only about 110,000 tons of coal raised annually a large supply has to be obtained from foreign sources, which has led to a considerable trade between San Francisco and Newcastle, in New South Wales. A Bill passed the American House of Representatives some time ago placing coal on the free list, and it is believed that this Bill will be confirmed by the recently-elected Senate, as the majority of its members favour the removal of duty from raw materials.

The export of coal from New South Wales to San Francisco and other ports on the Pacific coast of the United States has steadily increased during the last few years. The low rate of freight, and the drawback of 3s. 1d. per ton allowed upon coal imported into the United States for the use of foreign and domestic steamships, are stated to be the principal causes of the increase.

The shipping facilities for coal at Newcastle. near Sydney are very great, and the tonnage of the port is often as large as that of Port Jackson.

The amount of coal mined in Canada for 1890 was 2,719,478 tons, and the output has increased fourfold during the last twenty years ; some of which enters into competition with New South Wales coal in the San Francisco market.

Many vessels bringing cargoes from British ports take coal from Newcastle, in New South Wales, to South America and other ports, or go in ballast to San Francisco and elsewhere to ship wheat, &c., for the British market. The following table shows that coal-mining is more profitable in New South Wales than in the United States :—

Country.	Coal per miner.	Wages per ton of coal.	Earnings of Miner per annum.
	Tons.	£ s. d.	£ s. d.
New South Wales	467	0 3 7	83 13 5
United States	347	0 3 4	57 16 8

Coal-mining in Australia is more remunerative to the miner than in America, owing to the accessibility of the carboniferous formations and the excellent quality of the coal.

The total value of coal raised per miner was £210 3s. in New South Wales against £139 in the United States. The value at the pit's mouth per ton was 9s. in New South Wales, and 8s. 4d. in the United States.

The coal-mines of New South Wales are by far the most important in the southern hemisphere. The coal is of such excellent quality, and the seams are so extensive and easily worked, that there is every promise for their future. The total area covered by the seams is estimated at 23,950 square miles.

Mr. Consul Griffin says : "By comparison, the coal from Newcastle, in New South Wales, is much denser than English Newcastle, and very nearly equal to the best Welsh coal. A ton of New South Wales coal would occupy nearly 6 per cent. less space than an equal quantity of British coal. New South Wales coal contains less sulphur than the British, and consequently, is not so liable to spontaneous combustion, or to affect the purity of the atmosphere as British coals." The Colonial collieries have until now enjoyed almost perfect immunity from marsh or light carburetted hydrogen gas, which renders the loss of life so appalling elsewhere.

The bituminous, semi-bituminous, splint, anthracite, and cannel coals of New South Wales equal in thickness and quality those found in any part of the world. There are also many deposits of petroleum oil. In fact, some of the highest authorities on minerals, both in England and Australia, are very decided in the opinion that New South Wales coal in many respects is better than the English coal, inasmuch as it is more adapted to steam purposes and richer in gas-giving products.

Although, in 1890, the Australasian colonies imported 7,054,293 gallons of American kerosene, there were 38,463 tons of kerosene shale exported from New South Wales to foreign countries, of which 2,563 tons were sent to the United States.

The quantity of kerosene shale raised in New South Wales was 653,041 tons to the close of 1891.

Mr. Griffin says : "New South Wales has for many years carried on a profitable industry in the manufacture of petroleum and paraffine out of the shale product, which exists in considerable quantities in parts of the Colony." It has been predicted for many years that the oil-bearing districts of the

United States would become exhausted, and that the bulk of the world's supply must hereafter be looked for in Russia and Australia. The kerosene shale in New South Wales covers a vast area, and the shale found at Eskbank is said to be the richest in the world. Considerable quantities of it are used in the large cities of the colonies for the purpose of enriching gas. It is also exported for the same purpose to Holland, Java, and the Pacific slope of the United States.

Dr. Heisch, public analyst of the districts of Lewisham and Hampstead, London, in his report upon the shale from Joadja Creek, in New South Wales, showed that its gas-producing power was extraordinary. The richest quality of Australian kerosene shale yields upwards of 150 gallons of crude oil per ton, or 18,000 cubic feet of gas, with an illuminating power of thirty-eight or forty sperm candles. Professor Chandler, Columbia College, New York, compared the kerosene shale-mine at Hartley, New South Wales, with grahamite from West Virginia and albertite from Nova Scotia, both of which are used for enriching gas, and found that the candle power of gas from the Australian mineral was 131·00 against 49·55 for albertite, and 28·70 for grahamite.

An excellent axle oil for railway carriages is obtained from the Australian shales, equal to that used in the United States and as cheap.

American mining machinery has of late years been largely introduced into Australasia from San Francisco—such as steam engines, furnaces, smelters, ore-separators, pumps, pumping gear, and rock-drills, as the experience of American miners in perfecting these machines has enabled them to do excellent work.

If the Australian Colonies had introduced the processes made known by the American experts at the International Congress of Metallurgy, held in America in 1890, there is no doubt that iron and steel manufactures could be made in due time in Australia to rival the productions even of the large rolling mills and furnaces of Pittsburg, Chicago, and other great iron centres, which have made America the first nation in the world in the amount of her iron products. Just as America has recently distanced the mother country in mining this most useful metal, so hereafter the United States may be distanced in the industrial race by the products of Australasia, owing to the immense iron ore deposits in that country, especially in New South Wales. Tenders are now invited for making in New South Wales 175,000 tons of steel rails from local ores for use on the Government railways. Large deposits of iron ore, equal to the best English hematite, have been discovered in New South Wales, often in the same localities as the coal and limestone suitable for smelting purposes. The want of proper metallurgical knowledge and appliances for the treatment of the ores has prevented the starting of rolling-mills similar to those in America, although the late Government Geologist reports on some of the iron ore deposits that where they occur convenient to coal and limestone they contain in sight 12,944,000 tons of ore, estimated to yield 5,853,000 tons of metallic iron.

New South Wales has extensive deposits of rich iron ores, associated with coal and limestone in unlimited supplies, suitable for smelting purposes, and for the manufacture of steel of certain descriptions. Abundance of manganese, chrome, and tungsten ores are also available.

Although there are large deposits of iron ore throughout New South Wales, they have not been developed, owing to want of capital and technical knowledge ; and nearly all the pig, bar, rod, plate, and sheet-iron used in the

G

foundries is imported. The efforts to establish iron-making in the Colony, have so far not been successful, though it possesses the requisites to ensure success so far as deposits of iron, fuel, and flux are concerned. Mr. W. Davis, of Mount Pleasant, Wollongong, who has had considerable experience in smelting iron ores, has, however, recently offered to supply the iron for 20,000 tons of pipes required by the Government, and he states pig iron could be produced in the Colony as cheap if not cheaper than it could be imported. Iron made in the Colony at present is not from ore, but from scrap, the quantity in 1891 being 4,125 tons, valued at £36,101. As it is estimated that 153,000 tons of iron ore are imported into New South Wales annually, Mr. C. S. Wilkinson, its late eminent Government Geologist, calculated that the amount of iron which the Colony could readily produce would furnish a supply for over thirty-five years.   There are three localities favourably situated for the establishment of smelting-works, namely, near Mittagong or Picton in the south-western coal-seam, on the Great Southern Railway line near Wallerawang or Lithgow, on the edge of the western coal-field, on the Great Western Railway, and near Rylstone also in the western coal-field on the Wallerawang-Mudgee Railway line.   The quantity of iron ore available for smelting works is estimated as follows :—In the Mittagong or Picton district, approximately, 8,234,000 tons, containing 3,684,000 tons of native iron ; in the Wallerawang district, 2,484,000 tons of ore, containing 1,212,000 tons of metallic iron ; and in the Rylstone district, 2,226,000 tons of ore, containing 957,180 tons of metallic iron ; or a total quantity of 12,944,000 tons of ore, containing 5,853,180 tons of metallic iron.   At one manufactory that was started, the metal treated was red silicious ore, averaging 22 per cent., and brown hematite, yielding 50 per cent. of metallic iron.   The total quantity of iron made was 49,651 tons, of the value of £383,565.

In one valley in the Blue Mountains, which is approached by a railway zig-zag of world-wide notoriety, resembling in construction the Marshall's Pass on the Rio Grande route in the United States, are now to be found collieries, smelting-works, and potteries, with abundance of kerosene shale, iron and limestone in the vicinity. It is not many years since this valley was first inhabited, and the present industries may be taken as evidence of what may be done by railway extension, in bringing to market the hidden wealth in the many gullies of the mountain ranges.   The late Rev. W. B. Clarke says of the formations in New South Wales : "It is not too much to say that no sooner are we off the carboniferous areas containing coal, than we are in the region in which gold and copper, and lead abound ; and passing from the sedimentary to the plutonic rocks, we can discover granites which, however barren externally, are within frequently charged with the ore of tin ; so that the three great geological divisions of our Colony are replete with mineral treasures that are practically inexhaustible."

In 1891 the value of the exports from the Australasian Colonies exceeded the value of the imports.   It is remarkable that in the year in which the value of wool and other produce fell so extensively the colonies should have been able to add £7,920,000 to the value of their exportations.   Last year Australasian imports were valued at £72,085,907 and exports at £72,719,277.   In 1890 the value per inhabitant of exports of domestic produce was in Australasia, £13 3s. 8d. ; in the Argentine Republic, £7 0s. 4d. ; in Chili, £5 10s. 5d. ; in Canada, £3 12s. 7d.; and in the United States, £2 17s. 9d. ; so that Australians are able to dispose of their raw products to a much greater value per head than the people in either North or South America.   In 1891 the exports of home products from Australasia amounted to £15 4s. 8d. per inhabitant.

The total value of agricultural produce in Australasia in 1890 amounted to £23,613,700, or an average value of produce per acre under crop of £3 6s. 10d. The value of the principal crops in Australasia in 1890 was as follows:—Wheat, £5,884,673 ; maize, £1,379,940 ; barley, £487,618 ; oats, £1,708,087 ; other grains, £67,437 ; hay, £4,317,359 ; potatoes, £1,827,869 ; other root crops, £1,094,039 ; sugar-cane, £1,416,419 ; tobacco, £24,957 ; grapes, £919,269 ; green forage, £772,215 ; hops, £85,593 ; orchards and market gardens, £3,046,082 ; other crops, £581,543.

Heavy duties imposed by the United States on the varieties of fine wool only obtainable from Australia must not only have a deterrent effect upon manufactures in the Eastern States, but prove prejudicial to commercial reciprocity between the two countries. Ten high-bred merino sheep were presented by George III to Captain John Macarthur, which were placed with superior rams and ewes procured in 1797 from the Cape of Good Hope. These sheep proved the true "golden fleece," they were added to from time to time, and at the end of 1891 their progeny had spread all over Australasia, numbering 116,041,707, and representing with the land upon which they were pastured a value of at least £400,000,000. There are many squatters whose present annual income is from £10,000 to £100,000, and one pastoral king, who owns some thirty stations in Victoria, Queensland, and New South Wales, secured in 1890 a net profit of £192,000.

The amount of money received from Europe for wool by the Australian Colonies since the foundation far exceeds that obtained for the precious metals. The long merino combing wools in New South Wales show the advance which has been made in recent years, and that Colony has hitherto been specially famous for its fine clothing wools which occupy a first-class position in the market. Although the price of Australian wool has recently declined, the fall has been only at about half the rate of the depreciation in British manufactures for the last fifteen years, and there has been relatively a smaller reduction in the sterling value of the colonial staple than in the world's production of almost all kinds.

Australia has followed the example of South American countries in shipping wool direct to the nations on the continent of Europe, instead of allowing them to obtain all their supplies through the London market. The value of the direct export trade of wool to the United States amounted in 1881 to £132,699 sterling, and in 1890 to £189,237, being a proportion of the shipments in each year of 0·8 and 0·9 respectively. The value of the export of wool from Australasia in 1890 amounted to £20,349,300 sterling, of which 30·5 per cent. was shipped from New South Wales, irrespective of the fact that wool belonging to it of the value of £2,892,220 sterling was shipped from Victoria, and that a large quantity was also sent for shipment to South Australia. In the wool trade of the United Kingdom in 1890, out of a total import of 649,908,000 lb., the imports from Australasia amounted to 418,702,000 lb., and 67,206,000 lb. were exported to the United States. The imports into Europe and America from Australasia rose during the period from 1880 to 1890 from 869,000 bales to 1,411,000 bales. The average value per bale of Australasian and Cape wools decreased from £20 5s. to £14 15s. during the nine years 1880–1888, and although the production rose by nearly 50 per cent., the total yearly value kept on an almost uniform level.

With a practically unchanged supply, the total value of the Australian wool clip in 1890 was £1,250,000 less than in 1889. In the distribution of wool sent to the United Kingdom in 1890, 665,000 bales were consumed by English manufacturers, 979,000 bales by continental manufacturers,

and 48,000 bales by American manufacturers. The proportion of wool
exported from Australasia the produce of New South Wales was 44 per
cent. of the whole. The wool clip of New South Wales has more than
doubled during the last ten years, whilst that of California has decreased by
11,000,000 lb.

The production of wool in New South Wales since its foundation has reached
in value the magnificent total of £196,790,000, and the annual return from
sheep, cattle, and horses to £35,920,600. The total export of greasy and
washed wool from New South Wales in 1891 amounted to 331,870,720 lb.
of the value of £11,312,980. In the Paris Exhibition of 1878, the Grand
Prix was awarded to Mr. E. K. Cox, of New South Wales, for samples of
wool produced on his lands in the Mudgee district.

There has been a large trade with Great Britain in preserved meats, and
frozen, preserved, and other kinds of meats were exported from New South
Wales to the value of £200,000 in 1891. As beef and mutton are now sold in
Sydney at less than half the price at which they are procurable in the Eastern
States of America, and as there is much surplus stock, it would be a good thing
if this abundance of fresh animal food were brought more within the reach of
the working classes in the Union, who, however, are better off in this regard
than the people of England were before frozen meat was imported by them.

In 1880 the number of horned cattle in Australasia was 7,863,000, as against
35,926,000 in the United States. In 1890 the number in Australasia was
10,949,524; in Canada, about 4,200,000; and in the United States,
50,331,042. Sir Roderick Cameron states that live cattle could now be profitably shipped to Europe at the low price for stock now ruling in Australia.
The exports of oxen and beef from the United States has greatly increased
during the past few years, notwithstanding the large quantities of frozen
mutton sent from Australasia to Great Britain, so that there appears to be
good markets in England for the surplus stock of both countries, as their
beeves and flocks have reduced the price of meat from two to three pence a
pound. The domestic export of fresh and frozen meats from Australasia in 1890
amounted to 1,025,552 cwt., and of salt and preserved meats, 152,761 cwt.
An immense value of meat product has been allowed to go to waste season
after season, which food would be very acceptable to other countries. Owing
to the enterprise of the late Mr. T. S. Mort twenty years ago, a large frozen
meat trade is now carried on with the mother country. New South Wales contains about one half the sheep in Australasia, whilst thirty years ago it only
had one-fourth, and it is estimated that there is a surplus of 60,000 to 100,000
head of cattle and 4,500,000 sheep, which in any ordinary year could be
exported without trespassing on the local requirements. There are several
frozen meat works in the Colony, and one of them recently sent away a first
shipment of 40,000 carcasses. The animals are killed in the country districts,
and the chilled meat forwarded by railway is found to be superior to that of
travelled stock, and is free from the large waste caused by privations when the
live animals are taken long journeys by road or rail. There are openings in
New South Wales for frozen-meat centres, such as those in Chicago, Omaha,
Kansas City, or St. Louis, so that the meat could be put into refrigerating
cars or vessels, and conveyed, still maintaining the same temperature, to either
the local or foreign markets. There is an excellent opening in New South
Wales for the introduction of proper machinery and the applied knowledge
of experts in the latest improvements at work in Chicago factories to
preserve for export beef, mutton, and pork by canning, chilling, smoking,
and dry and wet salting. The colonial exhibit of tinned meats at the

Colonial and Indian Exhibition was reported by the judges as extensive and excellent, and mostly superior in quality in every way to tinned meats from the United States the product of lean Texan cattle, from which the prime joints have been removed to supply the hotels and markets in the eastern cities, and "so only the inferior portions of an inferior animal are used."

There is a great market in Europe for frozen meat as Great Britain alone imported to feed its population in 1891 no less than 2,168,270 cwt. of salted and fresh beef, and 1,662,994 cwt. of mutton. In 1891, 3,323,821 carcasses of frozen mutton were imported into Great Britain, of which number 2,231,399 came from Australasia. As only 400 carcasses of mutton were imported from Australia in 1880, a great development in the trade has taken place during ten years. New Zealand mutton from cross-bred sheep is preferred to that of the Australian merino, but the flesh of the latter has firmness of texture and sweetness of flavour, and obtains a higher price than Argentine sheep, which also find a ready and lucrative sale in the United Kingdom. There are twice as many sheep sent to England from Australasia as from the Argentine Republic. In the beef trade of England, the chilled meat has of late years been preferred to frozen meat, and the perfecting of new freezing processes enables Australia to send chilled carcasses from the antipodes in as prime a condition as they can be obtained from America. The live cattle trade with England has been more profitable to Canada than the trade in dead meat, against which there has been a prejudice now being rapidly removed by the adoption of improved chilling process in Australasia. The cattle trade of Canada increased in the ten years prior to 1887 in value more than £1,000,000 sterling, the greater part of this trade being with the mother country, but it will be greatly interfered with by a recent proclamation with regard to the importation of live stock for fear of their bringing disease with them. During the last few years the export of live sheep and mutton from the United States has greatly decreased.

Twelve years ago frozen mutton was unknown in the English market, but now nearly 20 per cent. of the mutton used is imported in that state, and this is greatly due to the enterprise of Mr. T. S. Mort and other Australian merchants. Mr. Robert Hudson, one of the founders of the extensive works of Hudson Bros. at Clyde, near Sydney, and Superintendent of the Executive Commissioner's staff at the Chicago Exhibition, has recently obtained a patent for refrigerator cars constructed under his supervision, twenty-two of which are in use on the colonial railway lines conveying frozen meat in a most satisfactory manner for many hundreds of miles, as it is found by using his system " the grazier gets every ounce he fattens and the consumer gets his beef and mutton in its natural and healthy condition."

A magnificent block of buildings has recently been erected for Messrs. Geddes and Co. (Limited), on the North Shore of Port Jackson for the reception of pastoral produce, which will have all the best modern appliances for the frozen-meat trade. Mr. J. H. Geddes, who during a recent tour in Europe has given much study as to the best methods of exporting the large amount of surplus mutton and beef of Australia to the inexhaustible markets of Europe, so that there may be no waste, has recently written a letter to the press on this subject from which the following extract is taken :—

" As our association consists of many of the most prominent stock-owners of New South Wales, who originally co-operated with a view to the development of the frozen-meat trade, every possible attention has for long past been given to this question, and especially to chilling, receiving, grading, freezing, cold storage, shipping, freight, and disposal of in local market or in England ; and I feel convinced that the erection of small chilling and boiling establishments (inasmuch as they are only a third of the cost of freezing works) at the different country centres, connected by rail, and acting as feeders to freezing works at the port of shipment, is the only practical scheme for the disposal of our surplus mutton, and is the one most worthy of stock-owners' consideration ; and as companies have already been formed and works erected at Tenterfield and Narrandera (mainly through the zeal and energy of Mr. Robert Hudson), companies also being formed at Dubbo, Young, and Bourke, and are being now vigorously promoted at Wagga Wagga, Jerilderie, Forbes, Narrabri, and Gunnedah, besides being in contemplation at other centres, this scheme may be considered to have come into active operation.

While thoroughly grasping the immense importance of this great trade, I may mention that the freezing establishments now in existence, and the freezing preparations which will be completed by the end of the year of our association, will represent a capacity for manipulation in New South Wales alone of practically 1,500,000 carcasses per annum, almost equal to the respective exports of New Zealand and the Argentine Confederation, while Queensland which has imparted singular energy to the development of the frozen-meat trade, with works at Brisbane, Rockhampton, and Townsville, will represent a similar quantity of beef or mutton annually, and with Victoria exporting 100,000 carcasses annually, principally from Southern Riverina, the tide of frozen-meat export may claim to have fairly set in, and we may look forward to seeing in the near future a very large increase in this export trade from Australia. This Mr. Mort foresaw, and for this he laboured so indefatigably that he certainly shortened his days. Not only Australia but the whole world owes him a deep debt of gratitude, as in solving the problem—in his own words—" of supplying the over abundance of one country to make up for the deficiency of another, and the year of plenty to serve for the scant harvest of its successor, even to the most distant parts of the globe," Mr. Mort led the way for the frozen-meat trade of the world, and not only by his philanthropic views and his large personal expenditure in experimenting, but also by his untiring zeal, energy, and foresight, a world-wide frozen-food export trade has on his basis been successfully established exactly in accordance with his foreshadowings, and the one regret all must unite in is that he is not here to see the successful issue of the great labour of his life."

In 1880 the number of horses in Australia was 1,065,000 as against 11,202,000 in the United States. In 1890 the number in Australasia was 1,732,628 ; in Canada, about 1,100,000 ; and in the United States, in 1888, 13,663,294. General Von Kodilitch, of the Austrian army, says that the magnificent Australian horses make the very best for troopers in the world.

There are in Australia numerous tracts of level country, and the plains, although not generally as fertile as the treeless prairies of America which after cultivation have made Chicago so famous, yet contain large quantities of excellent land mostly heavily timbered with valuable hardwoods.

In New South Wales half the runs of the pastoral lessees is open to selection, but owing to the comparatively sparse population nothing occurs approaching the recent rush on throwing open the reservations of Cheyenne or Araphoe Indians, near Forderno, where 43,000 people fought for 12,000 farms. Although there is considerable friction between some squatters and the small settlers who select on their leased pastoral runs, this feeling is not so strong as the antagonism between the farmers and the " beef-barons " of Wyoming, Texas, and Colorado. Australasia and America are destined to be always the great producers of food as well as of wool and cotton for the nations of Europe, although the cheap labour of India now grows large quantities of wheat and cotton for the English market. Out of the 2,023,181,760 statute acres owned by the Australasian Colonies 126,877,289 acres only had been alienated at the end of 1890 ; so that there then remains unsold a balance of 1,896,304,471 acres in this immense public estate. The area at present leased in Australasia amounted to 810,408,894 acres, principally for sheep and cattle runs, while the extent of cattle ranches in Canada amounted only to 2,288,347 acres, showing that the extent of settlement for the pastoral industry is very small when compared with that attained in Australia. The squatter in Central Australia has sometimes to endure great privations during a dry season from the small and uncertain rainfall, but the boring for artesian wells should tap to a much greater extent the underground rivers which flow through immense tracts of the cretaceous formation in New South Wales. New Zealand and Tasmania have extensive snow-capped mountains, the frozen water from which, if required, could be utilised for irrigation purposes, as in the United States. On the Australian continent comparatively little snow falls, although the splendid agricultural land in the Kiandra district of New South Wales could be watered from the Snowy River, and settlements formed which should be made to outvie even those in the far-famed Utah Valley, if something like the intelligent perseverance of the Mormons was displayed by the colonial settlers.

The recently-formed Department of Agriculture in New South Wales, on the lines of a similar Bureau at Washington, has started an agricultural college like that at Guelph in Canada, and gives national prizes for orchards, farms, vineyards, and dairies; and, by lecturers, publications, and other means, is endeavouring to introduce the best methods of farming and horticulture in force in North America and elsewhere.

It must be admitted that the principles of agricultural science have hitherto received but scant recognition from the colonists, and a band of American farmers, fruit-growers, and raisin-preservers, with a knowledge of labour-saving implements and the latest appliances, might reasonably expect adequate success in New South Wales. There are now 84,924 persons engaged in agricultural pursuits in New South Wales, and their prospects are better than those of people similarly employed in Canada and the eastern states of America. Although there has not been much progress made of late years in settlement on the lands of the Colony, yet from 1862 to 1890 there were 227,794 individual selections of Crown lands applied for, amounting to a total area of 29,873,620 acres, of which, in 1890, there were still in existence 157,062 selections covering an area of 20,404,540 acres. Not a fourth part of the lands of the Colony has as yet been disposed of, and there still remains unalienated 151,123,999 acres. Under the Real Property Act in force in New South Wales deeds of grant are guaranteed by the Government on a simple system of registration devised by an Australian, and the difficulty which has arisen in the transfer of many Californian Mexican ranch grants is not met with by purchasers of land in the Colony.

The value of agricultural production per head in Australasia in 1890 was £6·3; and in settlements in America in 1887 (the last figures available) it was in the United States, £7·5; Canada, £7; Argentina, £5·8; Uruguay, £3·3.

The traveller on the railways over the great prairies of America passes through corn-fields extending for many miles and as far as the eye can reach, so that there are few spots not under cultivation; and an Australian cannot help contrasting these extensive crops with the scattered farms on similar plains in Australia, which only require the intelligent farmer to make them likewise produce as plentiful a harvest.

One of the things which most strikes the traveller on the Canadian-Pacific Railway, is the comparatively little land brought under cultivation in the Great North-West which can be seen from the railroad car, as the farmers are compelled to settle on lands far from the railroad, owing to many of the sections along the line being either free grants to the railroad company or in the hands of private speculators, who are waiting to secure the unearned increment obtained by the improvements of those settlers who have had to select land in the back country.

The principal crop in Australasia is wheat, to which half the tillage is devoted, and the average production per acre for the last decennial period was little short of 10 bushels, varying from 6 bushels in South Australia to 24·5 bushels in New Zealand, the smaller yield owing to favourable conditions often paying better than the larger. The average production of wheat per acre in the United States is a little larger than that obtained in Australasia, but greater attention is paid in America to the growth of the crop, and the best machinery to gather in the grain is more extensively used than by Australians.

The total yield of wheat in some years only is larger in Canada than in Australasia, but as the former has a larger population it has less for export. In 1890, the quantity produced in the United States amounted to 393,262,000 bushels, in Canada, to 40,527,562 bushels, and in Australasia, to 32,839,505 bushels. The consumption of wheat per head in bushels was for Australasia, 6·6 ; for Canada, 6·4; and for the United States, 4·7. Owing to the plentiful harvests in America, Russia, and Australia, the price of wheat this season is the lowest within the century, and it has declined per imperial quarter from £3 12s. 5d., in 1854, to £1 5s. 9d. in 1892.

The labouring population of Australia, owing to the cheapness of meat usually eat that article of diet at every meal, and therefore do not consume so much vegetable food as the workmen in America, who however have a much more plentiful meat diet than the artisans in Europe. Although rust in wheat is found in some parts of Australia it is comparatively unknown on the table-lands of New South Wales. Of late years the most favourable results have been obtained by a system of mixed farming, of growing wheat with sheep-farming in pastoral districts, where it was stated by the squatters wheat would not grow. Many years ago large quantities of flour were imported into Australia from California, but now the production of wheat in Australasia is as great as in California.

Much of the land now under lease to squatters is suitable for agriculture and should be utilised for that purpose, as a farming district would employ thirty families where sheep-growing requires only one. The falling in of many pastoral leases will shortly throw open a large quantity of arable land for agricultural settlement in New South Wales.

The average annual consumption of wheat in Australasia during the last ten years amounted to 21,447,000 bushels, and there was a surplus from the local yield available for export amounting to 8,305,000 bushels of grain, and the last transactions reported in the London market gives a higher price for it than for the best Californian grain. One point in favour of the occupier of new rich lands, under a suitable climate, is that the character or quality of the grain produced on them far surpasses that of the grain grown on lands long cultivated and highly manured, in order to force from them a large yield. The very manuring is one of the largest elements of the cost of agriculture in old countries on exhausted land, when compared with the mode of cultivation of farmers on the rich virgin soils of new countries. Again the operations of agriculture in these new rich lands are in themselves simple and comparatively inexpensive, partly from the character of the soil, partly from the dryness of the climate in the countries most favourable to wheat-growing, so that its cost is reduced to a minimum in Australia and America.

Owing to the great scarcity of provisions shortly after the foundation of New South Wales, the Governor placed himself with the rest of the community on half allowance, but now the finest wheat, slightly superior to Californian, is grown in New South Wales, averaging, in 1892, 16·70 bushels to the acre. Notwithstanding that New South Wales has good wheat land of unlimited extent, in 1891 only half of the quantity used was obtained from the soil of the Colony, so that there is a good margin for the farmer even in the supply of domestic requirements, although its bread-stuffs grown this year are valued at £1,000,000 more than in the previous season.

In consequence of the exhaustion of arable land in the United States, through a large and rapidly increasing population, there appears to be a much greater difficulty in obtaining good farms than formerly, and by the end of the present century it is estimated by Mr. C. Wood Davis, an American writer, that the selector will have to go elsewhere. He writes : " The uncultivable character of the lands of plain and mountain districts, and the rapid diminution of the unoccupied arable lands of the United States, have been clearly shown by the events following the opening for settlement of the limited and not over-fertile lands in Oklahoma country. When men who had failed to find satisfactory locations in California, Oregon, and Washington, retraced their steps hoping to secure land on which to found a home only to find in advance of them an army of would-be settlers, large enough to occupy a territory ten times the size of Oklahoma."

Large areas in Australia are leased from the Crown for sheep and cattle farming, much of which in the natural growth of the country should now be utilised for tillage, as the great want at present in Australia is a larger settlement of population on the land. This better use of soil suitable for agriculture would also give greater development to manufacturing industries, in making machinery and other appliances needed by the farmers, as the labour requirements of the squatter for sheep-farming are now comparatively small, owing to the fencing in of the runs of late years, and the substitution of boundary-riders for shepherds.

In New South Wales, the winter is so mild that the land may be kept constantly under crop, and lucerne is cut from four to six times a year in favourable seasons, and during one year two crops of maize may be grown. There is an excess in the production of maize over local consumption amounting to 3·1 per cent., which finds a ready market in the other Austra-lian Colonies. The average yield per acre in New South Wales of wheat, maize, and barley is greater than that in any other continental Australian Province, or in the United States, but the total consumption of grain of all kinds is 13·5 bushels per acre per head of population, while the produce is only 9·6. If swine breeding were carried on in New South Wales to the same extent as it is in the western states of America, the maize so prolifically grown could be used for feeding the hogs, and perhaps a fattening industry established similar to the one in Chicago, which has been so successful in curing hams, making lard, &c., for exportation. The amount of land sown with maize in New South Wales in 1892, was 174,577 acres which produced 5,721,706 bushels, or 32·77 per acre, of the value of £833,176 ; showing that the Indian corn crop was more valuable than in California, which by the last returns at hand had 160,000 acres under crop, yielding 4,396,000 bushels of the value of £553,750.

At the Philadelphia Centennial Exhibition in 1876 the Indian corn grown in New South Wales was awarded the international prize for maize owing to its superior quality even over the American article. The average production of maize per acre for Australia was 29·3 bushels, being about 5 bushels more than that gathered in the United States during the last five years.

The lucerne and grass crop in New South Wales had an area in 1892 of 19,861 acres, with a product of 45,867 tons.

The New South Wales Executive Commissioner to the Philadelphia Exhibition paid particular attention to the growth of the tobacco plant in California, and in his report argues that the difficulties which have been mastered there could be overcome in the same way in Australia, as the environment in both countries is similar, and the wide range over which the plant is grown in the United States ought to assure the most sceptical that there is nothing in its own nature to exclude it from the climate and soils of Australia. In the report on tobacco in the Indian and Colonial Exhibition, Messrs. Watt and Macarthy also say, that the "American weed is for the most part used in the preparation of pipe tobacco, and it is remarkable that in every case it is the product of a milder climate than that from which we obtain our cigar sorts. This would lead us to look to Australia and the Cape Colonies for the future supply of this class of tobacco. At present, the cultivation in these colonies may be said to have hardly got beyond its experimental stage, but there are not wanting many hopeful signs in regard to the future." More than half the tobacco produced in Australia is grown in New South Wales, which, in 1890, had 14,021 cwt. of leaf, or an average of 10·8 cwt. to the acre. There has been a great improvement in the quality of the Australian leaf during the last twenty years, but in 1891, unmanufactured tobacco of the value of £29,565, manufactured of the value of £42,239, cigars of the value of £505, and cigarettes of the value of £2,158 were imported from the United States. A large quantity of manufactured tobacco is also received from the United Kingdom, and the largest proportion of cigars from Germany, Hong Kong, the United Kingdom, France, Belgium, and the Phillipine Islands. Leading American tobacco factories are represented in Australia by manufacturing branches in Sydney, and Messrs. Cameron & Co., of Virginia in the United States, carried off the first prizes at the Sydney and Melbourne International Exhibitions, and their products at the latter exhibition were awarded a gold medal, and the Emperor of Germany's special prize of 1,000 guineas. Messrs. Dixon and Sons, a colonial firm, commenced the manufacture of tobacco in Australia in 1839, and they have a large factory in Sydney, and have also obtained many first-class prizes.

The number of acres under cultivation for tobacco has greatly declined during the last two years owing to few of the farmers possessing the necessary skill for the proper cultivation and preservation of the leaf, so as to make it equal to the American product. The produce, however, of the tobacco manufacturers who used principally foreign leaf in 1890 amounted to 1,915,040 lb. the work of several different establishments.

There were in 1890, 16,739 cwt. of leaf tobacco produced in Australia, at the rate of 9 cwt. per acre, against 7 cwt. per acre in the United States. There has been a great falling off in the production of tobacco leaf in New South Wales owing to the want of a foreign market, so that only very low prices could be obtained, and perhaps also owing to the want of that proper preparation which could only be given by American experts with long training.

Although little has been as yet done in New South Wales in the silk-worm industry the climate is very favourable, being similar to that of southern Europe. The mulberry-tree grows to great perfection on the Tweed River, in the northern district of New South Wales, supplying leaves from the end of July till April. Mr. Brady, who is a pioneer in this industry, states that he has for many years obtained a continuous hatching of silk-worms day by day or week by week. The rearing of silk-worms and collection of cocoons would find employment for many intelligent families, and experiments in

silk culture are now being made by the Government with a band of Italian
immigrants who found shelter in the Colony owing to the failure of the
Marquis De Ray's proposed settlement on one of the Pacific islands.
It is estimated that cocoons could be produced by them in New South Wales
at much less cost than they are in Italy, and samples of the silk already
obtained will be shown at the Chicago Exposition.

At the last Paris Exhibition Australian wine-growers were awarded the
grand prize and twelve gold medals, while the American producers were
awarded four gold medals. As, from the awards of the French experts, it
is evident that the soils of many different parts of New South Wales are
admirably adapted for the production of the best qualities of wines, there is
ample scope for a larger development of this industry, if suitable scientific
labour can be obtained for making wine and brandy adapted to the requirements of the European market. Samples of brandy sent from Australia
have received recently the highest praise from experts in London. During
the last ten years the product of wine increased in California by 9,500,000
gallons, while in New South Wales the increase was only about 330,000
gallons. It however appears that there has been a decrease in California
in 1891 as compared with the previous year of 4,000,000 gallons, whilst in
New South Wales there was an increase of 146,000 gallons. The average
production of wine in gallons per acre was for Australia, 170; for the United
States, 140; and for Chili and the Argentine Republic, 100, so that the
yield is much greater on the southern continent. The production of wine in
Australia in 1890 was 3,997,889 gallons, and there was also raised 13,237
tons of table grapes. Australia exported to Europe in the same year 816,523
gallons of wine, of the value of £63,318. Recent reports from experts state
that the samples of wine now produced in Australia are much superior to
those sent to Europe some years since, and are therefore becoming more
generally appreciated.

The wine presses of New South Wales have been yielding richly during
the past year, as the maturing of young vineyards has given a substantial
increase to the output of wine. New South Wales offers advantages for
viticulture second to those of no other country in the world, and there can
be no doubt that there will be a large increase in this industry in the future.
At the present time, however, the total area under vines is 8,281 acres, of
which 3,846 acres were for wine-making, 913,107 gallons being made.
California has given much greater attention to wine-making, and as a consequence had 200,544 acres of vines producing 14,626,000 gallons, and
there is room for a similar development in New South Wales, as its wines
have obtained the highest awards at International Exhibitions in Europe.
There were 3,694 tons of table grapes produced in New South Wales, but
no attempts have been made to manufacture raisins, of which 1,372,195 boxes
of 20 lb. each were exported from California. In South Australia excellent
raisins have been produced, and there is a good field in New South Wales
for the starting of this new industry by Californian experts, as good samples
have been manufactured in the irrigation settlements on the Murray River.

Although New South Wales, like California, is destined to be the greatest
fruit-producing state on its side of the Pacific, in 1890 it had only 28,746
acres under cultivation for orchards and gardens, which was, however,
more than in any other Australian Colony. No other colony in Australasia
has superior advantages to New South Wales for the growth of every
kind of fruit desired in the European or American market. It is affirmed
that in New South Wales, from sub-tropical lowlands to uplands bordering

on the snow line, the conditions of climate and soil are present for every variety of fruit; and it would appear that nothing else offers more remunerative return for so little outlay, so that there can be no doubt that the same rapid advance in horticulture will shortly be made in the Colony as has been made in California where the fruit crop now exceeds in value that of wheat. The soil in the Parramatta district, only a few miles from Sydney, is one of the best in the world for the cultivation of the orange, but the industry has not obtained such development as it has in California, principally through the immense population in the United States compared with that of Australia. In the Parramatta district are also grown apples, pears, peaches, nectarines, plums, loquats, quinces, persimmons, and other fruit. The orange-growers of California are indebted to the introduction of the "Australian Bug" or ladybird (*Vedalia Cardinalis*), by an American naturalist sent over for that purpose, for the ridding of their trees of a most destructive disease, which it is estimated had decreased the output by millions of dollars each year. Unfortunately the apple-trees in New South Wales have suffered by the introduction of the codlin moth in fruit imported from California, a pest which has done much harm to orchards in both countries. Some of the orange-trees in New South Wales are over sixty years of age and are still in full vigour, are not less than 40 or 50 feet in height, and measure nearly 6 feet in circumference, and over 10,000 oranges have been gathered from a single tree in one season. It is said on high authority that the orange groves of the Parramatta district are equal to any in the world, and that the trees are unsurpassed. The principal variety of orange grown in Australia came from Brazil in the early days of the Colony. The navel orange was brought from Batavia and afterwards was introduced into California as the "Australian Navel," where it has been rechristened the "Washington Navel." The mandarin or Chinese orange also thrives in New South Wales, especially in the valley of the Hawkesbury. Select land, suitable for orange-growing, can be obtained at from £10 to £15 per acre, while land for the same purpose at a much greater distance from the metropolis can only be obtained in California for from £20 to £60 per acre. A well-known orange-grower, Mr. W. H. M'Keown, of Roseville, Gordon, about 8 miles from Sydney, states that he realised from his orange-trees in one season fully £50 per acre. Cherries grown on the coastal range of mountains are regarded as among the largest and finest in the world. Passion fruit is grown in abundance, although almost unknown in California. Melons of all kinds are quite equal in size and flavour to similar varieties sold in the markets of San Francisco. Lemons are also largely exported from New South Wales, and of late years a very refreshing drink called "lemon squash," made with lemon juice and ground sugar has become a favourite and whole-some beverage during the summer months, and would no doubt prove a pleasant change from the mixtures often sold in the American drug stores. The condition in which fruit is brought to market has been of a rough and unsatisfactory character, and contrasts unfavourably with the nice wicker baskets and boxes used in the trade in San Francisco, but steps are now being taken to copy the best methods of packing obtaining in other fruit-growing countries.

In 1892 the orangeries of New South Wales covered 11,370 acres, of which 8,745 were productive and 2,625 not bearing, and the fruit gathered filled 694,500 cases, or an average yield per acre of seventy-nine cases. There were 16,606 acres under other fruit-yielding crops of the value of £200,790, being a yield of the value of £12 15s. 1d. per acre. Lemons and oranges can be placed on the New York market in the off season when they are unobtainable except in Australia. It is stated that in point of freight it would be cheaper to land oranges from Australia in New York than to carry them by rail from San Francisco.

Mr. Allen, a Californian expert at Mildura, who has been engaged to manage the fruit-preserving works, is surprised at the quantity of the local production. He says that the apricots are equal and the peaches are superior to any he has handled in California, the home of the fruit-growing and fruit-preserving industry. Major Dane, well known as a lecturer both in America and Australia, speaking of Mildura, says : " I unhesitatingly say that when you take into consideration the climate, the soil, which is of a very superior character, its naturally advantageous position for irrigation, and look at the work already done, it promises to surpass anything in America. The works are certainly on a larger and more substantial basis than any I have ever seen in the United States."

The Hon. J. Lyne, Minister for Public Works, in a recent speech stated that " he had only lately had the direction of water conservation or irrigation, and that he intended to prosecute it vigorously in two districts he knew of in New South Wales most suited for action in this direction. The prosperity of the colony has been checked in many districts by the uncertainty of the rain-fall, but when its rivers, now flowing to waste, are utilised, and the desert lands irrigated, many thousands could find employment on the land who are now congregated in the cities. Drought has been the one great drawback and danger to the interior plains of Australia ; but this, it is believed, will shortly be overcome by irrigation, as in many parts of India, California, and Utah, which although parched and sterile have been transformed into fertile lands by the impounding of waste water and distributing it over the soil. Large tracts of country could be rendered fertile if they could irrigate the fringes of their rivers both north and south. By that means they would have greater supplies of fruit, wheat, and vegetables, and all the other things they could produce in the Colony, and the Government were about to bring in a general Bill to enable any cor-poration or any number of persons who like to combine together to form irrigation settlements." The experience of American capitalists in similar works would be found very profitable if embarked in Australian irri-gation companies, and recently a band of Californian fruit-growers have taken up 300 acres of land at Mildura with that object.

Lord Jersey made a recent tour through the Colony over which he is Governor, and in a speech at Mildura, he is reported to have said :—" He had had an opportunity during the last day or two of seeing not far from there what irrigation could do. He had seen how the energy of two men had con-verted some almost useless land into what was now a garden, which in a short time would be a very fruitful garden, and he thought every credit was due to Messrs. Chaffey Bros. for what they had done. They had accomplished what no Government could do, they had set the example of what private indi-viduals could do, and do better than the Government, in turning barren land to profitable use. He knew they suffered here occasionally from dry weather, and yet at the same time they had those beautiful rivers running past their very doors. Well, if they could combine those rivers with their dry land in such a way as to make that land fruitful, they might depend upon it any number of people would take the opportunity of coming and making it their head-quarters."

Major Dane, in a lecture delivered in Sydney, stated "that Australia had an equally fine climate and more splendid soil than the countries of the Mediterranean, whereon the best fruits of the earth might be cultivated and bear crops at a season of the year when similar fruits of domestic growth are not obtainable in England and North America."

It is estimated that Australia spends annually £750,000 for dried imported fruits alone, and England imports dried fruits to the amount of £8,000,000 sterling per annum. There are many other profitable openings in New South Wales for the preservation of fruits and vegetable products by American processes for domestic consumption and export to other countries.

If the services of women, boys, and girls were utilised as much in the light work of the canneries in New South Wales as they are in California the industry should pay well, especially as, in addition to the heavy freights for carriage from Europe and America, there is now a protective duty of 2d. per lb. on preserves and canned and dried fruit, candied peel, and prunes, and 1d. per lb. on fruit boiled or in pulp, drained or dry, and almonds. Notwithstanding the large quantity of fruit imported into New South Wales, in some of the country districts cows and pigs are at times fed upon luscious peaches, apricots, nectarines, and plums, and thousands of tons of good vegetable food are lost through lack of available means of preservation. This waste might have been prevented if the American processes for fruit-drying had been brought into requisition. A similar state of things, however, obtained in California until modern preserving processes were adopted. A cannery was a few years ago established by Mr. Walter Lamb about 20 miles from Sydney on the model of the Californian workshops, which as a pioneer factory is doing excellent work, and a good article is turned out at a fair profit to the enterprising proprietor.

Of late years great progress has been made in the dairy industry of New South Wales, by the erection of creameries and butter factories and the use of the best modern machinery in them, so that there is a manufacturer in Sydney doing considerable business in making separators for the use of farmers. The cool storage chambers in many of the steamers have been used for shipments of factory butter to the English market, which has secured remunerative prices, and there should be a good opening for the development of this industry, as the quality is equal to the best Danish butter.

Several of the large European mail ships are now fitted with cool chambers for the preservation of fruits on long voyages, and it is believed that New South Wales will shortly follow the example of Tasmania in placing on the London, New York, and Montreal markets, large quantities of fruit which will reach England and America at times when fruit is not obtainable from domestic and other foreign sources. The fact has been recently pointed out that Australian oranges occasionally find their way to the Canadian market by way of London, and the opinion is that fruit can be profitably exported to Central Canada, and to the north-western portions of the United States. Although California relies for much of its tropical fruit on the Sandwich Islands, yet the pine-apple, banana, cocoa-nut, mango, and other similar fruits and nuts could not only be supplied from Fiji, and other groups of islands in the Pacific Ocean, but also from some parts of the Australian continent, and even from the northern parts of New South Wales.

If New South Wales followed the example of California and Utah by using the waters of its inland rivers, underground rivers, and snow mountains for irrigation purposes, much of the dry lands could be successfully utilised as in those states in America where there is a very small rainfall. There is now an excellent opening for the Californian expert to introduce into New South Wales the manufacture of raisins and prunes which of late years have become such a marked success for domestic use and foreign exportation, outrivalling similar products in American markets previously supplied from the shores of the Mediterranean.

The cultivation of the olive has been successful in South Australia, and Sir Samuel Davenport reckons that this industry could be made more profitable than even that of wool-growing. Some magnificent olive oil, free from the adulteration now generally found in it, was shown at the Colonial and Indian Exhibition from Menangle in New South Wales, so that an olive, industry should thrive in many parts of that Colony if managed in view of the experiments in South Australia and California.

The varied experiences of America in the development of the vast natural resources of a comparatively new country have already proved of great service to Australia, especially in improved appliances for agriculture and mining, but there still remains opportunities for the introduction into New South Wales of many tools and processes which have proved useful in developing agriculture, mining, and manufactures in the United States. In no branch of mechanical industry could the experience of Americans be of more value than in the work with the diamond drill in boring for water on the south-western and north-eastern districts of New South Wales, which, owing to their small rainfall, require an artificial supply on the pastoral runs and along main stock routes for travelling cattle. The Officer in Charge of Water Conservation reports that "there is a wide opening for the encouragement generally of artesian well-boring to the great benefit of the Colony, and particularly to the immense plains in the north-western portion of it, where the supposed cretaceous area embraces a territory of 45,000 square miles, or over 28,000,000 acres. There is a great opening too for any inventor that can devise a means for boring artesian wells at a cost that will place it within reach of all classes. As it stands, the expense, which may be roughly averaged from 30s. to 35s. per foot, limits the operations to the few. The cost in America which averages somewhere about 8s. has an important bearing on the progress and development of the work there." One Government artesian well near Bourke, in the south-western portion of New South Wales, known as the Native Dog Well is 475 feet deep, cost £1,000, and gives a supply of 2,000,000 gallons per diem, or 730,000,000 gallons per year of water reported by the analyst "as of a good description for irrigation purposes and suitable for all domestic purposes." This well would furnish a supply equal to a rainfall of 20 inches per annum over an area of 1,280 acres, which is the quantity estimated to be needed for irrigation purposes, and Mr. T. W. E. David, the Professor of Geology at the Sydney University reports :—" That it would be possible to irrigate at least one-sixth of the whole cretaceous basin, or about 6,500 square miles, by means of water obtained from artesian wells or bores, provided the water proved suitable for irrigation purposes." There are already about 100 artesian wells in New South Wales, yielding large quantities of water.

The Hon. Alfred Deakin (ex-Premier of Victoria) visited California seven years ago, and saw Messrs. Chaffey Brothers at the Ontario Irrigation Colony, on whose water supply £100,000 has been expended, which has since large avenues of trees, cable cars, and fine buildings ; and the outcome of his visit was the forming of two similar settlements on the banks of the

Murray River in Australia. When in America, Mr. Deakin also visited the different irrigation systems at work in the high uplands of Colorado, the river-flats of Arizona, the plateau of New Mexico, the valley of Utah, and the prairies of Kansas, but he states, that it was in Southern California alone that for an irrigation colony there is found the same kind of climate, and the same kind of general conditions as obtains on the Murray River. Lord Ranfurly, who is one of the largest settlers at Mildura, recently stated there that four years ago when he was in America the cheapest he could get an orange grove for was £350 per acre, while only from £40 to £50 could be obtained by the Mildura settlers for improved land, and he thought the success of the settlement in the past would be nothing to what the future would be as the first year's returns were better than he estimated. Messrs. Chaffey Bros. have been awarded a silver medal at the recent Horticultural Exhibition in London for the products of their Australian irrigation settlements, and this award by English experts should lead to a large Australian as well as foreign consumption, especially as Mr. Deakin states that without sending a single orange, or olive, or raisin across the sea there is a large market in Victoria, since these fruits to the value of half a million sterling are imported annually. The Mulgoa Irrigation Colony on the Nepean River, near Penrith, and about 40 miles from Sydney, will shortly work 10,000 or 11,000 acres, as £22,000 has been already expended on works and machinery as required by Parliamentary statute.

There were 23,106 acres returned as under irrigation in New South Wales during 1891. Very successful irrigation colonies have been formed by Chaffey Brothers, with all the benefits of their Canadian and Californian experience, on an area of 250,000 acres, at Mildura, in Victoria, with about 4,000 inhabitants. Out of 6,500 acres cultivated, no less than 6,000 acres are orchards and gardens, the raisin industry being the main one. There is a similar irrigation colony at Renmark, in South Australia, and the Water Conservation Branch, in New South Wales, is now preparing a scheme for similar settlements in that Colony. The two settlements contain 500,000 acres, on which upwards of 90 miles of main irrigation canals, and 140 miles of subsidiary channels have been constructed, and also the necessary pumping engines erected.

Near Wilcannia, with salubrity of atmosphere, and irrigation, there are beautiful gardens containing trees, whose prolific limbs have to be propped up; and at one station 1,700 lemons were obtained off one tree. In California, where, it is stated, land could once be obtained for a mere nothing, by irrigation the same land now fetches £150 per acre. A like result could, no doubt, be secured in the rich soil of great depth to be found at Wentworth, Wilcannia, and other places on the Darling River, especially as the land generally resembles that at Mildura, so that with water it should be made to produce from 10 to 50 tons of grapes to the acre.

During the past forty years, the supply of sugar in the world extracted from beet-root, has increased far more than the product from cane, so that in 1890, the quantities were from beet 3,630,000 tons, and from cane 2,118,000 tons. The quantity of sugar produced from cane in New South Wales is six times as much as is produced from beet-root in California, notwithstanding that three beet-sugar factories in the American State obtained £33,417 as Government bounty on an output of 8,069,566 lbs. During the last twenty years the bounty given in Germany to exported sugar, has caused the beet industry to increase by 645 per cent., and the manufacturer now obtains half as much again from the beet owing to improvements made in the machinery. Although of late years great improvements have also been made in producing sugar from cane, the most recent appliances are not used at many of the mills in Australia, or a very much larger result would be obtained in the crushing. It is stated in a report by Mr. Neville Lubbock that of the known quantity of 5,000,000 tons, about one-half is produced from sugar-cane, and one-half from sugar-beet. The superiority of the sugar-cane over the sugar-beet as a source of supply, may, however, be fairly assumed from the following important consideration, that, whereas the whole of the cane sugar in the world with the exception of about 200,000 tons is produced without any artificial assistance, such as protection or subsidies from governments, there is not, at the present time, a single pound of beet sugar produced anywhere in the world which has not the advantage of protection in the markets of the country in which it is produced, or of export bounties in the countries which export this description of sugar. There were exhibited for New South Wales at the Indian and Colonial Exhibition, white cubes, crystals, granulated, grey crystals, semigrany, and the ordinary brown second running. All the sugars exhibited were of a high class, and, like those from Queensland and Fiji, adapted to the requirements of the Australian market.

In 1892, the area of sugar-cane in New South Wales was: cut, 8,623 acres; and not cut, 13,639 acres; and the product 185,205 tons of cane. The sugar industry is firmly established on the northern rivers of New South Wales without the aid of coloured labour, but in Queensland Kanaka labour from the South Sea Islands has been introduced on the plantations, in the same way as Japanese labour was imported for the purpose into the Sandwich Islands.

Sugar is only grown in New South Wales and Queensland in Australia, and in the former colony 26,533 tons were produced by white labour; but coloured labour was principally used by the Queensland planters, and an Act has recently passed its Legislature continuing the introduction, under contract, of Kanakas from the South Sea Islands.

The great variety of vegetables to be found in the New South Wales markets are grown principally by Chinamen, who not only supply Sydney but many of the country towns and villages, near to which they cultivate well-kept gardens, and appear to make a good living.

Australia has no otters or beavers like those of Canada, whose furs are a great necessity for the cold climate they inhabit; but there are annually imported into England from Australia about 2,000,000 opossum skins, which are dried for coat linings, capes, muffs, carriage wrappers, &c. England also receives from 50,000 to 60,000 Australian wallaby skins, used for fine upper leather in boots, and the commoner sorts for imitation chamois leather. There are annually 60,000 wombat skins sent to England, as the fur is very close, strong, and durable, and many are dyed brown or black to be used for rugs and dress purposes. About 500,000 kangaroo skins are shipped annually from Australia, and these skins are mostly taken by America, and used principally for the best class of boots. Large quantities of rabbit skins are also exported from New South Wales, obtained in the extermination of many millions of this great pest.

Along the coast, and in the harbours and rivers of New South Wales, there are sixty families of fishes, comprising 348 species, and of these 105 are edible. Although there are so many varieties of excellent fish, the fisheries have not assumed anything like the same proportions that they have in Newfoundland, and on the Pacific Coast of North America. If some of the hardy Canadian seamen, with their smacks and appliances, could be induced to fish in Australian waters, there is no doubt that a rich harvest from the sea might be gained. Although there are many excellent eating fish in Australia, the salmon, the king of fish, is not yet caught in its rivers, though attempts have been made for many years to acclimatise it in some of the inland waters ; so that there is a good market for California and Columbia River salmon, especially if larger quantities of it could be sent fresh in steamers having chilled chambers.

The natural history of Australia has attracted the attention of eminent European and Australian scientists ever since the time when Sir Joseph Banks noticed the peculiar fauna and flora at Botany Bay, but it is only during the last quarter of a century that great progress has been made in the study of the large varieties of native plants, rocks, birds, mammals, reptiles, fishes, insects, shells, and corals. The flora of Australia is the most remarkable on the surface of the earth, as it contains many strange forms of vegetation. Australian marsupials have always excited interest on account of their peculiar character, differing so much from animals in any other part of the world, as the opossum is the only living species they resemble in America, though a recent discovery of Australian mammals in South America is considered some indication that not only Africa but the Antipodes were possibly parts of one vast vanished Antarctic continent. Australia is stated by the Rev. J. E. Tenison-Woods, to have amongst her animals a perfect representative series of animals on other portions of the globe, and that the continent is a true and well-defined zoological province, with species peculiarly her own. In Australia none of the leading orders of birds are wanting, and the special features are sixty species of beautiful parrots, peculiar mound-building birds, beautiful bower birds, and certain genera which have no parallel elsewhere. The lyre-bird, with its graceful plumage, should be the typical national bird of Australia as the eagle is of the United States.

There are few venomous reptiles in Australia, and few snakes as dangerous as the rattlesnake in America. Some of the butterflies rival the rare beauties of the South American forests, and all the familiar forms of European insects find their representatives in Australia.

The discovery of the Port Jackson shark (*Heterodontus phillippi*) whose dentition is like the fossil teeth of acrodus found in mesozoic deposits, and the duck-bill platypus, (*Ceratodos fosteri*), an existing ganoid fish, whose anatomy shows it to be a faint connecting link between lizards and fish, surprised geologists, who believed these species had long ceased to exist.

The emu and kangaroo, which are peculiar to Australia, form typical figures at each side of the shield on which is placed a fleece, ship, anchor, and wheatsheaf, with the motto " Advance Australia." in the same way as in California the grizzly bear is the representative animal in the state coat of arms, and its form is otherwise used in local artistic decorations.

There are already discovered 8,000 distinct species of Australian flora, a number exceeding those known in Europe, and Sir J. Hooker speaks of its high antiquity and organisation as well as of its remarkable richness.

The indigenous animals of Australia have not been exterminated by the advance of population to the same extent as in America, where the buffalo and the deer are now seldom to be seen, except in zoological gardens, and their horns are the only legacy remaining on the plains for the search of the Indian. Although marsupial skins are now largely sought after for rugs and leather, it will be many years before the kangaroo becomes as rare as the native animals in North America.

Scientists have found many problems in connection with the fauna and flora of Australia, and one animal, the duck-billed platypus or water mole, after much controversy, has only recently been proved to be a mammal, suckling its young, although laying eggs with shells like birds and reptiles. There are few dangerous animals or birds of prey on the Australian continent, and of the 630 land birds known in Australia, not more than 5 per cent. occur in other countries.

Whaling used to be a great industry in Australia, and several millions sterling worth of oil was exported from it; but it is now little pursued, except by the descendants of the mutineers of Her Majesty's Ship "Bounty," who are located on Norfolk Island under the supervision of the Governor of New South Wales. The visit of several whalers to the Antarctic Ocean in 1892 should secure much oil and bone, and perhaps lead to Sydney again becoming a principal depôt for the Pacific whaling industry.

Australia happily has had no difference with regard to her fisheries like the controversy over the capture of seals in Behring Straits, and though these animals are to be found in the Antarctic Ocean and on the Seal Rocks in New South Wales, they are not now often disturbed.

Australian natural history, apart from its own beauty and variety, is rendered doubly interesting by being so distinct from that of other provinces, and many problems in zoology will no doubt in time be solved with its aid through the investigations of naturalists, who have been surprised at various anomalies.

There are few edible plants and fruits native to New South Wales known. Extinct aboriginal tribes consumed many plants ; but the knowledge of some of these esculents and medicinal varieties has perished with them.

Perfumery may be prepared from the essential oils of many of the Australian plants. The American collector would find an interesting study in ascertaining the amount of floral variation under cultivation which may arise from hybridisation, and the process of perpetuating interesting varieties.

There are in New South Wales thirteen genera and sixty species of salt-bush plants, which in dry seasons are very nutritious, and supply to stock the place of grass and other products. The vegetation of New South Wales, viewed from a utilitarian or a scientific standpoint, appears to have no finality in the development of its resources or in the application of them to the purposes of art. The cultivator may obtain ornamental double flowers ; and an Australian orchid called the rock lily, the waratah or native tulip, the gigantic lily, and the Christmas bush are now transplanted to the home garden, and grow there with care almost as well as in their wild habitation.

Specimens of Australian tree-ferns, and other large plants are shown at the Chicago Exposition.

A plant used by the aborigines, and called by them "*piluri*," possesses properties stronger than tobacco, and is said to produce a luxurious and dreamy sensation. Many Australian plants, gums, and resins, have medicinal properties, and are known in Europe, such as the bitter bark of *alstonia constricta* and the native sarsaparilla ;· but few professional men have devoted much time to testing the value of the native medicines and antidotes. The properties of the *eucalyptus globulus* have been celebrated through out the world, and the leaves of some eucalypts have wonderful healing properties, while the volatile oils with which they abound is likely to prove highly efficacious as a febrifuge. Although in the leguminous plants alone the properties are very varied, some being astringent, some purgative, some narcotic, and some even poisonous, the whole order of the myrtaceæ is, to a greater or lesser extent, anti-scorbutic, astringent, and sudorific.

The iguana genus of American lizard is not connected with the Australian species, which has certain peculiarities of its own. Crocodiles are only found in tropical Australia; but there is evidence of the existence of large species at one time in New South Wales. Australian beetles are easily distinguished from those of any other country. Australia is rich in shells, which are much prized by collectors, as they differ from those of other countries in a marked manner, and are in many cases beautiful in form and colouring. The marine fishes of New South Wales contain two distinct fauna, one belonging to the temperate regions and the other to the tropics, and the fishes on the east coast are very different from those on the west, though the genera are about the same. Several species of trigonia survive nowhere else but in Australia; but traces of them are found in the miocene beds. The Sydney rock oyster has a fine flavour, and is free from the copperish taste of those found in tropical countries. In Australian natural history there are representative forms of every department of animal life to take the place of animals in other countries.

The number of flowering plants in New South Wales approaches 2,600, and there are 1,200 species in the neighbourhood of Sydney alone. Most of the trees and plants of other countries are also flourishing in the Sydney Botanic Gardens in the open air. New South Wales possesses valuable timbers, resins, gums, oils, and barks for exportation, and the trade which has already commenced in these products will largely increase.

Australia has been styled a country of contradictions, both as regards her fauna and flora, but the most striking peculiarities of the great southern land are fast disappearing owing to the clearing of the forests and the introduction of economic plants from all parts of the world which are changing the face of nature, not always to its improvement as two garden plants introduced from America are troublesome weeds. Many of the wild flowers in New South Wales do not possess sweet perfume but all are beautiful, and some of them, such as the large Australian tulip or waratah and the *Boronia Serrulata*, native rose, are gathered near Sydney in their native loveliness, and are much prized. The Australian eucalyptus, of which New South Wales alone has about fifty species, on account of its sanitary qualities, is now attracting great attention throughout the world, and the large number of blue gum trees (*E. globulus*) successfully grown in the streets of the towns in California proves that the climates of both countries are very much alike. One of these gum trees seen by the late Anthony Trollope, was stated by him to be 480 feet in length, surpassing altogether those world-famed productions of California, which have for a while been regarded as the kings of the forest.

The Revd. Dr. Woolls, F.L.S., says, regarding the great economic value of Australian woods to the world:—"Some of the species, more widely diffused, are becoming more and more valued for the strength and durability of their timber, the texture of their bark, and the properties of their resins and volatile oils. Some are valuable for building purposes, railway sleepers, fencing, naves and felloes of wheels, staves for casks, piles for bridges, and, in fact, for anything where endurance is required. The 'ironbarks' and 'mahoganies' are among the kinds best known for their strength, and for the long time they resist the influence of heat and moisture, but of late years the 'spotted-gum,' the common 'blue-gum,' and the 'tallow-wood' have come into greater favour, because they are more easily worked, and afford useful materials for artificers."

Mr. Thomas Taslett, timber merchant, and Surveyor of Forests to the Admiralty in London, reports respecting the timbers of New South Wales at the Colonial and Indian Exhibition as follows :—"A careful study of these during the inspection gave the impression that the Colony abounds in hard, heavy, strong wood, suitable for engineering and architectural works ; that a fair quantity would make good furniture, while the remainder could well be adapted for local and general purposes."

Australia has not many woods of light weight that are easy to work as fir and pine, and most of the red cedar and Moreton Bay pine have been cut down in the settled districts. The Australian timber-getter generally fells trees regardless of the season of the year, and ships them in their wet state, so that if the American drying process were adopted the hardwood could be made much more suitable for market.

There are many valuable woods in Australasia, such as the Jarrah of Western Australia, which is sometimes called mahogany, and is stated to be impervious to the cobra, and, therefore, admirably adapted for piles placed in water, and no doubt much more suitable for wharves and bridges than the softwoods of America.

Trees are frequently met with in Australia over 400 feet high, and one fallen giant was measured and proved to be no less than 480 feet high, but the girth of these trees is not so much as that of the Californian giants in the Yosemite Valley. In the hollow, however, of one of the valuable Huon pines in Tasmania, the Governor and seventy-eight other persons dined, and this tree is very tall, as well as broad, as it is over 300 feet high.

There are no less than 136 species of eucalyptus in Australia, of which fifty-three are found in New South Wales, and they are conveniently grouped according to their barks, such as ironbarks, stringybarks, &c. The bark of some species of eucalyptus may be utilised for covering . rustic buildings, the manufacture of rope and paper, and the preparation of door-mats, and matting in general, whilst leaves of all kinds yield volatile oils, differing in their essential properties, and available for combustion, perfumery, and tonic beverages. It is now generally believed that the eucalypts absorb malaria, and have powers of exhalation favourable to health. Hence the sanitary effect of these trees, in common with other kinds of myrtles, is highly important, and in the opinion of eminent authorities they prevent, in a great measure, the prevalence of ague. There are about eighty species of acacia indigenous to New South Wales, and of these some are highly esteemed for their wood, gums, and bark. The bark of the " black and green wattle " is much used in tanning, and the gum which exudes from it is made into the gum-arabic of commerce. The resin of the grass-tree abounds in piric acid which is used extensively as a yellow dye, and on the basis of indigo for green colour.

Baron F. von Mueller, who has devoted many years to the study of Australian botany, has compiled a long list of plants suitable for thread, rope matting, and other textile fabrics, many of which would be used as commercial products, if the necessary skilled labour and machinery were available for their growth and manufacture.

There are twenty-one State forests in New South Wales, covering 97,724 acres. The timber reserves number 945, and cover an area of 5,459,937 acres. The value of the timber sawn from reserves in 1890 was £670,050. The American softwoods are popular in the colonies on account of their being more easy to work than most of the native timbers, but Australian hardwoods are remarkable for great size of beam and great toughness and durability in which they have no equals, as one of them, the grey ironbark has a resistance to breaking equal to 17,900 lb. per square inch, being greater than that for English oak and for teak.

The five colonies on the Continent of Australia annually import timber from the outside world of the value of over £2,000,000 sterling, and in 1891, Sydney received 105,162,863 superficial feet of rough and dressed timber, for which £91,000 was paid as duty.

There are Forest Conservancy Departments in South Australia, Victoria, and New South Wales, and in the last-mentioned Colony, alone, about 5,500,000 acres have been reserved for the operations of the Department.

New South Wales in 1891 imported from the United States, dressed timber to the extent of 2,166,588 superficial feet, and rough timber measuring 26,011,989 superficial feet, and from Canada 5,586,133 superficial feet of lumber. The vessels bringing softwoods from North America ought profitably to obtain return cargoes of the hardwoods in Australia suitable for road-making, as owing to their use the streets of Sydney are now much superior in formation to those of San Francisco and other American cities in which cobble stones are principally used.

The Director-General of Forests for New South Wales estimates that at the very least, double the quantity of the so-called softwoods of commerce will half a century hence be necessary for Australian requirements ; and that the supply from foreign sources will not be equal to the demand, for the following reasons : "First, because the present source of supply, America and the Baltic chiefly, are, gradually, but surely (to use a homely phrase), killing the goose which lays the golden egg, and second, because owing to the natural increase in the populations of the countries, especially of America which forms our largest and most important field of supply, the time will and must come when what each land can produce in the way of useful timber will be required for its own people."

New South Wales has a very great diversity of soil, and climate, and there can be no question that the capabilities of its forest lands for the successful growth of the pine and softwoods of Europe and America is a matter beyond all doubt, but there is greater wealth contained in the many different hardwoods extending over a greater part of the colony.

Mr. J. Ednie Brown reports : "The timbers of Australia, especially those of New South Wales and Queensland, we know are of immense variety, both in their quality and in their fitness for specific constructive purposes. We have timbers with great specific gravity, and others apparently as light in weight as is some of the 'deal' of the northern hemisphere. For such purposes as railway-sleepers, jetty and bridge piles, and other out-door work, both above and below ground, and in water our timbers are second to none in the world, and for these uses are largely drawn upon." The Director of Forests further says: "We state unhesitatingly that with suitable soil and situation of which there is no lack, both the coniferæ and hardwoods which produce the favourite timbers of commerce can be successfully grown in Australia. Not only this, however, but it is our opinion that owing to the advantages which we possess here in regard to both soil and climate, we can grow such timbers to a marketable size in less than half the time necessary in the natural habitats of these trees." This testimony of a Canadian, who besides extensive experience in his own country held the position of Conservator of Forests in South Australia for several years, and did much valuable work in connection with arboriculture there, is most valuable in connection with the future of the timber industry of New South Wales.

PACIFIC COLONIES AND PACIFIC STATES.

DURING the last decennial period, the Pacific Colonies on the Australian Continent have surpassed in several directions the Pacific States of America, such as in increases to population, growth of pastoral production, and expansion of manufacturing industries, whilst the four American States have exceeded the four Australian Colonies in progress in agricultural settlement, railway construction, and in mining output.

A comparison of the present condition of the Western States of America with that of the Australasian Colonies, shows that the resources of the groups of settlements on both sides of the Pacific Ocean are somewhat similar, and that owing to the discovery of gold in California in 1849, and in New South Wales two years later, the rapid progress made by them finds no precedent elsewhere in the history of the world.

The area of the four British colonies is 1,970,771 square miles, being more than four times as great as the area (469,015 square miles) of their neighbours on the opposite shore of the Pacific.

The census population during the last two decennial periods was as follows :—

	1881.	1891.	Increase. 1881-1891.
Pacific Colonies (New South Wales, Victoria, Queensland, and South Australia)	2,107,204	2,986,788	879,584
Pacific States (California, Nevada, Colorado, and Oregon)	1,296,187	1,978,633	682,446

During the decade, 1870-1880, the increase to population in the settlements on either side of the Pacific was nearly the same; whilst during the decade, 1881 to 1891, the addition to the inhabitants was in the four colonies in Australia 187,000 more than in the four settlements on the Pacific slope of the United States.

Mulhall gives the amounts for wealth per head of population of the Australian Pacific colonies, and the American Pacific States as under :—

New South Wales..... £483 per inhabitant.
Victoria ....£337   ,,
Queensland ....£330   ,,
South Australia ......£413   ,,

Total £1,563

California............ £350 per inhabitant.
Nevada........ ...... £230   ,,
Colorado .... £160   ,,
Oregon .... £150   ,,

Total........... £890

Mulhall therefore, shows the average wealth of the American citizen on the Pacific slope to be £222 10s., whilst he also estimates the British colonist on the Australian Continent to own £390 15s., or more than half as much again as the inhabitant of the wealthiest part of the United States.

The Australasian Colonies have made far greater progress in sheep and cattle farming than the Pacific States of America, as since 1880 there has been a large increase of stock in the four British Colonies of New South Wales, Victoria, Queensland, and South Australia against a decrease of nearly 100,000 in sheep, and only an increase of 775,801 in cattle in the four American States of California, Colorado, Nevada, and Oregon. The increase in swine in the four Australian Colonies, however, only amounted to 37,000, whilst there was found to be a decrease of 312,000 hogs in the four

American States. Although there are half a million more horses in the Pacific Colonies than in the Pacific States the increase in the four states was 13,000 larger than in the four colonies. .

SHEEP.

	1880.	1890.	Increase.
Pacific Colonies (New South Wales, Victoria. Queensland, and South Australia)	59,147,595	93,780,352	34,632,757
Pacific States (California, Colorado, Oregon, Nevada)	9,741,269	8,754,000	987,269 (decrease)

CATTLE.

	1880.	1890.	Increase.
Pacific Colonies (New South Wales, Victoria, Queensland, South Australia)	7,322,094	9,824,283	2,502,189
Pacific States (California, Colorado, Oregon, Nevada)	2,496,199	3,272,000	775,801

SWINE.

	1880.	1890.	Increase.
Pacific Colonies (New South Wales, Victoria, Queensland, South Australia)	743,515	780,437	36,922
Pacific States (California, Colorado, Oregon, Nevada)	1,087,754	775,000	312,754 (decrease)

HORSES.

	1880.	1890.	Increase.
Pacific Colonies (New South Wales, Victoria, Queensland, South Australia)	1,008,497	1,446,039	437,542
Pacific States (California, Colorado, Oregon, Nevada)	435,866	860,000	424,134

The Pacific States of California, Colorado, Nevada, and Oregon have made more progress in tillage than New South Wales, Victoria, Queensland, and South Australia, as the increase in acres under crop for wheat was more than five times greater, and for maize or corn over three times greater than in the opposite settlements. The American States had 265,000 more acres under cultivation for wheat than the Australian Colonies, but the latter had an excess of 90,900 acres under crop for maize, as will be seen from the following tables :—

WHEAT (in acres.)

	1880.	1890.	Increase.
Pacific Colonies (New South Wales, Victoria, Queensland, and South Australia)	2,974,310	3,162,359	188,049
Pacific States (California, Colorado, Nevada, and Oregon)	2,345,873	3,428,000	1,082,127

MAIZE OR CORN (in acres).

	1880.	1890.	Increase.
Pacific Colonies (New South Wales, Victoria, Queensland, and South Australia)	271,557	300,909	28,352
Pacific States (California, Colorado, Nevada, and Oregon)	100,905	210,000	109,095

The returns of the number of hands employed in manufactories are not taken in Queensland, in Australia, or in Nevada, in America, so that a comparison can only be made between three settlements on each side of the Pacific. There are now much more than twice as many persons engaged in making goods in the Australian settlements of New South Wales, Victoria, and South Australia than in the American ones of California, Colorado, and Oregon, and the latter, during the last decennial period, have made but slight progress in manufacturing industries compared with the former, notwithstanding that there are more Chinamen employed as cheap labour in various trades on the Pacific slope than in Sydney, Melbourne, and Adelaide.

MANUFACTORIES (hands employed.)

	1880.	1890.	Increase.
Three Australian Colonies (New South Wales, Victoria, and South Australia)	74,345	117,493	43,148
Three American States (California, Colorado, and Oregon)	51,040	52,297	1,257

The numbers of hands employed in manufactories are taken, for the Australasian Colonies, from returns of Government Statisticians in Australia, and for the Pacific States from Porter's " The West, from the Census of 1880," and King's " Handbook of the United States," published in 1892.

The Colonial Treasurer of New South Wales stated that the number of persons now employed in the Colony in manufactures was 42,000 against 32,000 in mining, 42,000 in pastoral pursuit, and 82,000 in agriculture.

There has been a wonderful extension of railway communication both in Australia and in America during the last ten years. The extent of lines laid in the four Pacific States of California, Colorado, Nevada, and Oregon has been much greater than in New South Wales, Victoria, Queensland, and South Australia, on the other side of the ocean, principally owing to the commercial intercourse between the eastern and western states of America being carried on by railroads more than it is on the Continent of Australia, where the greater proportion of trade between the various colonies is conducted over the ocean in a mercantile marine, which consists of many more vessels with far more tonnage than those employed on the American Pacific coasts.

RAILWAYS (miles).

	1880.	1890.	Increase.
Pacific Colonies (New South Wales, Victoria, Queensland, and South Australia)	4,881	9,050	4,169
Pacific States (California, Colorado, Oregon, and Nevada)	5,102	10,808	5,706

The Governments of the Australian Colonies have been charged with borrowing too much money for railway extension; but it will be seen that in the Pacific States private enterprise has constructed during the last decade over 1,500 miles more of railroad lines.

The land in the settlements on both sides of the Pacific Ocean contains the largest developed deposits of minerals in the world, especially of the precious metals. This fact has made them great mining centres, the large yields from which have attracted population from all parts of the globe. The total value of minerals raised in Australasia to the end of 1890 amounted to £427,776,035, and during 1890 minerals were raised to the value of £12,262,934; but the total outputs for the four Pacific States and the four Pacific Colonies cannot be given, as the complete returns from the American settlements are not available. There are much larger outputs of coal, tin, and kerosene shale in the Pacific Colonies than in the Pacific States, as large quantities of these useful minerals are shipped to California for use . in American manufactories.

The Pacific Slope produces most of the precious metals mined in the United States, and the value of the gold and silver obtained in one year, according to the returns for 1890–1, amounted to £3,373,826 more than the output for the four Australian Colonies :—

	Gold.	Silver.	Total.
	£	£	£
Four Pacific States	4,352,083	6,911,784	11,263,867
Four Pacific Colonies	5,053,160	2,836,881	7,890,041

The production of gold in New South Wales, Victoria, Queensland, and South Australia is greater by £701,077 than in California, Colorado, Nevada, and Oregon; but the value of the output of silver in the Pacific Colonies was less by £4,074,903 than in the Pacific States.

In the foregoing comparison only the four principal colonies on the Australian mainland have been contrasted with the four leading States on the opposite Pacific shores; and the figures for Western Australia, New Zealand, and Tasmania are not, therefore, included in any of the totals given for the several industries. These three British colonies in Australasia, in addition to the amounts quoted, had mined £63,669,581 worth of minerals they owned 23,092,530 live stock, and they had 1,636,179 acres of land under cultivation, so that their present condition would bear favourable comparison with that of Washington Territory and other prosperous American settlements on the Pacific Slope whose great progress also has not been dealt with in this short review.

AUSTRALASIA AND CANADA.

THERE is no British possession with which Australia has greater sympathy than Canada, as there are now many similar political and commercial problems affecting the interests of both countries. Forty years ago the late Rev. Dr. Lang, a leading Australian legislator, predicted that if Canada left the maternal side Australia would be found in her company, and there can be no doubt that the example of one country will always have a great influence on the other. A quarter of a century ago Canada set Australia an excellent example by the federation of Upper and Lower Canada, and it is hoped that Newfoundland—"the first-born colony of Great Britain"—will shortly be found in that union.

Nearly 400 years ago John Cabot, with his genuine English sons sailed from Bristol Bay, and they were the pioneers of colonisation on the northern continent of the western hemisphere. Captain Cook, some years before his discovery of New South Wales, took soundings in the River St. Lawrence, opposite the French encampment, and afterwards assisted in the capture of Newfoundland, so that this great circumnavigator helped to lay the foundations of the British Colonies in both North America and Australia.

The seven provinces in the Dominion of Canada in their area, population, and political institutions more nearly resemble than any other country the seven colonies of Australasia, and the returns from the census recently taken afford materials for a comparison between the two largest possessions of the British Crown.

The Australian travelling through Canada sees in her present condition a resemblance in many ways to Australia, before that feverish spirit of 'enterprise set in which has made Australians more like the go-ahead citizens of the United States than the steady going Canadians. Prior to the discovery of gold in Australia the great bulk of the colonists had to work very hard for a living, and had therefore to practice much economy, just as the French Canadians are compelled to be thrifty at the present day, owing to the small returns from farming and other industries. During the last quarter of a century both the Governments and the peoples of the Australasian Colonies have pursued a more enterprising policy than that found in Canada to-day, and consequently they have secured much greater development in nearly every branch of industry than has been obtained in the Dominion during the past decennial period. Australians were once often reproached by visitors with not being enterprising enough, but some writers now urge that the colonists have been too speculative, and should have " hastened slowly" to get rich, so that they would find it impossible to satisfy both kinds of critics. Although no doubt some of the speculations in Australasia, in which colonial as well as English capital has been embarked, have not recently secured the large dividends hoped for by the investors, yet the money has been used in opening up great natural deposits, and those who succeed the pioneers will reap much of the benefits of the preliminary work which had to be performed, as has been found the case in other countries besides Australia.

The following tables give estimates of statistical writers respecting the relative wealth contained in Australasia and Canada, and as one of these comparisons was made sixty years ago and the other a few years since they well illustrate the progress made by the two countries during the last half century, and show the Australasian Colonies to be richer communities than even the Dominion of Canada :—

Pebrew's Estimate in 1833.

	Australasia.	Canada.
Capital or Wealth	£3,000,000	£62,000,000
„ per inhabitant	£75	£68
Earnings „	£12·5	£19·4

Mulhall's Estimate in 1888.

	Australasia.	Canada.
Capital or Wealth	£1,373,000,000	£980,000,000
„ per inhabitant	£370	£196
Earnings „	£40·2	£26

Porter, in his work on "Progress of the Nation," made in 1851 the following prediction with regard to progress in Australia contrasted with what would take place in Canada; but the conclusion arrived at by him has not been verified, no doubt greatly owing to the discovery of gold in New South Wales shortly after the prophecy was made. He said: "According to present appearances and the knowledge we have obtained concerning the nature of the country, it does not appear probable that Australia can ever become an agricultural country. It seems impossible that the Colony can ever assume anything approaching the importance of our North American possessions [then Canada only] either in regard to productiveness or population." Since this prediction was written it will be seen by the figures to be found in this work that the ratio of increase in almost every industry has been greater in the Australian Colonies than in Canada, and that the island continent of Australia alone by the development of its varied resources bids fair to surpass, before the end of the present century, even the great importance of the Canadian Dominion.

At the time the first settlement was made in Australia by about 1,000 people there was a population in Lower Canada alone of 161,000 and 30,000 more in Nova Scotia, so that although the Dominion of Canada has now a population of 5,000,000 or about 1,000,000 more than in Australasia, the relative growth of the colonies at the antipodes has been much greater than those situated much nearer the mother country, owing, no doubt, principally to the greater natural resources to be found within the borders of Australia and the adjacent islands. About fifty years ago the British Colonies in Australia and Canada had powers of government given them by the granting of a local Legislative Council, consisting of many nominee members, but it is only since 1856 that representative institutions were allowed to the oldest of the Australian settlements, and then only after considerable agitation on the part of the colonists.

AUSTRALASIAN PROGRESS.

	1830.	1890.
Land in Cultivation (acres)...............	110,000	7,066,398
Horses.....................................	18,000	1,732,628
Cattle	390,000	10,949,524
Sheep	1,300,000	116,041,704
Export of Wool, value.....................	£65,000	£24,398,381
Shipping (tons)	57,000	15,542,248
Public Revenue.............................	£155,000	£29,922,897
Miles of Railway	Nil.	11,990
Population	70,581	3,899,177
Commerce (imports and e p rts) ...	000,000	£132,801,164

These figures exhibit the wonderful progress that has been made by Australasia during the last sixty years, which will be found to be far greater than the development of Canada, and would bear favourable comparison even with the growth of the United States, especially when it is considered that Australasia has been colonised not a third of the time that both the other countries have had European settlements within their borders. The trade of the Australasian Colonies with other countries in value now amounts to about £133,000,000, and the exports and imports are carried in 17,500 vessels conveying 15,500,000 tons. Australasia has constructed 11,990 miles of substantial railways connecting all the chief cities, and 43,598 miles of telegraph on poles conveying messages to all parts of the Australian continent. Her pastures now feed 116,000,000 sheep, 11,000,000 horned cattle, 1,700,000 horses, and 1,200,000 swine, and the increase to the crops during the last half century is much greater than what is found in the Dominion of Canada.

The material development of Canada has been greatly helped by the magnificent freshwater lakes and canals which have enabled the country to be opened up, even before the construction of railroads, and still provide an opportunity for much cheaper transportation than by rail so long as the season of navigation lasts, as these waterways are generally frozen in the winter time. The wild and rugged parts of Canada, although not suited for the farmer and agriculturist, provide, as in Australia, abundant employment for the miner and lumberman. The hardy Canadian backwoodsman should have his counterpart in Australia, where magnificent forests await only the adoption of skill, machinery, and other appliances like those in use in North America, but more adapted to working hardwoods.

Owing to its comparatively isolated position, Australia is not so much subject to the movement of population from the eastern to the western slope as America, and there is no such shifting of immigrants and native-born as has taken place from Canada to the United States, making in the New England States the increase of aliens much more than the increase of the native-born. Western Australia, although containing over a million square miles, has only 53,000 inhabitants, so that there is ample room for any surplus population to "go west" to the largest of the Australasian Colonies.

It has been stated by Mr. George R. Parkin, M.A., a distinguished Canadian, who recently lectured in the Australasian Colonies on Imperial Federation, "that with a circumference of about 8,000 miles, and a diameter of more than 2,000 miles, it is very doubtful if Australia can ever have a great city more than 200 or 300 miles from the sea-shore." In reply to this statement it can, however, be urged that the conservation of water in Riverina, by damming in times of flood, and the tapping of underground waters in the extensive cretaceous formations of the back blocks, should hereafter lead to great settlement for agriculture on the immense plains near the banks of the Murray, Lachlan, Murrumbidgee, and Darling Rivers, from which a second Chicago, in the interior of Australia, may be evolved. In the Bourke district alone, over fifty water bores have been recently sunk, and more than two-thirds of them have proved successful, and many are yielding wonderful supplies of excellent water, even to 4,000,000 gallons per diem. Mr. Parkin, in contrasting Canada and Australasia, has also pointed out that Australians are different to Canadians in having to endure a greater intensity of summer heat, in not having large rivers and lakes, and in having to guard against droughts, but he affirms very justly that the British people are finding comfortable and prosperous homes in both countries.

There should be in the future a much larger commercial intercourse between the intelligent and industrious communities of the seven fair provinces of the Canadian Dominion and the inhabitants of the seven colonies of Australasia, as at present there is no direct regular steam communication and much of the trade across the Pacific is conducted in sailing vessels.

After the meeting of the British Association for the Advancement of Science, held in Montreal, in 1884, it was proposed that a meeting of that society should be held in Australia in her centennial year ; but as this could not be arranged, it is hoped that it will be possible for a similar conference of scientists to be held in Sydney at some future time, and that Canada will be fully represented by her learned men.

The route from England to Japan by way of the Canadian Pacific Railway, is asserted by Sir G. B. Powell, M.P., to be thirty hours shorter than the United States route, and he states that the new route should gain an annual trade with Asiatic countries of £120,000,000, and that England would subsidise the line at £60,000 for carrying the mails to China. It took the Red River expedition, under Colonel Wolseley, three months by water to reach Fort Garry in Winnepeg, but now the same place can be reached by land in a few days in a comfortable Pullman car, and the whole, distance from the Atlantic to the Pacific passed over in about a week. From London to Yokohama the distance, by crossing Canada, is about 10,060 miles or nearly 1,000 miles less than by New York and San Francisco ; and it is reported that the Canadian Government will give a subsidy of £25,000 for carrying the mails to the east by the Canadian-Pacific Railroad and Steam Company, the crews of whose steamships belong to the Royal Naval Reserve, as they may have to serve in these vessels as armed cruisers in times of war. If similar large steamers to those now trading from British Columbia to China and Japan, were employed between Vancouver and Sydney, numbers of Australians would doubtless make the tour to Europe, at least one way through the Dominion, and a real federation of interests effected by greater interchange of social and commercial relations would be created between Canada and Australia.

Considering the extent and wealth of Canada and her nearness to the mother country it is remarkable that a more extensive development of the great natural resources of the Dominion has not been made since its colonisation so long ago. This slow growth is no doubt due to 200 years of misgovernment and strife prior to the present century, but there is no doubt that there is a great industrial future before her, especially in developing the resources of Manitoba and British Columbia in the far west. The people of Canada must be warmly commended for the just manner in which they have invariably treated the Indians in their territory, as in this respect they have shown an excellent example to the people both of Australia and the United States. The Canadian people generally have also exhibited to the world by their management of home life patterns of domestic economy which the inhabitants of other new countries might well imitate. Although much corruption in political circles has recently been exposed, the community as a whole is remarkable for that regard to temperance and observance of the Christian Sabbath which are so noticeable in the cities of Toronto and Ottawa. Quebec and Montreal are inhabited largely by French Canadians, who display more markedly the characteristics of the Gallic people than the inhabitants of Ontario.

The early settlers in Australia had terrible difficulties to contend with, but nothing like the toil and suffering of the pioneers in Canada, who besides contentions among themselves had, in the early days, to fight with hostile Indians, and to endure the effects of an inhospitable climate. Canada has been the scene of many conflicts between the English, French, and American forces, but Australia happily has never been made the theatre of European war.

Many parts of Australia and Canada in which settlement was first made were covered with heavily-timbered forests, and the sowing of crops involved much labour to the early pioneers who had not as now access by railroad to the immense treeless plains to be found in the interior of both countries. Before the opening of the plains between Winnipeg and the Rocky mountains numbers of Canadians, consequent on the lessened demand for labour through improvements in agricultural machinery and other causes, went to the prairies of the United States, or obtained employment in towns at manufacturing industries for which they obtained higher wages.

The population of Canada numbered 4,829,411 at the last census, and shows that during the decade there was an increase of 504,601, or 11·66 per cent., which was less than was expected from natural increase of births over deaths alone, and only half the number of inhabitants gained by Australasia during the same period.

The great struggle between man and nature, and between one foreign nation and another in Canada has impressed its mark on the native literature more markedly than the less heroic occupation of Australia. The tragic expulsion of the Arcadians immortalised by Longfellow in "Evangeline" has no parallel happily in Australian history, and local poets have fortunately no grounds on which to base a similar description of rural happiness being despoiled.

From the days of the first Stuart King to that of the Grand Monarch the old cities of Canada, such as Quebec and Montreal, furnish many historical reminiscences of alternate English and French occupation very interesting to the traveller, and which have no parallel on the Australian continent. There are no racial differences in great masses of the people to be found in Australia, like those which have obtained in times past between the English and the French in Canada. At the present time the publications issued from the Government Printing Office at Ottawa have to be printed in the English and French languages, owing to large numbers only understanding the latter tongue.

That Australasia is in advance of other countries in the relative wealth and income of its population is proved by contrasting the following estimate made by Mr. Coghlan for Australasia in the year 1890 and Canada in the year 1888 with the following figures for the colonies, which do not include the value of Government property:—Private wealth, £1,169,000,000, being £189,000,000 more than Canada; wealth per head, £309 against £196 for Canada; state income per head, £7·8, more than four times that of Canada; and the private income per head was about double that in Canada. The wealth of Australasia, exclusive of unsold lands and public works, is also estimated by this Government Statistician to have been at the end of each twenty-five years during the century from the foundation of New South Wales as follows:—In 1813, £1,000,000; in 1838, £26,000,000; in 1863, £181,000,000; and in 1890, £1,169,000,000.

Mr. Coghlan has estimated the value of the productions of each Australasian colony to be as follows:—New South Wales—Agriculture, £4,131,400: pastoral, £13,359,800; mining, £5,003,900; dairy farming, £2,887,600; forests and fisheries, £1,843,000. Victoria:—Agriculture, £7,520,300; pastoral,

£6,041,300; mining, £2,384,200; dairy farming, £3,606.600; forests and fisheries, £519,700. Queensland :—Agriculture, £2,233,200; pastoral, £5,984,200; mining, £2,518,000; dairy farming, £989,100; forests and fisheries, £615,600. South Australia :—Agriculture, £3,569,700; pastoral, £2,176,300; mining, £381,000; dairy farming, £770,400; forests and fisheries, £275,500. Western Australia :—Agriculture, £366,900; pastoral, £500,200; mining, £94,300; dairy farming, £134,200; forests and fisheries, £295,800. Tasmania:—Agriculture, £962,700; pastoral, £748,300; mining, £357,700; dairy farming, £380,300; forests and fisheries, £329,700. New Zealand :—Agriculture, £4,829,500; pastoral, £7,110,500; mining, £1,523,800; dairy farming, £1,830,200; forests and fisheries, &c., £600,500.

The export of the pastoral product of Australia shows less variation in quantity than the agricultural, forest, mineral, and fisheries products of Canada, although Australian flocks and herds are sometimes decimated by terrible droughts, when runs in the rainless country lose many thousands of their sheep. The Australasian colonies contained in 1890 on their pastures, 116,041,707 sheep or nearly forty-seven times as many as Canada; 10,949,534 cattle, or more than twice as many as Canada; 1,205,782 swine, or about 45,000 less than Canada; 1,732,628 horses, or about 630,000 more than Canada. The eastern provinces of Canada export to England an immense quantity of live stock, and there is not the same necessity for shipping dead meat as exists in more distant colonies, as cattle can be conveyed alive on the short voyage from America to the British Isles, although even then there is sometimes a large percentage killed by the tossing of the vessels in rough weather.

Pastoral properties in Australasia, have been valued at £242,653,000, and the live stock depastured on them at £116,776,000. The staple of Australasia during the last decade brought remunerative rates in England, and the recent increased direct communication with foreign states by magnificent steamers is now opening up markets for colonial produce in other directions. The wool production of the Australasian Colonies is larger than that of any other country, and in 1890 the export value of the fleece was £20,349,300 The annual return from the pastoral industries has been valued at £35,920,600.

The number of vessels entered and cleared from Australasian ports increased from 10,496 of 2,819,728 tons, in 1861, to 17,629 of 15,542,248 tons, in 1890; the latter tonnage being about half as much again as in Canada. The vessels registered in the ports of the different colonies, at the close of 1890, numbered 2,782 of 393,311 tonnage. The Governments of the British Colonies in Australasia, owned in the year 1890-1 a net-work of railways, 11,990 miles long, being only 2,014 miles less than the length of the railroads in Canada, which however are not nearly all Government property as is the case in Australasia, but principally in the hands of private companies, such as the Canadian Pacific Co., which took over their lines from the State. The traveller may now ride by rail from Brisbane to Adelaide, and traverse in a few days comfortably the long distances between the capitals of Queensland, New South Wales, Victoria, and South Australia. The railways in Australasia greatly promote settlement in the interior, and give back a proportion of net receipts for capital and cost of 3·01 per cent., being about twice that given in Canada.

There are now in existence 125,000 miles of ocean cable of which 90,000 are owned and managed by British people. In 1890 there were 86,012 miles of telegraph wires connecting almost every town in the Australasian group, and the lines of ocean cables bring the colonies into direct communication with each other and the nations of Europe. A cablegram from Melbourne to London passes over 13,695 miles of wire of which 9,287 miles consist of submarine cables. There are nearly three times as many messages per head of population in Australia as in Canada, and the length of lines is nearly half as much again.

In 1890 there were 86,012 miles of telegraph wires in Australasia being 19,559 miles more than in Canada, and 13,112,830 telegrams received and despatched, about three times as many as in Canada. The Australasian Colonies are only surpassed by four other countries in the extent of telegraph wires, and by five others in numbers of messages and in no other land do the messages bear the same high rate to population.

The amount of revenue obtained per head of population is far higher in Australasia than in any other country, and more than three times what it is in Canada, as the total sum received for the year 1890-1 was £29,922,897. The percentage of revenue derived from taxation to total revenue was 38·1 in Australasia and 79·2 in Canada, and the percentage of interest on public debt to total expenditure was 24 in Australasia and 26·1 in Canada.

The amount of deposits in the Australasian Savings Banks is more than three times as much as in Canada, notwithstanding the thriftness of the Canadian people, who, however, have not had nearly so much money at their disposal as fell to the lot of the people of Australia. The deposits in the Australasian Banks of issue were £111,015,162 against £28,372,398 in Canada in the year 1890. The paid up capital reserves and deposits of banks in Australasia amounted to £138,000,000, or £37 per head of population, against £40,000,000, or £8 per head in Canada, and £1,030,000,000, or £16 per head in the United States. There has been considerable shrinkage in the market value of the paid-up capital of Australasian bank shares during the past two years, which even now stand however at a total premium of 71¼ per cent., notwithstanding that the directors are not, for some time past, actively seeking to extend the operations of these institutions. The gross public debt of Australasia was in 1891, £192,565,327, against £59,606,727 for the Dominion of Canada; but the difference in these amounts is principally due to the Australian Governments still holding nearly all the railway, tramway, and telegraph lines, which is not the case in Canada.

Canada has built a magnificent railroad across the American continent which has brought Yokahama three weeks nearer to London than it is by the Suez Canal, and which should prove of great service to the Australian Colonies, as besides being the shortest route to the far East, it would be most important were the Suez Canal closed against traffic in time of war.

The construction of the Canadian Pacific Railway across the Rocky Mountains into Vancouver was a noble work for 5,000,000 people to undertake and complete. It would, however, have been better policy for the Canadian Government to have retained for the State this great national work under the management of independent commissioners, as has been the case in Australasia, whose colonies as a rule own all the lines and reap the advantages from the increased value of the adjoining public land.

The great railway through Canada from the Atlantic to the Pacific not only opens up the vast wheat fields of the north-west in Manitoba, but also affords to the traveller glacier scenery, covering nearly 40 miles square, on "the backbone of the continent," with a peak 8,000 feet high, surpassing in grandeur even the famous mountains of Switzerland.

I

The Canadian Pacific Railway is the longest continuous line in the world being 4,315 miles in length, nearly three times as long as the main trunk line from Adelaide to Brisbane which has been constructed by the Australian Governments, without giving large subventions in money and grants of land to a private company as was the case with the Canadian Government.

Both in the United States and Canada the expense of railroad should be much more than in Australia owing to the necessity there for sheds many miles in length to keep the rails free from snow and ice. The capital cost of the railways in Canada was £163,843,294, and the cost per mile £11,703 against £10,030 in Australia. The net revenue per train mile in Australia was 2s. 1½d. against 1s. 4d. in Canada so that the railways are now securing a better result for the outlay than in the Dominion.

Winnipeg, as the portal to thousands of miles of illimitable stretches of fertile prairie lands, should, from its position, hereafter become a second Chicago, but its progress during the past decade in population has been exceeded by Broken Hill, a mining township in New South Wales.

Sir G. R. Dibbs, the Premier of New South Wales, during his recent visit to England, in a letter to the London *Economist* on the financial position of the Australian Colonies compared with that of Canada, said: " The railways in the United States and Canada have a great advantage of being constructed of one gauge, which is not the case in Australia."

The number of letters sent through the post offices of the Australasian Colonies was reckoned approximately to be 172,596,000 or an average of 46·2 letters per inhabitant against 21·91 per inhabitant in Canada.

The revenue in 1890 from post offices in Australasia was £1,256,774, being nearly double that in Canada, and the amounts derived from this source is considered to be the best criterion of the respective use made of this method of communication and as a test of intelligence of the people. The number of newspapers posted was 96,309,000, or nearly twenty-six for each inhabitant so that the residents scattered throughout the country districts of Australia should be well informed in the news of the world, especially as local papers are transmitted free or with only a half-penny postage.

The sum of £1,984,063, being £115,129 more than in Canada, was spent in 1890 from public funds of the Australasian Colonies on primary education alone, for 832,898 children at 7,287 State schools, which had a daily attendance in them of 426,924 pupils. There were, however, owing to the larger population, 165,925 more children attending school in Canada than in Australasia, but denominational schools are subsided by the Government in Canada, which is not the case in any of the colonies except Western Australia. The percentage of persons over ten years of age who can read and write increased from 76·75 in 1861 to 88·67 in 1881, and this gratifying result with the fact that persons signing the marriage register with marks has greatly decreased, being only 2·19 to every hundred married, goes to prove that the educational systems of the Australian colonies are becoming more effective in their operations.

Ontario has a population of nearly 2,000,000, and it is renowned for the intelligence and moral status of its people. The value for the taxable property in Toronto, "the Queen City of the West," and the metropolis of Ontario, is not, however, half so great as the assessed value of property within the Sydney municipality in New South Wales.

Toronto was settled by " United Empire Loyalists" who left their homes in the revolted American colonies, and have done a noble work in the settlement of Ontario, as its present satisfactory condition is greatly due to these people and their descendants. It was proposed at the end of last century to ship these loyalists to Australia, but the English Government did not agree to the suggestion, wishing to retain in Canada such valiant defenders of the remaining British possessions in North America.

The nomenclature on the maps both of Canada and Australia shows that such places as Sydney, Hawkesbury, and Bathurst were probably named in both countries in honour of the same English noblemen, which however has led to much confusion in the minds of those who are not well acquainted with American and Australian geography, and led to many mistakes being made in transmitting correspondence and otherwise found to be very undesirable.

The imports from Canada to Australasia, as recorded in the statistical registers of the southern Colonies, only increased from £71,455 in 1881 to £85,746 in 1890; and there were no exports direct to the Dominion recorded in 1881, and only £70 worth in 1891, so that the trade between the two countries is capable of much direct development, instead of by way of San Francisco as principally carried on at present.

The imports from the United Kingdom into Australasia increased from £25,662,180 sterling in 1881 to £28,163,348 in 1890; and the exports from £24,342,422 in 1881 to £28,200,563 in 1890. The percentage of imports from Australasia to the United Kingdom to total from British possessions, amounted in 1881 to 29·5, and in 1890 to 30·5. The imports from the United Kingdom into Canada amounted in 1890 to £9,062,855, and the exports to the United Kingdom from the Dominion to £10,073,686 ; so that the trade of Australasia with the mother country `is three times as much as that of Canada.

The total trade of the Canadian Dominion, including merchandise, specie, and bullion in 1890, was £45,543,205 ; but the increases in the value of the imports and exports during the past decennial period affords a striking contrast to those of Australasia. The total foreign trade of Australasia, compared with that of the countries in North America; was £20 2s. 4d. per inhabitant against £8 15s. 8d. for Canada, and £5 13s. 8d. for the United States; so that the people in the southern colonies carry on with other countries commerce of nearly four times the value for each inhabitant than the residents in the States, and more than twice as much as for those in Canada.

The proximity of Canada to the United States has caused its trade relations to be more complicated than is the case with Australia. Earl Grey has urged that the Canadian Dominion should not merely throw open its markets to England, but to the United States as well, by the adoption of a freetrade policy ; whilst Professor Grant argues that the mother country should make a preferential arrangement within the Empire, which would only be required as a temporary measure, and would really lead to the freetrade relations which are desired with the United States.

There has been a gradual increase in the value of exports from Canada the produce of her fisheries, and if suitable steam vessels and cool chambers were provided, no doubt there would be as continuous a demand for fresh salmon in Australasia, as there is now for the tinned article. The coasts of Australia, however, abound with a plentiful supply of other varieties of fishes, and similar vessels and appliances to those used on the coast of Newfoundland would reap a rich harvest from the sea of such delicious fish as schnapper, which, though plentiful off the coast, now brings a high price in the Sydney market, owing to there being few deep sea fishermen in New South Wales.

At Vancouver in 1886 there was only a single house, now there are 20,000 inhabitants, owing to its being the terminus of the Canadian Pacific Railway. There can be no doubt that in time Vancouver will become a great commercial centre, as there is now great activity in building displayed round the shores of Puget Sound. A large quantity of lumber has been shipped by the Vancouver Sawmill Co. to Australia, as in 1890 it sent 850,000 ft. to Sydney alone, and it is regretted that the depression in the building trades has prevented a greater use of these excellent softwoods at the present time.

The Mayor of Vancouver has recently intimated to Captain' Rounding, of Sydney, who is endeavouring to promote trade between British Columbia and New South Wales, that there would be a considerable demand in Canada for the surplus beef and mutton of Australia, as the requirements of the people of British Columbia exceed the local supply.

The total value of minerals raised in Australasia for 1890 was £12,262,934, or at the rate of £3 5s. 7d. per inhabitant. New South Wales produced over 40 per cent. of the output of minerals, which amounted in value to £5,003,903, or £4 10s. 10d. per inhabitant. The value of production in minerals is larger now than in 1852, the time of the first gold discovery; though the amount of that precious metal raised is much less, as the decrease from the auriferous deposits is more than made up by increases in the production of silver, copper, tin, coal, kerosene and other minerals.

There was a large output of Canadian minerals in 1873, especially of silver ore and mineral oils, but there was a great falling off the next year. The value of gold raised in Canada up to the end of 1888 was £11,410,708, and the output in Australasia in 1890 was over three times as much as in British North America.

The value of agricultural produce in Australasia, in 1890, has been estimated at £23,613,700, and the area under crop is more than five times as large as it was thirty years ago. The value of agricultural production per head in 1890 in Australia was £6·3, against in 1887 £7·0 for Canada, and £7·5 for the United States.   .

The average acreage of tillage per head of the Australian population was 1·1 in 1861, 1·4 in 1871, 2·0 in 1881, and 1·9 in 1890. Since 1861 there has been nearly a five-fold increase in the area sown with wheat, but several of the colonies of late years show a decrease, and it is estimated that in 1890 there was a production of 32,839,505 bushels; so that after deducting what is required for local consumption, a balance remained of 13,735,574 bushels for export to other countries.

Australasia in 1890 produced 32,839,505 bushels of wheat, more than four-fifths of the yield for Canada, and the consumption of flour from the crop per head of population is about the same quantity. The crops in Australasia also produced 15,805,324 bushels of oats, 2,787,726 bushels of barley, 8,902,101 bushels of maize, and 931,096 bushels of other cereals, 562,653 tons of potatoes, 1,282,471 tons of hay, 96,516 tons of sugar, and 3,997,189 gallons of wine.

The duties levied on articles such as agricultural implements, carpets, and pianos, are higher in Canada than in Victoria, which latter colony, however, imposes a much greater rate than those charged by the other Australasian Colonies, and that recently passed by the New South Wales Parliament is the lowest of any of the settlements.

The orange is the great commercial fruit of New South Wales, in the same way as the apple is that of Canada. The growth of the citrous fruits is found more profitable around Sydney than that of other varieties, such as apples and pears, which, however, are found to be plentiful in the same orchards.

The well-known maple sugar of Canada cannot be produced at a price approaching cane-sugar in Australia, but it has an agreeable flavour and is acceptable when made up in sweetmeats.

The annual export trade in apples from Canada to Great Britain amounted in value to £907,614, and from Canada to the United States to £272,360. As the fruit seasons vary in Australasia and Canada, the semi-tropical Australian orange might be exchanged for the Canadian apple, which is best produced in a cold country. The Peninsular and Oriental Steam Navigation Company have undertaken to provide in their magnificent steamers to carry away from Tasmania, for the present season, a teeming harvest of fruit, which is expected will include 300,000 bushels of apples. It has been urged that "the business of Australia, together with producing abundance for its own population, is to supply the millions of Europe and America with the fresh fruit which for half the year their own orchards, orange-groves, and vineyards do not grow. That means virtually duplicating the supply of fresh fruit consumed in the northern hemisphere, and for meeting this great demand the Colony of New South Wales has a capability that is not surpassed by any country in Australia or the world. From within 14 miles of Sydney can be drawn all the fruits yielded by the cold clime of Britain itself, while within that range and extending to the limits of the Colony are to be found the soil and temperature that will produce every fruit besides that is grown from north to south of Europe."

The dissimilarity of the vegetation of Australia and Canada is even illustrated by the fact that the honey from Ontario, though excellent in quality, is different from that produced in these colonies, which is darker in colour, owing to being principally gathered from flowering trees and shrubs of the eucalypti at any time of the year which is not the case with other plants.

The expenditure on public works during 1890 was in Australasia £10,536,634, and in Canada £2,126,140, or five times smaller than in the Southern settlements ; and these figures afford a striking illustration of the progressive lines on which the Australasian Colonies have been governed during the past ten years, compared with the greater caution exercised by the Dominion Government in borrowing money to carry out works for opening up the country.

NEW SOUTH WALES AND CALIFORNIA.

A COMPARISON between New South Wales and California, the acknowledged wealthiest state of the Union in natural resources, and the one which she greatly resembles in geographical features and general capabilities, will be one of the best ways of illustrating to our enterprising kinsmen in America the resources of their neighbours on the other side of the Pacific. It cannot but be also interesting to contrast the progress of two settlements one of which in the year 1849 elected to be governed by the democratic articles of the United States, whilst the other has worked under the principles of the British constitution.

For many years the city of Sydney, the capital of New South Wales, was styled "the Queen of the Pacific," as a tribute to her magnificent harbour and commercial greatness. The title has also been claimed for San Francisco on account of its excellent situation and wonderful progress. The future emporium of the trade of the Pacific has yet to be determined, and in the commercial race Port Jackson will be found a worthy competitor with the harbour at whose entrance is the famous "Golden Gate." When La Perouse visited California and afterwards New South Wales, on his ill-fated expedition in 1778, he found the former settlement a Spanish colony under military rule, and arrived just in time to be at the birth in Sydney of the infant Australian state. Although California was colonised at the end of last century, it was not until the finding of gold in 1848 that it advanced with rapid strides, and the same fact is true concerning New South Wales. Gold has been found as early as the year 1841 near Sydney, by the late Rev. W. B. Clarke—the father of Australian geology·—but on reporting the circumstance to the Governor he was entreated not to publish his discovery for fear of its effect upon a crown colony. Had this discovery been made known it would have prevented the departure for California of thousands who in 1849 unwittingly left greater deposits of the precious metal behind them, and also have drawn much earlier a large stream of emigration to the Australian shores. Proper development of the resources of New South Wales cannot be said to have commenced till after the gold discovery in 1851, and the consequent granting of free institutions to the Colony which took place in 1856. The Colonies of Australia have been "precipitated into a nation" by the discovery of vast mineral wealth within their borders, and when containing a larger population there is no doubt that much greater quantities of the precious metals will be unearthed. It is not likely or desirable, however, that such great disturbances of business relations will ever happen again as what took place in California and New South Wales on receipt of the tidings of the first gold discoveries.

California is reckoned, on account of its situation, to be the wealthiest state in the Union, in the same way that New South Wales is proved to be the richest of the Australasian Colonies. The extent of New South Wales is 310,700 square miles or 198,848,000 acres, and that of California, 155,980 square miles or 101,350,400 acres, or only about half that of the Australian Colony.

Sir George Dibbs, in a letter to the London *Times*, shows the progress made in New South Wales by the following figures :—"The value of primary industries—that is, the products of stock, agriculture, mines, and forests—during 1881 was £20,000,000, while ten years later it had risen to £28,750,000 sterling. The weight of wool exported in· the year firstnamed being

140,000,000 lb., while in 1891 the quantity was 332,000,000 lb. The general exports in 1881 were valued at £16,308,000, and in 1891 at £25,944,000. Taking the exports of domestic produce alone, the value in 1881 was not quite £12,000,000, and last year the total was more than £21,000,000, notwithstanding the fact that prices had fallen more than 20 per cent. during the interval."

The most sterile of the lands of New South Wales are the great depositories of its mineral wealth, and exhibit how singularly favoured this country is in its varied resources. Adequate attempts have not been made to work the auriferous rocks of the Colony, and much of the land taken up was only for speculative purposes. The practical experience of the American mining expert has been already found invaluable in Australia, especially for the treatment of silver ores. Although, as in California, the production of gold in New South Wales has declined since the first discovery, the value of other minerals won has greatly increased, so that the amount now yearly obtained for silver-ore is greater than ever received from the auriferous deposits. The value of minerals raised in New South Wales to the end of 1890 amounted to £80,456,039.

The colonies which have been formed by New South Wales, both on the mainland and in the neighbouring islands, are very prosperous, and the progress of Victoria, one of the settlements, has been so great, principally owing to its large deposits of gold, that it seemed at one time as if even the prosperity of the parent colony would be surpassed; but the resources of New South Wales, both in natural and acquired wealth, are so varied and substantial that its supremacy is now well assured.

New South Wales during the last decade has increased in population over 50 per cent.; the number of children receiving instruction has also increased by one half; the number of sheep has increased from 37,000,000 to 62,000,000, growing a clip of wool which has risen in weight from 140,000,000 lb. to 332,000,000 lb.; the output of coal has grown from 1,769,597 tons to 4,037,929 tons; the external commerce of the colony has increased in value from £34,000,000 to £51,000,000.

During the last decennial period, New South Wales has surpassed California in the increase to its population, in sheep and cattle farming, in mining, in the number of hands employed by manufacturing industries, in both imports and exports by sea, and in the money deposited in the banks. The American State, however, has made greater progress in agriculture and the construction of railways which convey its wondrous growth of fruits and grain to eastern markets. The pastoral industry of New South Wales has developed wonderfully, its fleece having more than doubled during the last ten years. The wool grown in California, on the other hand, has been decreasing in volume, and now amounts to only 35,000,000 lb., about one-tenth of the yield in the Australian colony. The growing of grain and fruit has, however, developed to a far greater extent in California, as the total value of crops in New South Wales only amounted to £4,131,000 whilst in California, for cereals, hay, and root crops, &c., the estimated value is now over £14,000,000.

It is believed that by the proposed Government irrigation scheme now being considered, large quantities of grain and fruit can be produced from what has hitherto been only waste land, as has been done by similar means on the arid country in California. The Director of Agriculture states that the present annual agricultural export of £200,000 per annum could, under favourable circumstances and judicious encouragement, be raised to several millions sterling, and that butter could be shipped in winter and cheese in summer to successfully meet the requirements of the English market. Butter was exported from New South Wales to the United Kingdom valued at £18,914 or about half the exports of that article.

There are vast tracts of good arable lands in the unsettled districts of New South Wales which will be fertilised by the waters of Riverina under the Government irrigation proposals for locking the Darling River, and by the underground wells of the extensive cretaceous formation now being extensively and successfully tapped by artesian boring, so that there should be much more agricultural production in the future.

The geographical advantages possessed by Australia will be seen by noting the position which the continent occupies, not only to North and South America, but also to the island colonies of New Zealand, Tasmania, and Fiji ; to the Pacific ports of North and South America, India, China, Japan, and the other Asiatic ports; and also to New Guinea, New Caledonia, Borneo, Sumatra, Java, and the various groups of islands in the Pacific and Indian oceans.

New South Wales occupies the premier position for commerce in Australasia, and the magnificent shipping facilities of Port Jackson for the large export carried on in pastoral produce, and of the adjacent harbour of Newcastle for the shipment of coal, make the Colony the southern centre to which the growing trade of the world principally tends. Sydney is situated in the centre of the richest coal region ever known to man, and from this metropolis is principally shipped wool, frozen meat, hides, and tallow the produce from the pastures ; gold, silver, copper, tin, and coal, from the mines ; and corn and hay from the farms.

The coast line of New South Wales, although not so long as that of California, is indented by a number of excellent harbours, some of which must, in the course of time, become great shipping ports, and one of them is now being improved for that purpose by prison labour.

The number of sheep in Great Britain has decreased by nearly 5,500,000 since 1870, and is now only half that in New South Wales alone, notwithstanding the increase of population in the mother country. There should, therefore, be a great market for the excellent frozen mutton which can be readily shipped to London by the immense vessels now trading to that port.

The trade of the American State and the Australian Colony in 1890 was as follows :—

	Imports.	Exports.	Total.
New South Wales	£22,615,004	£22,045,937	£44,660,941
California	£10,612,181	£20,833,333	£31,445,514

The volume of trade in Sydney amounted in 1891 to £35,500,000 against imports and exports in Melbourne amounting to £31,500,000 sterling. In point of value the trade of Sydney surpasses that of any port in Great Britain except that of London and Liverpool. For many years past Sydney has doubled its volume of trade every ten years, and if it continues to advance at the same rate in fifteen years its trade will be equal to that of Liverpool, and in twenty years to that of London. The Dominion of Canada with five times the population has not so large a volume of trade as New South Wales, and there is not a colony or dependency of the British Empire which has a commerce equal in value to that Colony. The imports and exports of New South Wales amounted during 1891 to £51,327,417 against a trade of nearly £38,000,000 for Victoria, or a sum of £44 17s. 8d. as against £32 18s. 6d. per head of population. New South Wales exported in

1891 £21,103,816 sterling worth of its growth or manufactures, or £18 9s. 3d. per head ; whilst Victoria exported only £13,026,426 worth, or £11 7s. 2d. per head. The export of wool alone from New South Wales reached £11,000,000 sterling against £3,750,000 from Victoria.

California has been described as the second largest of the United States, and greater in extent than the combined area of New England, New York, and Pennsylvannia, or than Great Britain and Ireland with several German states thrown in. Twenty years ago the population was about the same in California and New South Wales, but owing to a rapid influx of emigrants from the Eastern States California in 1880 had 113,486 more inhabitants. The census population however of New South Wales in 1891 was 1,132,234 and of California in 1890 1,208,130. At the beginning of the decade, therefore, the population of California exceeded that of New South Wales, but since that time the Australian colony has obtained a much larger accession to its numbers than the American settlement. The returns show that the increase of population in New South Wales during the last decennial period was 37,232 more than in California, so that there has been a larger influx of emigrants into the British Colony, which at the end of 1891 had 1,165,300 inhabitants.

Nearly all the residents in New South Wales are of British descent, whilst a very large proportion of the people of California have come from nearly every European country, bringing with them not only the good qualities but also the errors, vanities, and prejudices of the races to which they belong. Although a small number of foreigners is no doubt beneficial to a new community, as they bring with them a knowledge of the arts or industries of their native lands, yet the presence of a large proportion of persons unacquainted with the English language, and without much training in working free institutions, is less desirable, both in America and Australia, than that of those who have received political education in a similar English speaking community.

The population of Sydney during the last decade increased nearly three times as much as that of San Francisco, and in 1890 Sydney had 383,386 inhabitants or 84,389 more than San Francisco, although the latter had nearly 10,000 more residents in 1881 than the metropolitan district of New South Wales.

The Town Hall in Sydney is often used for high-class concerts, given by local Leidertafels and other Musical Societies. This hall contains one of the largest organs in the world, played by Mons. Wiegand, a performer of the highest European repute, whose recitals of classical music are attended by large and appreciative audiences several times each week, as he is under a permanent engagement with the city authorities.

As the extent of New South Wales is twice that of California, while the population is about the same in number, there is much more room for the immigrant in the former place than in the latter. Californians acquainted with raisin, olive, and prune production ought to obtain a remunerative return for their capital and knowledge in New South Wales, where these industries should prove as successful as they have done in California.

The mountains of California resemble the coast range of New South Wales, both in geological conformation and in being the matrix of vast mineral wealth ; both ranges too are crossed by railways, in the face of great natural obstacles. For over thirty years after the foundation of the Colony the Blue Mountains running north to south, at a distance of 20 to 120 miles from the sea, were deemed impenetrable, and the settlers were limited to the land abutting on the coast line, but the discovery of a passage across the dividing range opened up vast plains admirably suited for agriculture and pasturage, and did as much good to the Colony as the expeditions of Captain Frémont did to California in its early days.

The rivers of New South Wales draining the country on both sides of the Blue Mountains, make the Colony the best part of Australia. These rivers are larger and more important than is generally represented, and by the removal of obstructions are now greatly improved so as to admit of extended inland navigation. Early navigators believed the coast line of New South Wales, like the opposite shores of America, to be nearly destitute of good harbours, and, therefore, not well adapted for carrying on maritime pursuits. Several fine ports have however since been discovered on the Australian coast, one of which, in the number and tonnage of the vessels entering it, rivals that of Sydney. Port Jackson is generally acknowledged by visitors to be in the beauty of its conformation superior to the magnificent road-steads of San Francisco or New York, and to be also the finest natural dock in the world.

The climate of New South Wales resembles that of California, and the clearness of the atmosphere in both countries attracts the admiration of visitors from other climes. The rapture expressed by the early navigator Magellan at for the first time seeing the constellation of the Southern Cross, which he recognised as the emblem of the Christian faith, is shared by the astronomer in contemplating the wonders of the celestial system as revealed in this new hemisphere. Owing to there being few extremes of heat or cold in New South Wales, the workman is enabled to labour in the open air, and the traveller to camp out in the bush at night, in most parts of the Colony all the year round, without contracting disease from exposure. The Pacific Ocean has such an influence on the mean annual temperature of the City of Sydney that it is much warmer in winter and cooler in summer than the inland towns. The great extent of New South Wales enables immigrants to settle in a district with a hot or cool climate as is most congenial to their previous habits of life. Both in New South Wales and California there are some places in the far interior where the heat is intense in the summer-time, but there is no district in the Australian Colony whose mean temperature is higher than that of places with such ominous names as Death Valley, Funeral Mountain, and Furnace Creek, some 70 or 80 miles eastward of the Sierra Nevadas.

The mean temperature of Sydney is 63 degrees, and of San Francisco 55 degrees; and although the Australian city has not the most.equable climate, yet it is not troubled with most disagreeable fogs coming from the Pacific Ocean, which are found specially injurious to new comers in the American city.

Vital statistics show the natural increase by births over deaths in New South Wales to be 22·33 per 1,000 whilst in the United States it is 22·8, and the death-rate in 1890 amounted to only 15·10 per 1,000 in Sydney, against 18·1 in San Francisco, which is much lower than Chicago, New York, or Montreal.

There are twice as many Indians in California as Aborigines in New South Wales, and the local tribes in both settlements are inoffensive compared with other savage races in the Rocky Mountains and Polynesia. The red man has received greater consideration in California than the black native in the Colony, though attacks on Australian settlers were not to the same extent as those on the immigrants crossing the plains from the eastern states to the Pacific slope at the time of the gold discovery.

Australians could learn many lessons from the experiences of their Californian neighbours in some of the problems which have received attention on that side of the Pacific, especially with regard to foreign immigration, agricultural production, free education, socialism, syndicates, taxation, and land legislation. Both countries have experienced seasons of depression after long periods of prosperity; but even now there is no doubt that they are the two richest communities founded in modern times. California, from the first financial depression in 1854 to the mining scare in 1887, had many experiences in over-speculation, which it would have been well for Australians to have known and noted, as it might have prevented their being recently victimised by monetary institutions similar to those which had suspended payment in San Francisco several years previously. The Government of New South Wales is now endeavouring to prevent future loss from failures of land, building, insurance, and other financial companies, by an enactment similar to that in force in New York, regulating the operations of all societies receiving deposits from the public. Although at the present time New South Wales is suffering from the "booming" of land syndicates, the gambling spirit has not been nearly so rampant in Sydney as it was in San Francisco in years past. In Australia there is, however, much betting carried on by what are called professional "bookmakers" in connection with horse-races and other sports at holiday gatherings, which have not only demoralised numbers of young men, but also greatly injured these out-door amusements.

A stately slowness was once said to be the characteristic of the people of New South Wales; but recently they have been charged with being too fast in entering on public works and private undertakings. But the boundless natural resources of New South Wales will ever enable it to hold a leading position on the roll of British settlements, in the same way that California must continue to be one of the richest states in the Union. There is no doubt but that the great enterprise in agricultural and horticultural industries displayed by Californians of late years might be advantageously copied by Australians. Our Trans-Pacific neighbours could also learn many lessons from the social and religious life of New South Wales, the people of which have more of the steady characteristics of an old established Anglo-Saxon community than the large foreign population of San Francisco. The Australian native-born in New South Wales now number more than two-thirds of the population, and form a rapidly-increasing new and promising nationality, even though there are many "larrikins" to be found in Sydney as there are "hoodlums" in San Francisco. Unlike Americans Australians are very fond of all out-door English sports, and perhaps in danger of too eager a pursuit of athletics rather than of too earnest attention to the attainment of true intellectual excellence; but this may be through want of discretion on the part of some educators in giving the passion for all kinds of amusements an undue encouragement. The results of the examinations held for many years past by the local Universities, and the classification of the works of the students of the Sydney Technical College by the examiners of the Science and Art Department of Great Britain and the City and Guilds of London Institute, prove that large numbers of Australians are not however behind English competitors in obtaining a satisfactory knowledge of literary, scientific, artistic, and technological subjects.

The University of California has an endowment of £1,458,000, and on its extensive property at Berkeley in addition to the ordinary branches it has departments of mining and agriculture and has an attendance of 400 students, or 78 less than at the Sydney University. This latter institution received in 1890 a Government endowment of £18,634, and has also obtained from time to time many large private bequests, one of which amounted to £200,000. The statutory school age is in New South Wales from 6 to 14 years, while in California it is from 5 to 17 years, so that the average daily attendance is larger in the American State, whose day and evening primary and high schools in San Francisco are conducted without charge to the students, and are consequently well attended by many who would otherwise become "larrikins" or "hoodlums," as is now unfortunately the case in New South Wales where the law should be altered so as to require youths leaving the primary school to attend free evening classes in high and technical schools, until they reach at least 17 years of age, when the habit of study thus acquired might be found continuing throughout their early manhood. The expenditure per head on public schools is much larger in the Pacific States and Australian Colonies than in any other parts of the world, and the cost per head is even greater in California than in New South Wales, as the appliances and furniture for use of the scholars are more perfect in the American State. The yearly expenditure on school buildings in New South Wales was, however, greater than in California, as many of the buildings in the latter are of wood, and not of substantial stone or brick as is the general rule in the Australian Colony; where however the fear of earthquakes throwing down solid walls does not obtain in the same way as is the case in San Francisco, owing to many accidents from this cause happening there. The private school attendance in New South Wales is 45,018, being double that in California, principally owing to the Roman Catholic Church in New South Wales founding and endowing a number of denominational schools in which instruction in religious as well as secular subjects is well imparted.

The charitable institutions of New South Wales are even of a more extensive kind than those in California, as they are adapted to almost every form of suffering in human beings, and are principally worked by a director of charities and committees of philanthropic persons who find even in this new community disease and poverty to be alleviated by the service of the Good Samaritan. Hearty responses given by the people of New South Wales to many appeals for help from residents in other lands evidence that, as a community, they are susceptible of much humane sympathy, and are not given up to selfish aggrandisement. Mr. Ben Tillet has recently expressed gratitude to the labour party in Australia, as the wages since the late London Dockers' strike had increased to them about £500,000 yearly, mainly owing to the opportune assistance given by Australians.

The great social problems now agitating the world, especially with regard to the relations of labour and capital, are discussed every week in somewhat the same way in the Sydney Domain as on the San Francisco Sand Block; but although the working classes in New South Wales at the last election returned over thirty labour members, who are about equally divided on the question of free-trade or protection, they have usually recorded their votes according to these convictions. There are grasping capitalists and soulless corporations in Australia as in America, but there is not yet that striking contrast between the wealth of a comparatively few millionaires and the great bulk of the masses that is found in the United States, as riches appear to be more evenly distributed amongst all classes of Australians.

There is no notorious principal political "boss" in Sydney, like the ex-saloon keepers who by bribery and corruption have played a considerable part in menacing the politics of San Francisco, to the great enrichment of themselves and the disturbance of law and order throughout California.

The number of licensed publicans in 1890 in New South Wales was 3,903, including 475 retailers of colonial wine. This is less than half the number of bar-keepers in California which was 9,373, but many of these are in underground "dives" which do not at all correspond in appearance to the Australian hotels, which occupy the best sites in the various streets. The number of persons to each taxed retail liquor establishment in New South Wales was 287, and according to population there are over three times as many public houses in California as in New South Wales, as in San Francisco there is one saloon to every 77 inhabitants. Public houses in New South Wales are required by law to close all day on Sunday and at 11 o'clock on week nights, and the practice of keeping the bar open all night and every Sabbath is not permitted in Sydney as in San Francisco, where it leads in certain parts of the latter city to disturbance and immorality. The people of New South Wales are not educated up to the point of seeing that the money spent in intoxicating liquors is worse than wasted, a conviction which has led to the passing of prohibition laws in several American States, and a consequent great diminution of crime. Sydney, however, would compare favourably with San Francisco in respect of the proper regulations against the ill effects of the liquor traffic, as it has been stated that in the latter place "the saloon is the great agency by which corruption in politics is fostered, and the power of the bosses maintained." Though drunkenness is one of the evils of Australian life as elsewhere, yet the great offenders against sobriety are found to be not the Australian born, and the inhabitants as a whole do not consume more beer, spirits and wine than the total equivalent in proof alcohol used by the residents in the United Kingdom. A recent report from the medical officers of the Australian Mutual Provident Society, however, shows that the percentage of deaths from intemperance of members of that institution from 1849 to 1888 was 2·06, against ·59 in the Mutual Life Society of New York, and ·76 in the Scottish Widows Fund, although there was a marked improvement shown in the Australian office during the last ten years of the period. The proportion of insane persons is about the same in both New South Wales and California, and the percentages are lower than those for Great Britain or the United States.

It has been pointed out by a recent American writer that the expansion is greater of late years in the growth in population and wealth in the urban districts than in the rural communities of every nation except Russia, owing to the latter not having reached that stage of social and industrial development which brings it about, and this conclusion if correct would be most complimentary to the residents of Australia, who deplore the great concentration in the cities of all the colonies.

The circumstances attending the colonisation on both sides of the Pacific have led to both Australia and the Pacific States of America being made refuges for a large number of the criminal classes from other countries— for example absconders from each other and récidivistes from New Caledonia. In California in 1880 the foreign born were 13 per cent. of the population, and they furnished 19 per cent. of convicts and 43 per cent. of the inmates of the house of correction.

Amongst the dangers besetting American institutions is the peril from promiscuous immigration, and a recent candidate for office in California warmly supports the platform of the American party that, " Congress pass an immigration law, whereby a *per capita* tax shall be levied upon and collected from all immigrants coming to the United States ; and that such tax be made large enough to restrain further immigration from all foreign countries, and all persons not in sympathy with our Government should be prohibited from immigrating to the United States." Australians are not, however, opposed to the coming of any of the white races, but object to the introduction of large numbers of coloured labourers as an inferior and servile race, and the Hon. Edmund Barton (Attorney-General), when moving resolutions in the Legislative Assembly, in favour of the Federation of the Australasian Colonies recently said :—" That everyone who had studied the history of the racial question in America would see that there were things stronger than State rights, and while some feared the immense power that would be invested in such a central federal legislature as was proposed might interfere with State rights, as was the case when the American Republican party determined upon the emancipation of the slaves, it would be admitted—acknowledging the good qualities of the negroes—that nature was deeper than reason, and one thing that had to be acknowledged was a natural racial antagonism, and an inherent belief that the white was greater than the black. He had always argued that the essence of the Federation of Australia, having regard to their destiny in shaping the future, was to preserve the white races and distribute amongst them the advantages which the riches of the country offered."

Although the amount given for wages to artisans appears in some respects higher in San Francisco than in Sydney, the greater cost of clothing and provisions would absorb any difference in the rates ruling in the two cities. It is estimated that the cost of living for a family is much less in Sydney than in the eastern states of America, and even cheaper than is the case in California, though in both cities the rents are higher than in the suburbs of Chicago and New York.

The private wealth of California in 1890 reached to £223,146,318 ; whilst the value of real and personal property in New South Wales, amounted to £412,184,000, or nearly double. California stands fifth among the United States in the assessed valuation of its real and personal property, as New York, Pennsylvannia, Massachusets, and Ohio alone surpass it. The assessed value of property *per capita* in San Francisco was about £217, which was only excelled by the amounts from Boston, New York, and Providence, but the value per head in Sydney was about twice as much as in the other Pacific city.

It is stated that the true value of the property in the United States has not yet been ascertained by the census officials, but they estimate that it is about £200 for each man, woman, and child. Australian returns show even more satisfactory figures as to the wealth per inhabitant in the colonies. Mulhall estimates the wealth per inhabitant in New South Wales to be £440 against £350 in California ; so that the total value of land, cattle, railways, houses, furniture, merchandise, &c., is much greater in the Australian Colony than in the wealthiest of the American States. He also gives the following amounts per head for the various branches of wealth in New South Wales :—Land, £181 ; cattle, £25 ; railways, £27 ; houses, £92 ; furniture, £46 ; merchandise, £23 ; and sundries, £89.

Of the estimated value of the private wealth of New South Wales in 1890, amounting to £412,484,000, the amount for land, houses, and permanent improvements, was £303,152,000 ; for household furniture and personal property, £17,950,000 ; for live stock, £34,664,000 ; for coin and bullion, £9,726,000 ; for merchandise, £17,864,000 ; for shipping owned in the Colony £1,910,000 ; for mines and mining plant, £18,340,000 ; and for plant employed in agricultural, manufacturing, and other industries not elsewhere included, £8,878,000.

The estimated public and private wealth of New South Wales is represented in the items hereunder as amounting to £586,700,000 by its Government Statistician :—

Value of railways, tramways, telegraphs, waterworks, sewerage, and other revenue yielding works	£44,958,000
Value of works and buildings not directly revenue bearing	20,313,000
Amount due for lands purchased from State	13,224,000
Public lands leased, but not sold	94,400,000
	£172,895,000
Municipal property	6,400,000
Total, Public Wealth	£179,295,000
Land	173,352,000
Houses and Improvements	129,800,000
Other forms of Wealth	104,253,000
Total, Private Wealth	407,405,000
Total Public and Private Wealth	£586,700,000

The revenue and expenditure of New South Wales is much greater than that of California, owing to a large extent to the fact that many revenue-yielding undertakings are carried on by the Australian Government and not by private syndicates as in America. The revenue proper for New South Wales in 1891 amounted to £10,036,185 or £8 15s. 6d., per inhabitant. The construction in New South Wales of railways, tramways, telegraphs, sewerage, water supply, harbours, bridges, &c., has caused a public debt of over £50,000,000 sterling, whilst the public debt of California in 1890 was only £526,588, but the Colonial Government did not give large subsidies of money and grant free land to private railroad corporations along the lines as was done up to 1880 to the Union·Pacific and other companies amounting to about 200,000,000 acres. New South Wales could readily dispose of the railways, and other revenue-producing property for which the debt has been contracted in liquidation of the whole of the liability incurred, and still have the great part of its territory not only unalienated, but greatly improved by the construction of these works. It has been estimated that the people of New South Wales during the past ten years have invested £158,000,000 in the Colony, equal to £1,580,000 per annum or much more than the imported capital.

New South Wales possesses an abundant supply of sandstone, granite, bluestone, flagging, marble, limestone, slate, fire-clay, and brick and pottery clays, and its metropolis is much more favourably supplied with deposits of local materials for substantial buildings than San Francisco. Sydney itself stands upon the Hawkesbury formation which contains thick beds of sandstone, whence building stone of the finest quality is obtained, which has rendered the erection of a magnificent city with thousands of substantial buildings on the shores of Port Jackson comparatively easy. The buildings in San Francisco till late years were constructed principally of wood, but most of those recently erected of that material for private residences are of elegant design and highly ornamental. The stone, marble, and granite for the residences of the millionaires on Nob's Hill had to be brought by railways long distances from other States, so that the cost of their erection appears very high to an Australian. The sandstone for the first City Hall in San Francisco was brought from Sydney, but recently stone quarries have been opened up about 30 miles from San Francisco to obtain material for the new Technical University at Palo Alto, which has been built and endowed by Senator Stanford at a cost of several millions sterling.

Sydney has been called "the city of 100 bays," and San Francisco was once styled "the city of 100 hills." Many of the steep sand ridges on the site of the latter town, had, however, to be cut down, there being scarcely level space enough in 1849 for the presence of 500 people, where now there is room for 1,000,000. A large part of the business is now transacted where the sea once flowed ; as 20,000,000 cubic yards of earthy material were removed to fill in the water front. Although the people of Sydney are justly proud of their noble harbour, yet in comparison with the pioneers in San Francisco they have had to do comparatively little to make wharves at which large vessels can discharge. Mr. Consul Griffin wrote concerning Sydney : " The city has about 176 miles of streets, and about six miles of wharves. The Circular Quay has a length of 3,100 feet. There are about 25 miles of deep water frontage suitable for wharves. ' The public buildings, parks, and gardens will compare favourably with those of the most celebrated cities of Europe. The University is the first in the southern hemisphere. The streets and thoroughfares are always crowded, and it is said that the principal business streets, such as George, Pitt, York, King, Sussex, and others, have as heavy a traffic every year as any other streets in the world. The average number of vehicles passing George-street near the Town Hall every day of twelve hours is 10,960, and the estimated weight in tons daily passing over the road 20,470. There are about 21,000 houses, and no less than 65 miles of sewerage works in the city." The paving of streets with wooden blocks is becoming general in Sydney. These blocks are made of Australian ironbark which is much more effective for the purpose than the soft woods of America which have been tried but found unsuitable in San Francisco and other cities in the States.

There are three graving docks, four floating docks, and five patent slips in Port Jackson, and one of the graving docks is said to be the biggest single dock in the world and as will be seen by the model shown in the Chicago Exhibition is for vessels drawing up to 32 feet of water, so that the largest war-vessel can be readily refitted when required.

Sydney, the Queen city of the Pacific coast, is a spot where colonial historic recollections cluster, as the site was chosen for the first Australian settlement, and as it has been the cradle of colonisation in these southern climes. Although there are no ivy-mantled castles or old cathedral ruins like those in Europe to gaze upon, yet the inquirer will find in the vicinity of the city many spots of more than local interest, such for example as the place where Captain Cook first landed at Botany Bay. In Sydney originated many expeditions of discovery through the Australian Continent conducted by brave men, many of whom perished in the cause of science and through the desire to reveal the interior of the continent to their fellow men. The principal street is named after George III, whilst the second one in importance is called " Pitt " after the great Commoner. The work done by other British states- men, and many of the early governors is also commemorated by the names to be seen at many a street corner. The early settlers committed a great blunder in laying out Sydney, especially as they had not so many local difficulties to contend with as the pioneers in San Francisco, owing to the steep gradients of its surrounding hills and the want of a proper water front. The site of Sydney is as admirably fitted for the erection of a great metropolis on the eastern seaboard of Australia as San Francisco is on the western slope of

America, and these cities should be the commercial centres of both countries on the shores of the Pacific. Near Sydney there are not only excellent quarries of sandstone, but also deposits of fine clay for pottery, and forests of excellent hardwood. The magnificent stone structures in Sydney favourably contrast in extent with much fewer buildings found in San Francisco, for which stone and granite had to be brought from long distances. Over the Tank Stream, whose once sparkling waters led to the settlement of Sydney on its present site, there have been recently built immense Government and commercial offices at a cost of many millions sterling. The new Post Office recently erected is believed to be even superior to any building used for a similar purpose in the United States, and illustrates the commercial progress of the city when contrasted with the first building used for the delivery of the mails and the several edifices erected since for that purpose. Although the Town Hall in Sydney has not cost anything like the amount expended on the City Hall in San Francisco, the Centennial Hall is the largest meeting place for citizens in the British Empire, as it will comfortably seat 5,000 persons. Two blocks of Government offices in Bridge-street are like the administrative buildings in Washington, though built of solid sandstone instead of marble. There are several hotels recently constructed in Sydney on the design of the American Coffee Palaces, which for size, style, and comfort are not surpassed by the famous Palace Hotel in San Francisco. In the many beautiful villas which dot the foreshores of Sydney the visitor is reminded that the citizens are not absorbed in amassing wealth, but endeavour to enjoy in their leisure hours the beauties and comforts of well ordered homes. Port Jackson is acknowledged by travellers to be superior even to the magnificent port of San Francisco, "the city of the Golden Gate," and the fine harbour of New York, "the Empire City." Port Jackson stretches 15 miles in one direction and 9 miles in another, and contains 12 square miles of deep water. It resembles in some respects in its conformation the harbours of San Francisco and New York, but unlike them it has innumerable bays and inlets, none of which are more than 2 miles in width from one jutting point of land to another. Sydney harbour has been described as the finest in the world, and is said to be even more beautiful than that of Rio Janeiro, although the city is not backed up so closely with mountains as that famed South American port, which is too far away from the industrial heart of Brazil for a good administration, and a new capital has therefore to be sought for by that republic.

The foreign vessels entered and cleared in New South Wales in 1891 had the following tonnage :—Germany, 257,107 tons ; United States, 183,718 tons ; France, 173,751 tons ; Norway, 107,223 tons ; and Chili, Sweden, Japan, Denmark, Italy, Holland, Belgium, Hawaii, Austria, and Nicaragua a total of 69,830 tons.

The annual exports and imports of New South Wales according to statistics amount in value to about £13,000,000 more than those of California, but it is probable that some of the produce of the American State is not reckoned in the figures for the external trade, as a large proportion of the goods is carried overland by railroad to other states and not shipped to foreign countries by sea as is mainly done in the Australian Colony.

All the conditions necessary for the formation of a great manufacturing city are to be found in the neighbourhood of Sydney, especially as there is abundance of coal even in the formations under the metropolis itself. It has one of the finest fresh-water supplies in the world drawn from the Nepean River at the foot of the Blue Mountains range. It possesses

K

inexhaustible pastoral, agricultural, and mineral resources. It has a noble harbour and a central geographical position in Oceana. It needs, therefore, only enterprise on the part of its capitalists, and the proper technical training of its artisans to make it rank as one of the great manufacturing centres in the world. It is, however, not to be expected that at present many manufacturing industries can be conducted in an extensive territory possessing not much more than 1,000,000 inhabitants with so many other remunerative employments open to workmen. As large quantities of buggy and carriage materials are sent to Australia by American manufacturers, it is remarkable that they have no branch factory in Sydney to construct these parts in the wholesale way and after the finished style they are made in the United States, but no doubt workshops will be started under a system of intercolonial free trade, as when the Colonies are federated there should be a much larger market for all kinds of Colonial buggies.

The number of manufactories of all kinds in New South Wales in 1890 amounted to 2,583 employing 46,135 hands. In California 43,799 hands were engaged in the manufactories, a large proportion of whom were Chinamen, as they are not mainly engaged as in Sydney in cabinet-making, but are also at work in manufacturing clothes, boots, cigars, &c. During the last decennial period New South Wales has made much greater progress in manufactures than California, although the latter has had a protective policy and employs Chinamen to a much greater extent and in many more trades. In 1890, 1,245 sewing machines were run day and night by Chinese, and 300 Chinamen were employed at one bootmaking establishment in San Francisco. Of the 75,218 Chinamen in California some 20,000 live in San Francisco, and are chiefly engaged in domestic service and manufactories where they receive what is good pay to them, and live comfortably on three dollars a week.

It is claimed that " San Francisco is a great seaport as well as the chief centre of the railroad west of the Rocky Mountains. It has received the greatest part of the precious metals amounting to a value of £416,660,000 turned out by the mines of California and Nevada since 1848. The owners of many of the mines lived in San Francisco, which has consequently been enriched by their large returns. While the Comstock lode was in its most productive condition from 1871 to 1877, it possessed the most active of all stock markets. It has one-fifth of the population and one-third of the wealth of the coast, as well as most of the banking capital, rich mines, and railways. Amongst citizens it can count fifty millionaires. To it belongs in great part the manufactories of the slope, and it has the only sugar refineries, paint mills, glass works and glass furnaces, as well as the largest rolling mill, foundries, machine shops, woollen factories, and factories for the production of clothing, shoes, gloves, harness, cigars, furniture, carriages and wooden ware. The neighbourhood of the city is more thickly populated, and has a more valuable yield of agricultural produce relatively to area than any other part of the slope." San Francisco, it will be seen from this description by a local writer, is a splendid city; but the capital of New South Wales has surpassed it during the last decennial period in most particulars, as in a somewhat similar way the Golden Gate city distanced the progress of Sydney in previous decades.

Estimated by the annual value of its ratable property Sydney now stands as the second city in the British Empire, Melbourne ranking third, so that these Australian capitals now surpass in wealth many cities very much longer founded, and with larger populations.

During the last ten years the assessed value of property within the boundaries of the Sydney Municipal District has doubled, and the amount per head of population in 1890 was £457 11s. 2d. for Sydney against £217 8s. 9d. per head declared from the city assessment in San Francisco; which latter amount is 6s. less for that city than in 1880.

The capital value of property in Sydney in 1890 was £51,237,600 against £50,170,756 in San Francisco. The annual value of property in Sydney was rated at £2,710,488, and in San Francisco at £1,076,176.

Considering the improvements made in San Francisco it is remarkable that the value placed on property by municipal assessors shows no increase during the past decade, although furniture as well as the building is taxed only in the Californian city; but it is improbable that the same rate of increase in the capital of New South Wales will be maintained during the next decennial period.

The capital value of property in Sydney in 1891 was £55,716,900, and the annual value £2,785,846. The capital value of the property in the suburbs of Sydney was £51,174,200, and the annual value £2,704,876. The capital value of property in country municipalities was £37,386,300, and the annual value £2,438,776. The total capital value of incorporated boroughs and municipalities is, therefore, £144,277,400, of the annual value of £7,929,498. There is only a small part of New South Wales now under municipal institutions; but the new Local Government Bill will render incorporation compulsory throughout the Colony, when, of course, the total amounts for assessment by rates will be much larger than at present.

Owing to the value of land having so largely increased in Sydney numbers of persons have removed to the suburbs to make room for many magnificent warehouses and commodious offices erected to replace the buildings constructed in the early days of the Colony, and consequently the increase in population in the city proper has only been from 106,580 in 1881 to 109,090 in 1891, although during the middle years of the decade the number of residents was considerably higher.

Several substantial public buildings have been recently erected or added to in Sydney, such as the Lands Office, costing £200,000; the General Post-office, costing £303,000; the offices of the Colonial Secretary and Secretary for Public Works, costing about £129,000; the Australian Museum, the recent additions to which alone cost £24,909; the Sydney University, of which the new Medical School alone cost nearly £70,000; and the Public Library, recent additions to which cost £43,000; and the Sydney Technical College, Technological Museum, and High School involving an expenditure of over £60,000.

There are £3,000,000 more in deposits in the banks of New South Wales than there are in the banks of California, notwithstanding that the latter institutions receive the great proportion of the monetary wealth of the whole of the Pacific Slope, and are noted for the enterprise with which they are managed.

In 1890 there were 2,263 miles of railroads in New South Wales and 4,250 miles in California. The lines of railways have increased during the last decennial period in New South Wales by 1,187 miles, and in California by 2,030 miles; so that construction has been greater than the increase in population in both countries, and the American State has built 843 more miles than even in the Australian Colony, although the people of the latter have been accused by financial critics of prematurely making too many lines.

There is a cable system over the heavy gradients in San Francisco not equalled elsewhere, which has been copied in Melbourne, where the streets are wide, and on the North Shore, near Sydney, over a steep gradient, but nothing near as great as those which have to be surmounted in the American city, whose extensive tram system is greatly admired by every visitor.

Kearney-street, in San Francisco, was widened from 45 feet 5 inches to 75 feet, at a cost of £120,000, by removing back all the buildings, which caused an addition in the value of property in two years of £800,000. It would be a good thing if some of the narrow streets in Sydney were treated in a similar manner, as the municipal authorities have paid much more attention to sanitary improvements than the removal of encroachments to the thoroughfares. The Australian in America is surprised at the facility with which substantial houses are removed from one place to another, or the manner in which buildings are raised by jack-screws, so that a story is placed under the original ground floor, and the removal of the roof obviated, with but slight interference to business. It is claimed that Market-street in San Francisco is perhaps the most impressive business street in the civilised world, but although the main street in Sydney in width and length cannot compete with that of San Francisco, yet in many ways it is more attractive, as on it are several churches, banks, and warehouses, which are not equalled by those to be found in the chief city of California.

Shortly after the foundation of New South Wales, a few cattle escaped from the small herds brought out from England, and increasing in their hiding place, became the nucleus of the live stock of the Colony. The horned cattle of New South Wales number 2,046,000, nearly two and a half times as many head as were returned for California.

Sheep-farming was introduced into New South Wales by Captain James Macarthur, and an illegal importation of pure Spanish merinoes from the flocks of George III, greatly helped an industry which has made Australia the true grower of the golden fleece, and the supplier of the greater part of the wool used in the manufactories of Great Britain. The sheep of New South Wales alone now number 61,831,416, being more than ten times as many as there are to be found in California, where the pastoral industry is being supplanted by agricultural settlement. Sheep have more than doubled during the last twenty years in New South Wales, whilst in California, there has been a large decrease. The product of wool in the Colony in the year 1891 amounted to 331,887,720 lb., of the estimated value of £11,036,018, whilst the produce of California, in 1890, was only 34,854,000 lb. Notwithstanding that many millions of rabbits eat much of the grass on the pastoral runs the number of sheep in New South Wales at the end of 1891, was 61,831,416, an increase on the previous year of 5,844,985. The proportion of sheep in Australasia was in New South Wales, 49·1 ; in Victoria, 11·1 ; in Queensland, 15·8 ; in South Australia, 6·1 ; in Western Australia, 2·2 ; in Tasmania, 1·4 ; in New Zealand, 14·3.

The total number of merino sheep in New South Wales was as follows :— Combing, 42.719,169 ; clothing, 17,533,291 ; long wooled and cross-bred sheep, 641,152 ; and crosses long wool with merinoes principally, 937,806;— of which the sexes and classes were : Rams, 975,548 ; ewes, 27,694,837 ;

wethers, 7,664,562; lambs, 15,496,469. In 1888 of the 216 pure-bred sheep introduced into the Colony, there were 178 American merinoes, and Mr. Alexander Bruce, the Chief Inspector of Stock, has recently reported favourably on the results of these importations.

There are 459,755 horses in New South Wales against 250,000 in California; and there is a great demand for "Walers" in India and other tropical countries owing to their being found able to endure the heat better than horses from cold climates.

The tallow shipped in 1891 amounted in value to £304,599, as when sheep are unsaleable they are boiled down for the fat, which sometimes gives a better return than when sold as meat in the local market.

The only kind of live stock in which the American State surpasses that in the British Colony is in the number of hogs, there being 400,000 in California, and 253,189 in New South Wales.

New South Wales and California possess mineral wealth of the most extensive and prolific kind exceeding that of similar settlements in either America or Australia, and it is noticeable that in each the precious metals and the most useful minerals occur in great abundance. Although California has produced a much larger quantity of gold than New South Wales, the rich deposits of silver, tin, copper, iron, and the extensive and easy worked carboniferous formations of the latter which contain the best coal render it more fitted for the extension of manufacturing industries.

The total value of the output of gold and silver in California was more than in New South Wales, but the product of economic minerals, such as coal, kerosene shale, and tin, is much larger in the British Colony, and large quantities of them are exported to San Francisco, for the use of American manufacturers.

The decennial value of minerals mined in New South Wales during the ten years ending 1841, was £81,275; ending 1851, £634,937; ending 1861, £14,276,687; ending 1871, £16,638,574; ending 1881, £23,441,890; ending 1891, £38,459,650.

Although the late Rev. W. B. Clarke discovered gold in New South Wales in 1841, at the request of the Government he forebore publicly announcing his discovery for fear of an injurious effect upon a penal settlement. On 3rd April, 1851, Mr. Edward Hargraves, who had been prospecting for nearly two months after his return from California, in a letter to the Colonial Secretary offered "to point out localities in which he had discovered gold in formations which resembled those he had worked in the Sacramento Valley." The formations in which gold is generally found extend over 70,000 square miles or a fourth of the Colony.

Mr. Harrie Wood, Under Secretary for Mines, says, in the last report of the Mining Department, with regard to the proper development of gold-mining in New South Wales: "When account is taken of the number of mines standing idle because we do not know how to treat the ore, and the value of the metals that are wasted in the treatment of ores through absence of the knowledge of the methods by which such metals could be profitably saved, some idea might be formed of the amount which our output of minerals might under favourable circumstances be reasonably expected to reach. There can I venture to think be little doubt that we stand in need of instruction in regard to the treatment of some of our ores, but there is much difference of opinion as to how that instruction is to be secured, if it can be secured at all. I regret to say no effective and economical method of treating our pyritous gold ores has yet been brought into general use, nor have we yet brought water to bear on any extensive scale upon the large auriferous deposits found to exist along some of our river banks. I may be unduly sanguine, but I cannot help thinking that if we were in a position to treat our auriferous deposits by the best methods our present output of gold should largely exceed the yields of the early years of our gold-fields, and that gold-mining if so conducted as to avoid the waste which occurs under our present mode of working would become so profitable as to attract all the capital necessary to develop it."

The aggregate value of the mineral products of New South Wales to the end of 1891 amounted to £86,760,768, the value of such products for 1891 was £6,395,561, being an increase of £1,391,658 upon the value of minerals raised in 1890. The total value of following minerals exported to the end of 1891 was: antimony, £115,798; bismuth, £36,641; oxide of iron and pig-iron, £2,647; zinc spelter, £5,988; limestone flux, £107,346; alumite, £4,888; manganese ore, £665; opals, £15,600; cobalt, £470; fire-clay, £55; lime, £958; marble, £2,577; building stone, £5,205; ballast stone, £713; grindstone, £311; slates, £351; sundry minerals, £54,683.

The number of miners employed in New South Wales, is 32,338, being much larger than the number in any of the Pacific States and territories, with the exception of California and Colorado, the two great mining centres for gold and silver, which have about 37,000 and 35,000 respectively. A lease to mine for gold is 20s. per acre per annum, and for silver 5s., and for authority to dig 10s. is charged to each miner of alluvial deposits or quartz reefs. The area in which metals and minerals are found in New South Wales is as follows:—Gold, 7,000 square miles; coal, 24,000 square miles; silver, 10,000 square miles; copper, 6,000 square miles; tin, 4,000 square miles; total about 110,000 square miles. The area of the Colony is 310,000 square miles, and including other minerals not mentioned two-fifths of the entire Colony is of a mineral-bearing character. The total amount of mineral production in New South Wales amounted to £86,760,768. Up to the end of 1891 the value of minerals raised in the Colony were gold, £38,633,488; silver (silver, silver lead bullion, silver and silver lead ore), £11,302,095; tin, £5,675,663; copper, £3,481,923; coal, £25,800,041; shale, £1,416,712, and other minerals, £441,846.

The total value of the gold produced in New South Wales amounted to £38,633,488, against £270,844,444 in California, and £342,031,743 for the whole of the Australasian Colonies. The amount of gold produced in New South Wales for 1891 was 153,336 ounces valued at £558,306, whilst the output in California amounted to £2,520,000, or nearly five times as much. If the extensive gold-bearing reefs of New South Wales had received a tithe of the intelligent development bestowed on similiar formations in California, there is little doubt that the result would be found more in favour of the mines of the Colony.

Professor David, of the Sydney University, in a recent lecture, said it was improbable that many at any rate of the alluvially worked gold-fields had remained undiscovered in New South Wales, but with increase of scientific knowledge and skill, not only would the yield of many of their mines which were now being worked increase, but hundreds of mines now abandoned would be reopened.

The wages accepted by gold-miners in New South Wales is about £2 10s. per week. Although the rate of wages is not the same for the Australian as for the Californian miner, yet in the Colony the hours of labour and the cost of living are not so great as in the State. Numbers of Chinamen obtain a living at alluvial or "placer" mining in both countries.

Although the total yield of gold in Australasia, since the opening of the mines in 1851 has not been so large as that of the United States since the discovery of gold in California, yet the value of gold and silver obtained in the colonies in 1890 was £8,869,906 against £4,166,666 for the precious metals mined in California. The modern system of gold-mining, both in Australasia and in the United States, is greatly changed, owing to its now requiring a large amount of both skill and capital to work the alluvial and rock deposits, as the old "placer" diggings are becoming extinct. There would be a good opening in New South Wales for those capitalists in Californian hydraulic mining whose operations have been suppressed by recent judicial decisions in that State. Mount Morgan, in Queensland, "a mountain of gold," returned 3 to 12 oz. of gold to the ton, and has half a million tons of ore at the mine, accessible for treating. It is considered the richest gold-mine in the world, as over 60,000,000 oz. of gold from it have been found to assay 99⅒ per cent. of gold, and the remaining three-tenths was copper with a trace of iron, so that it is the richest native gold hitherto found. The mine has sometimes given yearly more than a million sterling beyond the cost of its working, although the gold is so finely distributed in the earth and rocks as to be seldom seen by the naked eye.

In the gold-drifts in various parts of New South Wales small grains of platinum have been found, but it has long been known that it occurs in the beach sand on the north coast between the Richmond and the Tweed. Platinum has recently been found in a lode formation near Broken Hill, and assays show that it is present in lodestuff up to 1 oz. per ton. In the gold-bearing veins in the Silurian, Devonian, and granite formations, ores of lead, especially of galena, are frequently found. Sometimes the ores are contained in matrices of fluorspar and barytes.

The quantity of silver and silver lead ore exported from New South Wales to end of 1891 was valued at £11,302,095, of which £3,484,739 worth was mined in the latter year. The total quantity of silver produced in California amounted to £5,416,666, being less by one-half the output in New South Wales.

The output of silver in California in 1891 amounted to only £193,939 whilst the output for New South Wales was £3,619,589, or nearly twenty times as much. Although the gold production has been much greater in the American State, the silver output is much less than the Australian Colony. Notwithstanding many of the silver mines in New South Wales were idle owing to the difficulty of treating the ore, the value of the export of silver and lead for the year 1891 exceeded that of any previous year, and exceeds that of 1890 by £857,035. With a full knowledge of the treatment of every variety of argentiferous ore there can be no doubt that the output from the silver mines might be greatly augmented. The quantity of ore raised in the Broken Hill and Silverton district during 1891 was 471,101 tons valued at £3,960,676. During the year the Sunny Corner Co. raised 35,270 tons of ore and smelted 39,046 tons, which produced 404,006 oz. of silver, 4,048 oz. of gold, 344 tons of copper, and 25 tons of lead, total value £104,565, leaving 10,847 tons of calcined ore at grass, valued at £7,300. At the old Nevada Mine 1,700 tons of ore were raised of which 1,020 tons were sent to Lithgow for treatment, and 680 tons were smelted at the mines, producing 110 tons of copper matte valued at £3,080.

Antimony to the value of £115,798 has been mined in New South Wales, but as there is at present but little commercial call for this mineral it has obtained scant attention from the miners. There is a large quantity of ore ready for mining in the antimony lodes, but the result from a shipment last year was not satisfactory, owing to the low price in the market. The ore, which is enclosed in a quartz matrix, consists of oxide and sulphide of antimony, and occurs in regular bunches at times of considerable size.

Tin to the value of £271,412 was exported from New South Wales in 1891, of which £75,395 worth went to the United States, and there has been a steady annual export to that country, as very little is mined there. The tin-mining industry in New South Wales is a very important one, as although tin has only been mined during the last sixteen years, there was a total production up the end of 1891 of the value of £5,675,663, and during that year there was an output valued at £133,963.

Working of the numberless copper lodes in New South Wales has been recently much retarded by the low price ruling for that metal. The total value of copper ore raised in New South Wales alone up to the end of the year 1891 amounted to £3,481,923 ; but the output in 1891 only reached a value of £119,195, owing to the low price of the mineral, through the large output in some of the United States.

The vast and easily accessible carboniferous deposits in New South Wales are elements of commercial and manufacturing greatness far superior both in certainty and value to the possession of the largest auriferous tracts. From the strata of New South Wales there has been already mined coal to the value of £25,809,041, and during the year 1890 the colony produced 3,060,876 tons, valued at £1,279,089, being a much greater amount than obtained from the mines of California. The principal customers for New South Wales coal are Victoria, California, South Australia, Hong Kong, China, Java, and Singapore, the United States alone taking 182,692 tons, valued at £102,205. In his work on the " Sedimentary Formations of New South Wales," the late Rev. W. B. Clarke has proved by the fossils found in its coal-measures that these seams are of the highest commercial value. The output of coal for 1891 was of the value of £1,742,795, and exceeds that of 1890 by 977,053 tons in quantity and £463,707 in value. During the year the exports to intercolonial and foreign ports, and the home consumption also show a satisfactory increase. The exports to intercolonial ports and the home consumption were larger than in any previous year.

The area of the coal-measures in New South Wales is about 23,950 miles, which are mined by ninety-six collieries employing 10,820 miners. The native kerosene shales are nearly as good as the American article, and are procured at about the same cost.

There are in New South Wales several magnificent limestone caves, which rival in beauty and extent of chambers abounding in stalagmites and stalactites the far-famed underground caves of Kentucky. Other large deposits of lime have not yet been brought into requisition for agricultural purposes in the same way as is done on the farms in England.

There were 56,010 tons of kerosene shale mined in New South Wales, in 1890, of the value of £104,103, the greatest part of which was shipped to the Netherlands, Spain, Italy, Brazil, the United States, India, and other countries for the purpose of enriching gas, as Dr. Heisch states that the gas-producing power of the Joadja mineral is extraordinary. Seams of petroleum oil, cannel coal, or kerosene shale occur in the coal-measures in several districts widely apart. The shale yields on an average about 115 gallons of crude oil which contains over 60 per cent. of fine kerosene oil, and its gas producing capabilities amount to over 80,000 cubic feet of gas with an illuminative power of from thirty-eight to forty candles. The export of kerosene shale from New South Wales in 1891 was 34,652 tons, of the value of £101,288, of which 2,571 tons, of value of £7,437, were sent to the United States.

Zinc ores are known to exist in various localities in New South Wales, but they have not yet been commercially worked. In the Broken Hill district, for example, the great silver-lead lodes pass into argentiferous zincs below the water level. In all probability, before long, the zinc will be conserved instead of being eliminated, as is done at present. The value of the zinc is twice that of the lead with which it is associated, and zinc production will be added to the industries of this important district.

Although attempts to work the cobaltiferous manganese oxide in the Port Macquarie and Bungonia districts have been without success, a most important discovery of cobalt ore has been recently made near Carcoar on the great western railroad, and the developments of these deposits are very promising. The great increase in the value of tungsten ores has lately brought them into notice. No deposits of nickel have been found in New South Wales, but traces of oxide of nickel occur.

New South Wales takes the lead of all the other colonies in the production of minerals, with the exception of gold, and besides silver, tin, copper and coal, it has a number of other minerals, such as titanium, wolfram, molybdeum, cobalt, manganese, sulphur, arsenic, antimony, bismuth, graphite, &c., some of which are now being worked. Chromic iron and manganese ores have been found in considerable quantities, but as yet it has not been found possible to work them profitably. Many thousand tons of chromic-iron ore, salt, and borax are shipped from California, but similar deposits are not yet worked in New South Wales.

New South Wales may be divided into three regions, viz., the coastal district which contains the river valleys well known as rich lands, whose fertility is traceable to the alluvial soils and rich deposits brought down from the mountain sides by the mountain streams ; the table-lands, 2,000 to 4,000 feet above the sea, where are found the best wheat-growing lands ; and the great plains with a small rainfall and a soil once thought only fitted for pastoral purposes. These sparsely-populated districts, however, cover a geological formation which is a reservoir of underground water, and if artificial wells were made to tap this supply these plains could be made as fertile as irrigated California and Utah, and the home of a large population. The present Land Act is framed on lines of great liberality, and agricultural land may be taken up on the payment of a deposit of 2s. per acre, and pastoral lands on still easier terms. Large areas of agricultural land, temporarily leased to the squatters for pastoral purposes, will no doubt be thrown open for selection in a few years, and a good opportunity thus afforded to those desirous of becoming farmers, and obtaining homesteads like those in the United States, under the law signed by Abraham Lincoln.

New South Wales is divided, according to its natural features, into the Eastern, Central, and Western Divisions, and land is obtainable as follows :—
(1.) By a free selection before survey in the eastern and central divisions, at the rate of £1 per acre, payable under a system of deferred payment; in the eastern division the minimum area to be selected is 40 acres, and the

maximum 640 acres; in the central the maximum is 2,560 acres. (2). By additional purchases of the same areas, and under like conditions, after the completion of the conditions of residence upon the original selection. (3.) By purchasing at double the price above mentioned, without the condition of residence, the maximum area being 320 acres. Government land is also sold at auction, the upset price being £8 per acre for town, £2 10s. for suburban, and £1 5s. for country lots. The area sold is not to exceed 200,000 acres annually, and the maximum area is 640 acres. The total land alienated, or in process of alienation, at the end of 1891 was 45,731,964 acres; the total of land under lease was 132,425,623 acres. The Central Division, which contains some of the best agricultural land, is at present principally a sheep walk, but there is no doubt that when the present leases to the pastoral tenants expire in a few years time much of these areas will be devoted to the purpose of tilling. Along the Darling River, from Bourke to the Murray River, there are enormous tracts of grain country of excellent alluvial soil. Unquestionably, in fairly moist seasons, good crops could be raised without irrigation, and with irrigation of course any cereal crop could be grown. New South Wales has immense agricultural resources, nevertheless the culture of the soil has been almost neglected in favour of other industries not requiring so much persistence.

The mountain and western districts of New South Wales contain an area of 44,800,000 acres, eight-tenths of which is capable of growing some crop or other. The northern table-lands contain tracts of the richest volcanic soils in the world. The wheat-fields of Tenterfield produce as much as 40 bushels per acre of splendid grain. Inverell is one of the richest agricultural centres in the world, with a vast expanse of deep chocolate loam of volcanic origin. There is in the Bathurst and Mudgee districts a vast area suited for agriculture, and extremely fertile chocolate soil in the basaltic formations of Orange. In the southern table-lands there are not only agricultural resources, but also immense stores of coal, gold, silver, copper, tin, antimony and diamonds, as well as an abundant supply of timber. The whole region is below the snow-line. This is a decided advantage to the growth of crops and the rearing of sheep and cattle, though perhaps not so fortunate as far as the conservation of water is concerned, and for carrying out schemes of irrigation. Although New South Wales has occasionally harassing droughts yet these are nothing to be compared with the disastrous tornadoes or blizzards and droughts with which the American farmer has to contend.

It is estimated that out of a total area of 195,882,150 acres in New South Wales not more than 5,000,000 acres are totally unfit for cultivation or occupation, so there is ample room for the farmer under somewhat similar homestead laws to those obtaining in the United States, excepting those applying to desert or irrigated lands which should now be adopted in the Australian Colony.

Owing to the expense of carriage agriculture has not received proper development in New South Wales; but the great lines of railway now being formed will afford, as in California, cheap and expeditious transport for produce. Statistics for 1892 show that in New South Wales there was grown of wheat, 3,963,668 bushels; of barley, 93,446 bushels; of oats, 276,259 bushels; of maize, 5,721,706 bushels; of potatoes, 62,283 tons; and of hay, 209,417 tons.

Large numbers of American agricultural implements are used in Australia, but there are many excellent local makers of machines which are perfected so as to be adapted to meet colonial requirements.

There has happily not been the same litigation over land titles owing to conflicting grants in New South Wales as over the Mexican grants in California, and it would be, therefore, a good thing if the provisions of Torrens' Real Property Act, of which a South Australian colonist was the author, were adopted by Californians so as to settle conflicting claims and to facilitate the transfer of land.

In 1890 the number of acres under wheat in New South Wales was 333,233 against 2,427,008 acres in California, so that there should be a much better opening for the farmer in the former place. As in all new countries the soil of New South Wales had to be analysed and experimented upon to ascertain its suitability for various kinds of crop, and it has been found that nearly every product of other lands could be readily grown there.

There are in New South Wales about 25,000,000 acres capable of producing annually without irrigation 10 bushels of wheat per acre. This would give a yield of 250,000,000 bushels per year, of a value at the rate of 3s. per bushel, of £37,500,000 sterling. In good seasons there would be, perhaps, twice this area capable of growing wheat. The acreage under wheat in 1891 was 356,666 acres, and the production, 3,963,668 bushels, or an average yield of 11·11 bushels per acre, or of the gross value of £827,073, which is not a fifth of the value of the Californian yield from the much larger area under cultivation. Last season little short of 4,000,000 bushels of wheat were produced, but at the rate of 6½ bushels per head, which is the average consumption in New South Wales, almost an equal amount of imported wheat was needed to supply the requirements of the people. Owing to the favourable season there will be a good wheat harvest in New South Wales in 1892, and it will have nearly sufficient grain for its own requirements, and thus save from half to three-quarters of a million sterling, the average annual payment to its neighbours for wheat and flour. There is an excellent opening for an extensive production of this cereal such as is pursued on the great prairies of America, and large tracts of similar land could be now utilised for that purpose on the plains of Riverina, which is destined to be the future granary of New South Wales and perhaps of Australia.

Maize or Indian corn, although cultivated to a much greater extent in New South Wales than in California, is not as acceptable as an article of diet to Australians as it is to Americans. Australian maize obtained the first prize at the Philadelphia Exhibition of 1876, so that it must have been superior to the domestic article, although America is famous for her Indian corn which is indigenous to the country.

The cultivation of oats is greatly neglected in New South Wales as only 25 per cent. of the amount consumed is produced in the Colony, and a large supply has consequently to be obtained from New Zealand, but the duty on agricultural produce in the new tariff has interfered with this trade and will no doubt stimulate local growing. In 1892 there were only 12,958 acres of oats under crop which produced 276,259 bushels, or an average yield per acre of 21·32 bushels. Oat-growing is carried on to a much greater extent in California, where 1,943,000 bushels of the value of £226,666 were produced.

The number of sugar manufactories in New South Wales in 1890 was 33. The quantity of sugar produced was 530,660 cwt., and of molasses, 1,074,080 gals. from 20,446 acres of cane under cultivation on the northern rivers by white labour. Returns show that the cane grown in the Colony produced 59,433,920 lb. of sugar against 9,000,000 lb. obtained from beet grown in California.

It was believed that the Corinth vine had not proved a success anywhere except in the Morea and Ionian Islands, but the currants grown in Australia and shown at the Colonial and Indian Exhibition were of such good quality that they could hold their own with any imported into England. The dessert raisins, zante currants, and sultana raisins displayed in the South Australian Court compared very favourably with the best qualities usually sent to England. At the Mildura Irrigation Settlement the trees of the muscat, gordon, and zante currant have a surprising display of fruit, and very good samples have been already obtained by the settlers.

There is a direct communication from New South Wales by subsidised mailships not only with England, but also with France, Germany, and America, and for the warm weather in the northern hemisphere when large quantities of fruit are consumed oranges and lemons could be easily shipped from Port Jackson as most of the orangeries are in the vicinity of Sydney, and the supply greatly exceeds the local demand, so that there is a large surplus available for exportation.

Mr. Griggs who has had many years experience in the Californian irrigation colonies says: "In Mildura the land is given to the settlers, £21 an acre is a mere nothing when the return is considered. In California such land would readily sell at £100 per acre. The future of Mildura is the surest thing in the world. There is no better climate in the world for grape-growing." The exhibits of local products at the last Horticultural Show at Mildura comprised apples, pears, peaches, apricots, quinces, lemons, passion fruit, gooseberries, figs, grapes, currants, almonds, melons, tomatoes, potatoes, onions, pumpkins, squashes, vegetable marrows, cucumbers, mangroves, beet, parsnips, carrots, scorzonera, kohlrabi, ukra, sweet corn, peas, leeks, garlic, wheat, barley, oats, rye, maize, millet, broom corn, and lucerne.

It is stated that on Australian irrigation farms wine vines when fully grown should produce from 300 to 400 gallons an acre. Instances of 1,500 gallons per acre are recorded. Orange groves give returns of from £50 to £200 an acre. Other fruits are estimated to give a yield to the value of from £25 to £50 per acre. From a quarter of an acre Mr. C. Trevatt, gathered over £40 worth of strawberries, and he also received £1 per tree for nectarines.

The excellence of the native wines proves that New South Wales, like California, is admirably suited for the cultivation of the vine, and the wines of the Australian Colony were classed by the most competent judges in the high category of "Grands vins" at the Bordeaux Exhibition in competition with the best American wines. About 913,107 gallons of wine were made in New South Wales during the year 1891, but this industry has secured a far greater development in the American State which produced 14,626,000 gallons. An expert in the new system of fermentation of wine on the French plan so as to improve and secure a greater uniformity in the quality, after visiting California, is under an engagement with an Australian vigneron. Many medals for wine were also obtained by the Australian colonies at the exhibitions in London of 1864 and 1884. A large amount of capital has been invested in the Australian colonies in grape culture, and the vineyards produce wine with qualities sufficiently pronounced to cause them to find favour in foreign markets. The heavy wines produced hitherto, such as sherry, port, and Madeira, which were growing out of favour in Europe, have been added to by the growth of light wines.

The great variety of fruits to be found in the Californian markets are also grown in New South Wales, whilst it much resembles the American state in the cultivation of that golden fruit, the orange. In 1890 there were 11,288 acres under cultivation for this fruit, yielding 11,562,000 dozen, or about 1,330 dozen per acre; but 3,000 dozen can be obtained from fair sized trees in full bearing in the Parramatta district.

Australians would do well to imitate the example of Californians in utilising more the water of the rivers for agricultural purposes. Two irrigation colonies have been formed on Victorian and South Australian sides of the Murray River by Messrs. Chaffey Bros. guided by their American experience, but in 1890 only 23,106 acres were returned as under irrigation in New South Wales.

The area under orchards and gardens in New South Wales amounted to 28,746 acres, in vines 8,281 acres, and in orangeries 11,370 acres, so that a considerable quantity of fruit is grown for domestic consumption; but it is hoped, by the extension of artificial irrigation and the adoption of cool chambers for preserving fruit on long voyages, that increasing shipments to foreign markets will be made, especially as the necessary steps are now being taken by the Australian Governments and many private companies, so that the favourable climatic seasons of Australia over those of other countries may be better utilised in supplying the fruit requirements of European and American markets.

The trade of New South Wales has been more profitable than that of any other Australian settlement, as owing to its great variety of climate it occupies the premier position in production, and after supplying its own people it has yearly a large surplus of products for export to other countries; so that it is hoped that more interchange of commodities will result from the display of its products at the Chicago Exposition.

The Pacific States of America and the Pacific Colonies of Australia now especially afford points of resemblance in their configuration, history, and resources; and the Chicago Exhibition renders opportune a comparison between their progress in the last decennial period, which has been greater than during any previous decade.

California, the wealthiest state in the Union, and New South Wales, the oldest and richest of the Australian Colonies, may be said to be opposite each other on the shores of the Pacific Ocean, and their history, population, climate, mineral, pastoral, and agricultural wealth present many features which can be specially contrasted more readily than with any other settlements of the American or Australian continents. In endeavouring to make a comparison between the various settlements in North America and Australasia, it has been found necessary to use any recent statistics that could be obtained; but the returns for the countries in North America were not procurable in as complete a form as those for the Australasian colonies, which have permanent Statisticians appointed by the several Governments. The figures for the primary industries in the following table are for New South Wales in 1890 and California in 1887, but the prices of the live stock have been calculated at the same rate in both countries, in order to obtain as near as possible a correct estimate of the annual production from the pastoral industry in the American State.

STATISTICS of New South Wales and California.

	New South Wales	California.
Production in Primary Industries ... ... £	26,725,700	26,069,224
Do Pastoral Industry ... ... £	13,359,800	2,909,474
Do Agricultural do ... ... £	4,131,400	14,116,000
Do Dairying do ... ... £	2,887,000	1,815,000
Do Mining do ... ... £	5,003,900	4,809,750
Do Forestry, &c. do ... ... £	1,343,000	2,420,000
Extent—Square miles	310,700	155,980
Population—Census 1891 and 1890	1,132,234	1,208,130
Do Increase, 1880-90	380,706	343,444
Do Principal town	383,386	233,959
Exports ... . £	22,045,937	20,833,333
Imports ... . £	22,615,004	10,612,181
Deposits in Banks ... ... £	40,390,159	37,294,207
Private wealth—Real and personal property ... £	412,494,000	223,146,318
Wealth per inhabitant (Mulhall's estimate)... ... £	440	350
Capital value of property in principal town... ... £	51,237,600	50,170,756
Annual assessment „ „ „ ... ... £	2,710,488	1,076,176
Wool exported—lbs.	631,887,720	34,854,000
Public School expenditure ... ... £	704,260	1,080,658
Do pupils	195,241	221,756
Gold—Total output ... ... £	38,633,478	270,844,444
Silver, &c. „ ... ... £	11,302,095	5,416,666
Copper „ ... ... £	6,023,431	Not given.
Coal „ ... ... £	25,809,040	„
Tin „ ... ... £	9,526,796	„
Railroads—Miles	2,263	4,250
Sheep—No.	61,831,416	6,000,000
Cattle „	2,046,347	850,000
Horses „	450,755	250,000
Swine „	253,189	400,000
Manufactories—Hands employed	46,135	43,799
Post Offices	1,338	1,368
Wheat—Bushels	3,963,668	29,121,000
Maize „	5,721,706	4,396,000
Oats „	276,259	1,943,000
Wine—Gallons	913,107	14,026,000
Sugar—lbs.	59,433,920	9,000,000
Urban population	516,019	495,086
Chinese	14,156	75,218
Aborigines	8,280	15,283
Population of chief town	380,040	298,907
Do Increase, 1880-90	159,175	55,038
Public debt—Colony or State ... ... £	51,010,433	526,588
Municipal debt ... ... £	1,628,203	1,100,275
Do Sydney and San Francisco ... ... £	710,000	375,258

STATISTICS of Australasia and Canada, 1890.

	Australasia.	Canada.
Area—Square miles	3,161,457	3,456,483
Do Density of population—Square mile	1·21	1·45
Population—Census, 1891	3,809,895	4,829,411
Do Increase, 1881-91	1,067,345	504,601
Do do per annum	3·34	1·10
Revenue ... £	29,922,897	8,308,318
Expenditure £	31,035,390	7,498,757
Debt (Net) £	190,947,813	49,483,585
Imports £	68,001,986	25,387,133
Exports ... £	64,799,178	20,156,072
Do Domestic Produce £	49,288,882	17,761,997
Imports from United Kingdom £	28,163,348	9,062,855
Exports to United Kingdom £	28,200,563	10,073,686
Tonnage entered and cleared £	15,542,248	10,328,285
Deposits in Banks of Issue £	111,015,162	28,372,398
Do Savings' Banks £	17,873,888	4,581,386
Do do per head of population £	37 0s. 0d.	0 17s. 8d.
Annual accumulation 1861-88 (Mulhall's estimate) £	17 10s. 0d.	5 10s. 0d.
National earnings, per head ,, £	2 2s. 0d.	1 6s. 0d.
Wealth—(Mulhall's estimate)—1888.		
Land £	533,000,000	282,000,000
Cattle £	104,000,000	80,000,000
Houses £	239,000,000	127,000,000
Furniture £	120,000,000	64,000,000
Railways £	94,000,000	151,000,000
Ships £	1,000,000	6,000,000
Merchandise £	65,000,000	21,000,000
Bullion £	24,000,000	4,000,000
Sundries £	193,000,000	245,000,000
£	1,373,000,000	980,000,000
Per inhabitant £	370	196
Railways—		
Passengers carried	103,191,359	12,821,262
Merchandise carried—Tons	12,632,011	20,787,409
Miles open for traffic	11,990	14,004
Capital cost £	113,768,038	163,843,294
Receipts £	9,694,748	9,759,130
Expenses £	6,265,869	6,856,948
Net Profits £	3,428,879	2,903,015
Net return on Capital	3·01	1·77
Population per miles of line	316	370
Emigrants from United Kingdom, 1815 to 1889	1,663,389	1,987,247
Public Schools—Expenditure £	1,984,063	1,868,934
Do Pupils attending	832,898	998,823
Wool exported £	20,349,300	49,097
Wheat crop—Bushels	82,830,505	40,527,562
Mineral Products—Value of Annual £	12,262,934	3,958,333
Post Offices—Revenue £	1,256,774	671,586
Do Letters, &c., per head	46	21·91
Telegraph lines—Miles of wire	86,012	66,453
Do Messages sent	13,112,830	4,231,958
Public Works—Expenditure on £	10,536,634	2,126,140

STATISTICS of four Pacific Colonies and four Pacific States, 1890.

		New South Wales, Victoria, Queensland, and South Australia.	California, Colorado, Nevada, and Oregon.
Wealth per inhabitant (Mulhall's estimate)		£390 15s.	£222 10s.
Population—Increase, 1870-1880		565,965	562,662
Do do 1881-1891		884,731	682,446
Do	1870	1,541,239	733,525
	1880	2,107,204	1,269,187
	1890	2,986,788	1,978,633
Maize—Acres...	1880	271,557	100,905
	1890	300,900	210,000
Wheat „	1880	2,974,310	2,345,873
	1890	3,162,359	3,428,000
Cattle—No.	1880	7,322,094	2,496,199
	1890	9,824,283	3,272,000
Sheep „	1880	59,147,595	9,741,269
	1890	93,780,352	8,754,000
Swine „ ...	1880	743,515	1,087,754
	1890	780,437	775,000
Horses „	1880	1,008,497	435,866
	1890	1,446,039	860,000
Gold output in 1890-1		£5,053,160	4,352,083
Silver „ „		£2,836,881	6,911,784
Mineral production „		£10,287,062	Not given.

INDEX.

M

Sydney : Charles Potter, Government Printer.—1893.